Lives in Play

WITHDRAWN

Lives in Play

AUTOBIOGRAPHY AND BIOGRAPHY ON THE FEMINIST STAGE

Ryan Claycomb

UNIVERSITY OF MICHIGAN PRESS : *Ann Arbor*

First paperback conversion 2014
Copyright © by the University of Michigan 2012
All rights reserved

Published in the United States of America by
The University of Michigan Press
Manufactured in the United States of America
⊚ Printed on acid-free paper

2017   2016   2015   2014   5   4   3   2

A CIP catalog record for this book is available from the British Library.

Library of Congress Cataloging-in-Publication Data

Claycomb, Ryan M., 1974–
    Lives in play : autobiography and biography on the feminist stage / Ryan
Claycomb.
        p.   cm.
    Includes bibliographical references and index.
    ISBN 978-0-472-11840-3 (cloth : acid-free paper) — ISBN 978-0-472-02853-5
(e-book)
    1. American drama—Women authors—History and criticism.   2. Feminist
drama—History and criticism.   3. Autobiography in literature.   4. Biography in
literature.   5. Feminism and literature—United States.   I. Title.
    PS338.W6C57   2012
    812.009′9287—dc23   2012011045

978-0-472-03598-4 (pbk. : acid-free paper)

PREFACE

In the spring of 1998, performance artist Karen Finley stood on the steps of the Supreme Court after arguments for *National Endowment for the Arts v. Finley et al.* and told the world that Senator Jesse Helms had been sexually harassing her through his political attacks on her and other artists—Holly Hughes, Tim Miller, and John Fleck—now known as the NEA Four. After being denied government funding from the NEA in 1990 based on "general standards of decency," the four autobiographical performance artists filed suit on First Amendment grounds, winning damages in 1993 in the amounts of their proposed grants. The case generated a great deal of publicity on both sides, with conservative politicians like Helms taking the offensive, while arts and free-speech advocates rallied behind the performers. The NEA (under the Clinton administration) appealed the lower courts' verdicts, and the case went to the Supreme Court in 1998. When the verdict in that now infamous case came down against the artists that summer, Finley interrupted her autobiographical show *Return of the Chocolate-Smeared Woman* to hold a press conference, a blurring of the lines of life writing and life, of making history and of history making. Finley's coplaintiff in the case, Holly Hughes, would go on to perform her account of the trial two years later in her show *Preaching to the Perverted.* In that moment, feminist and queer performance stood at the center of the spotlight in the national conversation on art, in large part because of the very political work that these performers were undertaking in their performances. These artists performed narratives of their own lives largely to open up a conversation about the language that constituted constructions of sex, gender, and sexuality; the cultural nerve that their performances hit tells us just how important that political work was, and it indicates in clear terms the significance of the autobiographical narrative strategies that structured this art.

The 1990s saw the culmination of a practice of staged feminist life writing—women's theatrical performances of real lives—that began with the growth of feminist theater and performance art during the women's rights movement of the 1960s and reached its peak during the so-called Culture Wars of the 1980s and 1990s. I was fortunate enough to find myself situated within a particular nexus of creativity and power, one where I could witness, and in small ways contribute to, this practice. In the summer of 1998, Jennifer Ambrosino, producing director for The Theatre Conspiracy (TTC)—a Washington, D.C., feminist theater company for which I served as literary manager—joked that she was tired of directing plays about real people, that she wanted a little fiction in her life. And no wonder. She was at that point directing a staged reading of Allison Pruitt's *The Trial of Susan B. Anthony* for the Source Theatre Festival in Washington, D.C., had just finished with TTC's run of Timberlake Wertenbaker's *New Anatomies* (a life of fin de siècle iconoclast Isabelle Eberhardt), and had helmed Lynn Kaufman's *Shooting Simone* (about Simone de Beauvoir) the season before. And I had experienced the same phenomenon. As coordinator for TTC's Emerging Women Playwrights Series that summer, I read more than fifty scripts from around the country, and of these, at least fifteen were biographically oriented. One of them, Jamie Pachino's *Theodora: An Unauthorized Biography*, became a featured reading for the series. In addition to the four feminist biography plays that either Ambrosino or I helped produce, the Washington area hosted Studio Theatre's production of Suzan-Lori Parks's *Venus*, the Source Festival's *Soulmates: The Passion of Petra Kelly*, by Nancie Carraway, and Horizons Theater's partially improvised *In Good Company*, which featured several historically prominent women, all produced within a short span in the late 1990s.

The Theatre Conspiracy was a small company of theater artists, many of whom were friends of mine from my undergraduate days. The first iteration of the company was articulated as a "Generation X" project and was driven by queer male artists who were riding a boom in queer theater inspired by the activist prominence of ACT UP, Queer Nation, and Queer Campus, and of theatrical successes like Tony Kushner's *Angels in America*. When the core members of that company began to go their separate ways, a small group of women who had been peripherally associated with it seized the opportunity to refocus the group and over the course of the six years during which I was involved, from 1995 to 2001, developed a commitment first to presenting "women's voices" and eventually to a more self-consciously feminist paradigm. My involvement was serendipitous. I was beginning graduate school in English, was interested in drama and theater, and was being exposed to a vibrant body of feminist theory and criticism, and so I was called on by my theater friends to join dramaturgical efforts for the first production of the newly reconstituted company, Kaufman's *Shooting Simone* (discussed in chapter 4), about the relationship between Simone de Beauvoir and Jean-Paul Sartre, and the challenges to de Beauvoir's feminist philosophy that this relationship embodied. I then joined the play-reading committee that chose *New Anatomies* (discussed in chapter 6) and ultimately took up leadership of that group and literary management duties the following summer with our Emerging Women Playwrights Series.

When I left the company just before it disbanded in 2001 to focus on the research that would eventually become this book, I realized that I had been witness to a pretty heady moment and that these years and the political and intellectual commitments that guided them would continue to guide my work for the foreseeable future. I realized that the feminist artistic practice to which I was directly contributing was as intellectually potent as what was happening in my graduate school classes, and my commitment to writing about and teaching texts and performances by women has only strengthened in the decade following, as the "heady moment" of feminist activism and scholarship in the 1990s has to some degree quieted. Yet women's voices continue to at once demand attention and at the same time benefit from the additional focus and energy that scholarly criticism can contribute.

The credit for this project must be shared with a number of women and men who inspired and fostered it through artistic practice, intellectual support, and the sheer conviviality that makes any scholarly work easier to undertake. At the outset, there was TTC, particularly Jennifer Ambrosino, Tricia McCauley, and Ann Mezger. To the three of them I owe much of the inspiration for this project, as well my thanks for years of friendship. I am grateful to Brian Richardson, Susan Leonardi, Catherine Schuler, Susan S. Lanser, Jackson Bryer, and Laura Rosenthal for both the guidance that kept this project on the rails and the freedom to let it occasionally jump the tracks. A particular thanks is due to that community of friends and emerging scholars among whom the project first took shape: Erin Sadlack, Leslie Jansen, Erin Kelly (who first introduced me to the suffragist statue at the National Statuary Hall), Jason Rhody, Lisa Rhody, Brian Eskridge, Natalie Bailey, Dave Eubanks, and Steve Severn, all of whom read drafts and listened to endless talk about the difference between performance and performativity, and especially to Eric Berlatsky, whose feedback at every stage, from dissertation proposal to book revision, was invaluable.

I am also grateful to the communities of scholars with whom I have had the pleasure of working: at George Washington University, particularly Christy Zink, Rachel Riedner, Mark Mullen, Phyllis Ryder, Heather Schell and Randi Kristensen; and at West Virginia University, particularly John Ernest, Katy Ryan, Donald E. Hall, Timothy Sweet, Pat Conner, Tom Bredehoft, Jay Dolmage, Adam Komisaruk, Marilyn Francus, Lara Farina, Elizabeth Juckett, Kirk Hazen, and Lisa Weihman, whose feedback on various drafts put me over the top on completing the book. I also want to thank the Women's Project and Productions in New York City for access to its archives, Holly Hughes for giving me access to the script of *Preaching to the Perverted,* and especially Terry Galloway for her warm support and smart responses to every single query I sent her way. Thanks also to LeAnn Fields and her colleagues at the University of Michigan Press not only for their continued guidance on this project but for their long commitment to bringing an important body of feminist theater criticism (a body I am honored to join) to the forefront of theater scholarship.

Finally, a particularly warm thanks to my family, especially my spouse Ann. I am grateful for every bit of support offered and given, and I hope to keep repaying her as her own artistic practice comes to fruition.

CONTENTS

INTRODUCTION : Lives in Play

Over the last decades of the twentieth century and into the twenty-first, performances that draw their material from the lives of real women have been very near the center of feminist theatrical practice. A broad range of reasons can be mustered to explain the phenomenon, many of which start with but move beyond the 1970s feminist slogan "the personal is political." But amid the growing trend of confessional narratives and theories of gender performativity that took root in the 1990s, that maxim no longer suffices to account for the complexities of women's lives transformed into life stories and live performances. In her recent study *Autobiography and Performance*, performance scholar Deirdre Heddon traces the changing shape of the ways in which "the personal is political" has morphed in the last four decades. First and foremost, she notes that with the proliferation of life narratives onstage (particularly autobiographical solo performances) the form has become conventionalized, moving from the fringes of resistant theater and art making into a more recognizable place within a traditional commercial theater economy. "The solo work," she writes, "demanding a versatile performance, is considered the ideal window through which to showcase that versatility. . . . The hope is that the piece will be picked up and transferred to Broadway or, at the very least, lead to the performer being cast in another production."[1] Nonetheless, she maintains that the politics of the personal remains a crucial component of auto/biographical performances, particularly those doing overtly political work.

But something much more foundational is being played out in these performances: an engagement with the fundamental structures of gendered and sexed identity as it might be conceived both onstage and in the world. In this project, I take a perspective at once broader and more narrow than Heddon's, considering a slightly fuller scope of life-writing performances—including autobiographical performance art, as well as biographical plays—while taking a more focused view on the uses of these narrative strategies specifically for women's theater, a methodology that marries narrative theories and performance theories. Taken together, these three forms of staged life writing reveal a persistent, politicized inquiry into how gender roles, *as well as the very notion of the subject who takes on such roles,* are constituted, shaped, and presented through performance. This line of thinking specifically interrogates a critical tension between staged women's lives as either radically performative or reliably referential, between the performer as either constructed through discourse or as a politically potent speaking subject. In particular, I argue, feminist theater artists are frequently *performing real life precisely to reveal real life as performative,* and in doing so, they are prodding the cultural structures that define and enforce norms of gender, sex, and sexuality. Yet while this tension between "real life" and "performativity" has played out both on the stage and in the criticism on the subject, these two poles ultimately do not reliably divide out different sorts of performances. Instead, they reveal how in performance both the performativity of identity and the efficacy of the live, speaking body *together* create a rhetorical effect in which a feminist performer might represent a theatrical image of reality while at the same time complicating the structures of narrative, identity, body, voice, history, and community that define her very presence onstage.

Life Writing, Feminism, Performance: The Critical Triad

This confluence of feminism, life writing, and performance coincide historically with trends in literary and theatrical criticism that all come to bear on this constellation of forms. Indeed, each pairing of two of these discourses saw significant advances in both theory and practice in the last quarter of the twentieth century, many of them despite apparent contradictions. The period from the late 1960s through the 1980s, for example, saw a marked flourish in feminist theater and feminist life writing, as well as an attendant growth of foundational criticism that both encouraged and interrogated these trends.[2] This criticism identified, among other things, a dearth of attention to women's voices both onstage and in the pages of life-writing criticism.[3] Moreover, feminist life-writing criticism has called particular attention to the formation, representation, and reception of the gendered subject at the center of such narratives by critiquing the trope of the individual male who controls his own life such that it can be ordered into a coherent, linear narrative of which he is the center. Critics such as Leigh Gilmore note that centering the male subject taps into an Enlightenment epistemology of self that assigns an excessive degree of authority to the subject and his accomplishments and "authorizes some 'identities' and not others and links 'autobiography' to the post-Enlightenment politics of individualism to the post-Romantic aesthetics of self-expression or both."[4] Furthermore, this argument suggests, the monologic, univocal presentation of self that assigns the male voice the privilege of ordering experience according to his own values necessarily elides the fragmentary, fluid nature of identity (invoked by the very idea of the performative).[5] Yet when applied to women's lives, this individualistic formation of the coherent self has traditionally failed to center the woman as empowered subject but rather has positioned her as an object of observation. Even though, as Brownley and Kimmich point out, "Autobiography . . . requires that the writer lay claim to subjectivity," those writing women's lives must work against a long history of objectification of women's lives and women's bodies and must at once establish subjectivity and work to subvert the confinement of women within proscribed gender roles.[6] When these lives are brought to the stage, the issue is doubly problematic, since the body of the performer also becomes a site for potential objectification as an object of visual pleasure for the male gaze, while the focus on that the individual subject of life writing serves to erase the importance of community in telling women's lives.[7]

Feminism's critical contribution to our understanding of life writing, then, complicates each etymological component of the term *auto/bio/graph/y*. By problematizing on gendered lines the stable notion of a true narrative produced by a singular, coherent, and narratable Enlightenment subject defined primarily in relation to the public sphere, feminist criticism has brought a politicized valance to such a critical approach to selfhood—the *auto* of *autobiography*. In the second place, the "life" in question, feminist and other poststructuralist critiques of narrative self-representation have to unsettle the representational terms of life writing, understanding, as Sidonie Smith does, that "the autobiographical text becomes a narrative artifice, privileging a presence, or identity that does not exist outside of language."[8] And if this notion suggests that any notion of "truth" underlying an autobiography is a radically unstable concept, Gilmore suggests that its appearance of stability functions in service of a patriarchal hegemony. Here she follows Michel Foucault in situating confessional narrative in relation to power, asserting that the policing of "truth" represents a specific avenue for disciplining, deauthorizing, and even criminalizing aberrant self-representations and, by extension, the selves that produced such texts. She writes, "Insofar as writers systematically and historically excluded from the rewards of a thoroughly patriarchal and class-bound individualism produce texts that resist this ideology—even, as is sometimes the case, in the very act of trying to reproduce it—they are de-authorized through this failure."[9] What we see as a result of such critiques is a new attention to self narratives that represent the subject as discontinuous, fragmented, unreliable, and contingent, all ways of unsettling what both Gilmore and Smith identify as an expression of the Enlightenment project.

Yet if life writing has been exposed comparatively recently as being unreliably referential, theatrical representation has borne this critique for most of its theorized history. Indeed, despite a long tradition of historical life narratives told on the stage, little theory of staged life writing exists that attempts to recognize these paradigms precisely because "truth" is held to be especially undermined by the artifice implicit in performance. In other words, while traditional life writing has typically (though problematically) claimed a privileged relationship to truth telling—a purchase on historical reality unavailable to other genres—theatricality is often conflated (onstage and off) with inauthenticity, with telling lies. Common assumptions about life writing run precisely counter to similarly common perceptions of Western art-making theater.[10] The very roots of antitheatrical prejudice (particularly gendered prejudice) are planted in theater's unreliable reference to reality, an assumption reproduced in contemporary theories of art-making theater. Keir Elam, in his meticulous study *The Semiotics of Theatre and Drama,* identifies theatrical space and time as referencing a field decidedly other than its own reality, "a spatio-temporal *elsewhere.*"[11] Similarly, in their introduction to *Theatricality,* Tracy C. Davis and Thomas Postlewait identify the logic of this line of thought: "So, while the theatrical reveals an excessive quality that is showy, deceptive, exaggerated, artificial, or affected, it simultaneously conceals or masks an inner emptiness, a deficiency or absence of that to which it refers."[12]

Of course, more recent scholarship has solidly undermined the impact of conventional prejudices about referentiality in seemingly the incompatible generic categories of autobiography and theater. In performance studies, work in theater and anthropology by Victor Turner, Richard Schechner, and others has located important structural continuities between theater and ritual, the latter of which is invested not with the semiotic as-if of traditional Western theater but rather a very real sense of efficacy, the notion that what happens in the world of the performance has very real consequences in the "real world" that surrounds it, that ritual space and time are entirely coincident with actual space and time, and that theatricality is a function of the heightened reality of the ritual performance.[13] So while antitheatrical prejudice may tag theatrical performance with a sense of falsity, criticism over the last decades seeks to overthrow this prejudice, staking out theater's purchase on the real and the consequential. This attitude extends into early criticism of women's performance art, about which Jeanie Forte stakes out a particular claim to referentiality, asserting that "Women's performance art has particular disruptive potential because it poses an actual woman as a speaking subject."[14] And while Forte recognizes the contingency of that speaking subject as fractured and "in process," the idea of the "actual woman" persists in criticism from the 1970s and 1980s. So despite a sense that this is a naive critical position, we might locate a lingering common set of expectations about reliable referentiality by readers of autobiography and, by extension, of other forms of life writing.

This move toward understanding performance as a kind of truth telling, even as scholars move toward destabilizing the *auto* and *bio* of *auto/bio/graph/y*, has more recently forced critics to seek to reconcile the inverse discourses of the referentiality of life writing and performance. Marvin Carlson, for example, writes that in autobiographical performance "the role the actor now plays is a role that she claims as her own, but it remains a role, still deeply involved in both mimesis and representation."[15] Carlson here considers autobiography as it complicates performance, noting that it "at first glance seems to deny the traditional operations of mimesis and deproblematize the relations between actor, character and story, but in fact the machinery of representation guarantees that these operations continue to operate in important, if even less direct ways."[16] Yet while Carlson's account uses autobiography to pry open the operations of theatrical performance, less has been done to suggest how theatrical performances might problematize autobiography. When they do, they seem to function, as Jill Dolan suggests, to "reveal performativity."[17] Sherrill Grace expands on this notion, arguing that such plays and performances "use the facts of a personal story to make us rethink the concept of *self* and the relationship of *self* to other."[18] What is developing out of this emerging body of criticism, then, is a sense that discourses on the truth claims and fictionality of theater and life writing, respectively, have deconstructed the seemingly antithetical referential stances of each.

And yet while this critical dyad (and with it, the critical triad of life writing, feminism, and performance) has been slow to develop, the confluence of gender studies, performance, and *life* found a crucial confluence in the groundbreaking late 1980s work of theorist Judith Butler. Her influence revolves primarily around a handful of core concepts, specifically that gender is "an identity instituted through a *stylized repetition of acts*" and that the sexed body's corporeality can be construed "not as site or surface, but as *a process of materialization that stabilizes over time to produce the effect of boundary, fixity and surface we call matter.*"[19] These central claims have so revolutionized the discourse that we might easily say that performance has become the primary metaphor for gender in the critical discourse. The implications of Butler's argument, that gender is itself a fiction, an effect produced by language and performance—in essence, by a compulsory theatricality—have resonated deeply throughout the practice and theory of feminist theater, although those ideas were not formulated specifically in relation to theater.

In fact, theories of performativity itself have specifically *resisted* application to theatrical representation. In what is largely regarded as the origin of studies of performativity, *How to Do Things with Words*, J. L. Austin expressly excludes theatrical speech from the constitutive effects of performative utterances, asserting that theatrical speech derails the performative and renders such utterances "not indeed false but in general *unhappy.*"[20] He continues on to note that "performative utterance will, for example, be *in a peculiar way* hollow or void if said by an actor on the stage."[21] Indeed, Butler's early arguments suggested precisely this same exclusion:

> In the theatre, one can say, "this is just an act," and de-realize the act, make acting into something quite distinct from what is real. Because of this distinction, one can maintain one's sense of reality in the face of this temporary challenge to our existing ontological assumptions about gender arrangements; the various conventions which announce that "this is only a play" allows strict lines to be drawn between the performance and the life.[22]

And, although Butler acknowledges theoretical and theatrical "attempts to contest, or, indeed, break down those conventions that demarcate the imaginary from the real," for her these remain special cases of world building that still leave real-world gender modalities unchallenged.[23] Meditating on precisely this prejudice in these theories, Andrew Parker and Eve Kosofsky Sedgwick take issue with this particular special pleading against theatrical performativity, noting in Austin's logic in particular echoes of antitheatricalism that go back to Plato and observing that "what's so surprising . . . is to discover the pervasiveness with which the excluded theatrical is hereby linked with the perverted, the artificial, the unnatural, the abnormal, the decadent, the effete, the diseased."[24] This amounts to nothing less than a queering of theatrical speech, they suggest, which seems to indicate a particular affinity between performance and Butler's political goals for a queer performativity rather than the sharp distinction between performance and performativity that Butler described in 1990.

Despite this distinction on Butler's part, the notion that one's gender can be performed, or inflected by performance, has spawned powerful theatrical images in all sorts of performance practice, from the scripted drama to public performances of drag. In many cases, such performances predate Butler's theories. Bertolt Brecht's 1943 play *The Good Person of Szechuan* offers audiences a self-consciously critical look at gender code switching in the form of the female Shen Te, who spends much of the play cross-dressed as the male Shui Ta. And while Brecht's tactics themselves are hardly in service of a feminist politics, they lay the groundwork for a whole host of feminist performances. Caryl Churchill's 1978 *Cloud 9*—a play that David Savran has called "the locus classicus of genderfuck"— offers up a spectrum of cross-dressed performances, precisely to draw out the degree to which power and discourse define the compulsory performances of gender that Butler would begin to theorize a decade later.[25] Certainly, critics such as Moya Lloyd have critiqued a certain logic that comes with a persistent reinstalling of a volitional subject in the form of the actor who does drag in these ways, a misreading of Butler that indicates an authorial understanding of performativity that locates transgression in the intent of the person performing. Yet while such overtly theatrical gender play certainly bears no risk of crossing the line between the imaginary and the real, it does succeed overwhelmingly in making gender a "site of insistent political play," the very goal for drag performance that Butler identifies in 1991 in "Imitation and Gender Insubordination."[26] In short, then, while theatrical representation may represent Austin's unhappy performative, it simultaneously presents opportunities for the performer interested in transgressing gender norms.

The Performativity Lab

These ideas and confluences of discourse among life writing, feminism, and performance have finally come to greater fruition in just the last decade as more criticism has appeared theorizing the powerful potential of feminist life writing in performance. On the one hand, staged feminist life writing works as rhetoric simply by establishing the speaking woman as a viable presence in both the art-making world and the space of public power. However, as feminist politics and conservative responses to those politics evolve and become more sophisticated, fundamental questions of how gender is constituted and represented come to bear on these discussions of voices in public spaces. And in the last decades of the twentieth century, a more subtle use of life writing began to emerge. In short, recent feminist playwrights and performers seem to be drawn to bringing real life into performance in order to interrogate the performativity of "real life," and to reclaim radically subversive performative lives as part of a broader tradition of feminism across history.

In fact, it is important that we historicize these trends and note that such performances began to appear before and as theories emerged that complicated both the representation of the subject and the inscription of gender and sex on that subject. We might posit, then, a decidedly syncretic relationship between these performances and their critical articulations. Linda Montano's 1973 performance *The Story of My Life*, for example, was cracking open autobiographical narrative well before Estelle Jelinek observed, "[I]n 1976 when I was writing my dissertation . . . I found practically no criticism on women's autobiographies."[27] Similarly, WOW Café performers, and indeed many of the more traditional playwrights considered in this study, such as Pam Gems and Maria Irene Fornes, were creating stage work that tested the boundaries of gender, performance, and life before Judith Butler's work gained currency. These plays are doing more than merely providing raw canvases for those of us in the work of theory and criticism to explicate; instead, such plays and performances might be said to be theorizing performativity even as they test its potentialities and limitations, politically, ontologically, and rhetorically.

We must insist, therefore, on thinking about the politics of such performances in terms of both their reality status and their rhetorical goals, because these two vectors represent what I would argue is the central tension of such performances and the efforts to theorize them. There exists in these performances a constant negotiation between, on one hand, the radical potential of performativity as a site of persistent play, and on the other, the persuasive nature of specific authenticity effects that are predicated on the appearance of referentiality, underpinned by bodily presence and auto/biographical narrative. Sherrill Grace brings the performativity argument to a point in her 2005 essay "Performing the Auto/Biographical Pact," where she argues for a notion of "performative autobiographics," bringing together Gilmore's work on autobiographical discourse with Butler's sense of performativity and theatrical performance. She follows Jill Dolan in seeking out how performance might "reveal performativity" and Elin Diamond's claim that "when performativity comes to rest on *a* performance" it renders visible the social relations and "the concealed or dissimulated conventions" that prop them up.[28] Grace synthesizes these claims in auto/biographical terms, asserting, "This performance site is all the more open to discussion as performative when the subject of the play is auto/biographical because in these kinds of plays self-identity is performed, whether by the author as actor or by another actor, before both the author and audience."[29] In terms of a performative approach to the ontology of identity, then, we might find in performance radical (if compromised) illustrations of shifting identities in a range of genres—Kate Bornstein's autobiographical performances of a transsexual life in *The Opposite Sex Is Neither*, the cultural and sexual crossings of Isabelle Eberhardt in Timberlake Wertenbaker's biography play *New Anatomies*, or the transformative performances of race, gender, and culture in the work of Suzan-Lori Parks. These performances, as I will explore in the following pages, illustrate for us any number of possibilities for performing against the constitutive identities inscribed on our bodies in the world at large.

And yet such radical transformations of identity run precisely against the rhetorical uses of a feminist performance that seeks to assert the performing body as evidence of a life lived. Indeed, the very category of autobiographical performance depends on an assumption of an essentializing connection between the subject-who-experienced and the body-that-performs. But this connection suggests a persistent limit, at least rhetorically, to the usefulness of performativity as a tool for feminist (and queer) politics on the stage. In such cases, performances rely on the very materiality of the performing body, one that we might legitimately recognize as crucial to a feminist performance politics. It is one thing to theorize the contingency of categories, such a line of argument might suggest, but it is another thing entirely to use such logic to underpin a kind of nihilism about a politics of visibility for female bodies and voices in public places. Susan Bennett summarizes this line of thought in lucid terms: "The very quality of liveness accentuates the problem of the body for autobiography, displaying that body along an axis of . . . the signification of identity, not primarily the identity that the writer constructs for him- or herself as the autobiographical project, but the identity that is a production of the body's exteriority." She continues, "On the other axis is the signification of the body as archive, the literal vessel of a somatic history."[30] So between body, self, and history, life narratives in performance seem to pose yet another special case. Examples proliferate across genres as well, from Holly Hughes's performances of the National Endowment for the Arts (NEA) trials to the insistence on historical fact in several biography plays to the notion of a disembodied performance of absence in Sarah Kane's *4.48 Psychosis*.

Heddon navigates this tension cautiously, refusing to fall into either extreme position. She writes, "I do not want to assume any easy or transparent relationship between a lived life and its portrayal. . . . However, neither do I want to erase the *bio* [the referentiality to lived experience], for in all the performances I explore here, the *bio* is politically significant and is the reason for the performance."[31] She poses this deployment of life narrative as strategic and later proposes that "essentialist gestures were as strategic as others."[32] While this echoes of something like Gayatri Chakravorty Spivak's concept of strategic essentialism, it suggests the rhetorical bind that staging feminist life writing runs up against: it must complicate, and even explode, the Enlightenment subject, but at the same time, to do so risks undermining the entire political project at hand. It becomes imperative, then, to complicate this binary between performativity and referentiality, between discourse and materiality.

Can such a binary, consistently reproduced by the scholarship on life writing in performance, be deconstructed? To do so, we need to consider ways in which the efficacy of life narratives on the stage are not so much undone by notions of performativity and constructionism as they are in fact propped up by those claims. That is, we must acknowledge that Austin's unhappy performative is not precisely as histrionic as he (or Butler) suggests, while at the same time, the theatricality of such performances constantly calls into question how such a notion of truth value might be meaningfully imagined in the space of witnessed performance. Timothy Gould, in his essay "The Unhappy Performative," takes up this set of questions by returning to Austin's seminal work. Here Gould focuses not only on the elements of theatrical speech that makes such performatives "unhappy" but also on the communicative transaction that renders the performative utterance potentially meaningful as an illocutionary act—a speech act that actually accomplishes that which it describes, that *does something*. Gould notes that even in everyday speech acts the illocutionary effect of the performative depends on "uptake," some sort of audience agreement with the terms of the utterance. Saying "I'm sorry" or "I bet you a bottle of Scotch," he points out, is only literally effective as an apology or a wager if the utterance is accepted. In short, the ontological weight of a speech act in the real world depends on its rhetorical effectiveness. If the apology is insincere, or the wager is clumsily proposed, it will be rejected, and the effect will retreat from the illocutionary to "that sort of thing that Austin calls the perlocutionary force or effect of the utterance," a secondary, rather than constitutive, effect: perhaps irritation, anger, or suspicion.[33] Therefore, the performative takes on its power to constitute an action not only in the utterance but in the acceptance of that utterance by an audience. This fact not only shifts the ontological component of the performative back to the realm of the rhetorical; it also trains our eyes on the audience as the site on which the performative must be arbitrated. In this sense, the rhetorical construction of much traditional theater does in fact correspond to Austin's unhappy performative, in that it invokes Aristotle's suspension of disbelief as a precondition to the invocation of an alternate world in which the theatrical action takes place.

But life writing in performance has a more complex relationship with reality as we might conventionally understand it, if not in an ontological sense (as postmodern critics of life writing have shown), then at least rhetorically, because it claims that the world that it invokes is not an alternative, but rather the real world, be it a real past, as in biography plays, or a very *present* present day, as in much autobiographical performance. To make such a claim, of course, we must take as a given that any speech act can invoke reality (never a given in this postmodern climate). Nonetheless in pragmatic terms, certain utterances, despite their status as unstable language acts, do in fact participate in the real, constituting identities, actions, and experiences on their own. In the same volume as Gould's essay, Butler herself speculates on the nature of certain speech acts with the potential to inflict actual pain (pain signifying, from Elaine Scarry onward, our closest access to a prelinguistic real).[34] In "Burning Acts: Injurious Speech," Butler examines the particular performative force of hate speech and its illocutionary potential, a kind of act in which the name doesn't describe the thing itself—hate—but in fact performs it. Butler argues that the actual effects of such speech acts derive their power not from the utterance alone but in part at least from the context that utterance takes from its history, a history of violence that gives it its weight. She asks:

> Is a community of and history of such speakers not magically in-voked at the moment in which that utterance is spoken? And if and when the utterance brings injury, is it the utterance or the utterer who is the cause of the injury, or does that utterance perform its in-jury through a transitivity that cannot be reduced to a causal or in-tentional process originating in a single subject?[35]

She continues on to assert that "a performative 'works' to the extent that *it draws on and covers over* the constitutive conventions by which it is mo-bilized. In this sense, no term or statement can function performatively without the accumulating and dissimulating historicity of force."[36] Here the ability of the performative to constitute reality as we perceive it de-pends not only on "uptake," as Gould points out, but on a history and a community that defines simple intentional acts by a lone performer acting as an agent or speaking subject.

What makes life writing in performance so slippery in this regard is that, on the one hand, the rhetorical assumption about life writing is that the audience *will* read the narrative as true, and so an Austinian notion of uptake is not defused by the theatrical presentation of the narrative. And the force of history (as well as, in many cases, the "historicity of force") is precisely what such audiences use to measure the efficacy of such a nar-rative. And in witnessing and "buying" a performed life narrative, a kind of community is invoked and sustained (as I will discuss in detail in the next chapter). So Butler and Gould both identify in the illocutionary per-formative precisely what life writing in performance brings to the stage, despite its theatricality. What marks it off as a category is its reliance on a history, one that is ascertained as such by an audience, and that gives its performances of gender a constitutive thrust.

Yet, despite Butler's refusal to install a single, stable agent-as-subject, such a complex exchange of discourse is sometimes deployed precisely in service of presenting the image of a single speaking subject, which we might say is an example of a performative that "*draws on and covers over the constitutive conventions by which it is mobilized.*" In such cases, as I will explore in chapter 2, the performative-in-performance uses the em-bodied subject-in-service of a rhetoric of the stable self, so on one hand, a materialist deployment of the subject in performance depends on a constructivist assumption that underlies performance itself. On the other hand, more radical uses of performative identities—alter egos, multiple identities, and so on—still depend on the audience's reading of an embodied experience as a kind of history, no matter how flexible, in order to read it *as life writing*. Therefore, in order for radical performers to achieve a kind of efficacy in the performance of identities, they must depend on the audience bringing a decidedly essentialist, embodied notion of selfhood to the theater. That is, for an audience to read a radically constructed performance of selfhood as real, they must first accept the body of the performer as an essential verification of selfhood in the first place. So even as a "stable" presentation of gendered selfhood depends on the ontological underpinnings of performativity, a radical presentation of (de)gendered selfhood depends on the rhetorical uptake of an audience in order to achieve a reality status through its very construction. The performances that I consider in the following pages, then, variously play out the possibilities afforded within a spectrum of staged life narratives: from the radically performative, like Kate Bornstein's solo performance, to the rhetorically essentialist, like many biography plays that rely on the truth value of history for their political critique.

Indeed, as the push and pull of the ontological and rhetorical readings of life writing in performance seem to collapse into one another on such analysis, we find that key elements of such performances—narrative, identity, voice, body, history, community—rely on one another to achieve a sense of efficacy. Yet on an ontological level, none of these discourses alone is self-sustaining; their apparent stability always at least partially breaks down under scrutiny. Identity is revealed to be a discourse produced ex post facto; the narrative of a life is always subject to the unreliability of language; the voice in narrative is merely an effect of the rhetoric of identity; the body is a text on which discourses of sex, gender, race, and power are written; history oscillates between real events and the narrative used to shape them through ideologies of truth; and community is only ever defined by perceived discursive commonalities. Each element of this equation, then, is subject to radical construction, manipulation, and social control within matrices of power that operate beyond the control of any individual, let alone an individual actor as thoroughly historically disempowered as a woman performing in public.

And yet in staged life writing, these notions turn to another for their constitutive force and rhetorical validation, propping one another up, creating something of a closed circle, more theoretically sound than any of its constituent elements. That is, the pairing of narrative and identity serves to construct a voice that is made legible to an audience, and in the theater voice is intricately connected to the body that physically produces it. And while the performative relationship of identity to the body is one that is constructed in narrative terms, it is bolstered by a verifiable history. History, then, is archived in the body and reaffirmed within the community of performance. The corporeal archive, following this assumption, becomes the grounds on which identity is constructed, assigned political meaning, and shaped into efficacy by narrative, which in turn makes the body intelligible within a communal act of performance. If we break it down even further, the conceptual structure follows like this.

- Identity is constructed by narrative.
- Narrative is legitimized by history (which is itself a narrative).
- Narrativized identity constructs voice.
- Voice emanates from the performer's body in the present moment.
- History is archived in the body as past experience.
- The body is interpolated into a community constituted by performance.
- History is verified (or challenged) by that community.
- The body is rendered intelligible within that community by constructions of identity.

This may read as a tautology, where each discursive support ultimately might be deconstructed by the unreliability that pervades the entire rhetorical system. And yet as a political rhetoric of gender and sex, such an arrangement *feels* to both performer and audience like a construction that is coherent, stable, and particularly resistant to all but the most abstract of challenges to its veracity. This relationship, then, upholds the sense of rhetorical stability even as it reveals the instability of signification at every turn. Of course, every statement cataloged above must be unpacked and illustrated, and accordingly, these become the very terms of analysis for this study. Ultimately, I will argue that while the existing scholarship might suggest a *tension* between the radical gender performances afforded by an unstable, flexible notion of identity as a performative on the one hand, and a particular purchase on the real aided by a historical narrative verified by the performing body on the other, this dialectic is precisely what undergirds the political heft of life writing in performance, particularly for women's lives.

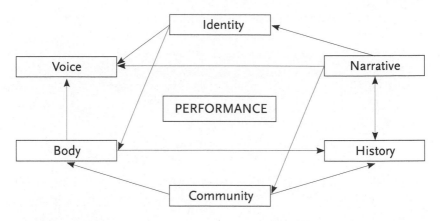

Defining the Terms

The axes on which this constitutive effect revolves will also serve as the key terms for analysis in this study—narrative, identity, voice, body, history, community. And of course, even as each of these concepts themselves are unstable, so are the very terms we use to describe them. So we must pause a moment to establish a few key terms.

Our understanding of life narratives in performance, for example, hinges on the uses of both "drama" and "life writing." Like many others who navigate the murky disciplinary waters between English, theater, and performance studies, I recognize that the boundaries between drama, theater, and performance are neither fixed nor uncontested. The traditional distinction between "drama" and "theater" is made between a written play and its live realization in the theatrical space, and the traditional distinction between "theater" and "performance" suggests, as Marvin Carlson puts it, that performance (or performance art) breaks down the notion of an "other" that "traditional theatre has regarded . . . as a character in a dramatic action embodied . . . by an actor."[37] Instead, performance artists "do not base their work upon characters previously created by other artists, but upon their own bodies, their own autobiographies, their own experiences in a culture or in the world, made performative by their consciousness of them and the process of displaying them for an audience."[38] Carlson's definition seems to set performance art and drama (via traditional theater) at odds with one another. However, any consideration of life narratives in performance must acknowledge that the autobiographical component of much performance art troubles the assumption of such a distinction between drama and performance. Therefore, allow me to broaden our working definition of *drama* to merely *a narrative composed for the purpose of performance.*[39] In this way, drama includes not only the traditional plays that we will examine in the chapters on biography plays but also the self narratives of feminist performance artists and the confrontation of self and other we see in oral history plays and performances.

Similarly, a simple definition of life writing might be reduced to what its name suggests: narrative writing based on the life of a historically verifiable person or people, living or dead. Here I divide the category into two primary subsets: autobiography, a first-person autodiegetic narrative of one's own life experiences; and biography, the narration of another's life experiences. At times, I will also mention a third form: performed oral history, a collection of narratives from a variety of perspectives that collectively form a more complete narrative than any of the individual voices that comprise it. Heddon treats this category as a form of autobiography, and others consider it under the rubric of documentary or verbatim theater, although Della Pollock makes a compelling case for it as a separate category.[40] Beyond this working definition, however, problems in defining life writing stem from the vague nature of the phrase "based on." As I have suggested, a huge body of work has been devoted to analyzing the truth claims of life writing, and still more work is being produced on this topic. I cover this subject more extensively throughout the book, yet I would argue that for my purposes here the label "life writing"—as opposed one such as "fiction"—works on a continuum. We will see some texts, such as Fiona Shaw's *Delirium of Interpretations,* that pay such meticulous attention to documentary accuracy that footnotes pepper the script, while more commonly, plays such as Joan Schenkar's *Signs of Life* or the work of Carmelita Tropicana openly indulge in tall-tale, fantasy, and outright invention. Nonetheless, the presence of a verifiable life narrative at the center of these texts qualifies them for examination in this study, especially given that the truth in such outlying cases is often less important than the reasons that the truth is being stretched, or the revelations that such truth stretching offers about more traditionally accurate narratives.

Because exploring the very nature of the construction of an identity in performance is precisely the aim of this book, the term *identity* itself must remain in flux at a broad level. But there are more particular iterations of identity in this study that do require more focus. Specifically, work on feminist performances necessarily invokes identity as a gendered category, and so establishing a definition of "feminist" performance becomes a necessary, if almost impossibly complex, task. Definitions set out by theorists and critics of the last decades range from the hopelessly broad to the maddeningly restrictive. Elaine Aston, in her *Introduction to Feminism and Theatre,* surveys the range of these definitions, from the useless "anything about women" to more specific ones such as those of Lizbeth Goodman. Goodman, for example, opens her study of contemporary feminist theaters by suggesting that feminist theater is a "political theatre oriented toward change, produced by women with feminist concerns." She elaborates on the component of "political change," though, by differentiating between "women's theater" and feminist theater. Here she follows Susan E. Bassnet-McGuire, who defines feminist theater based on seven specific political goals: "equal pay; equal education and job opportunities; free 24-hour nurseries; free contraception and abortion on demand; financial and legal independence; an end to discrimination against lesbians and a woman's right to define her own sexuality; freedom from violence and sexual coercion."[41] I find Bassnet-McGuire's definition (which, published twenty-five years ago, reflects the specific concerns of the second-wave women's movement) overly restrictive, and I contrast it to Janet Brown's more recent, broader, yet still instructive definition. Brown defines feminist drama by its "commitment to telling the stories of silenced and marginalized women, celebrating women's community and sense of connection through group protagonists, and expressing the moral concerns and societal criticism that arise from women's experience."[42] While Brown's third goal encompasses Bassnet-McGuire's definition, her first and second axes touch on concerns that are undoubtedly feminist but are less connected to immediate, concrete political action. Instead, they focus on some of the larger representational concerns of feminist artists and scholars. Ultimately, though, we must consider a definition of feminist theater that encompasses both a multiplicity of feminisms and a continuum of rhetorical emphasis on those ideologies. For example, while we may examine April De Angelis's *Playhouse Creatures* within the context of Bassnet-McGuire's seven demands, Suzan-Lori Parks's plays are far more concerned with racial politics than gender politics. Nonetheless, Parks's plays often take up the injustice of women's experiences as their grounds. Indeed, the title of Aston's more recent work, *Feminist Views on the English Stage,* shifts the attention from defining a playwright or even work itself as feminist and refocuses our attention on "feminist structures of feeling" and "feminist continuities and connections," terms that account for a wide variety of approaches to challenging the construction of "woman" or the roles and performances assigned to the bodies that we read through that construction.[43]

Furthermore, we must acknowledge the enormous overlap between feminist theater and queer theater, in terms of content, social position, and formal methodology. Certainly, playwrights and performers who self-identify as lesbian almost undoubtedly fit into both categories, and lesbian plays abound in this study. But given the critical debt of queer theory to feminist inquiry, and the degree to which queer theory has pushed feminist theory forward, I consider queer theories of representation as they illuminate feminist performances. For example, while Tim Miller and David Román's 1995 article "Preaching to the Converted" specifically describes gay and lesbian theater, its observations also frequently apply to feminist performances as well.[44] Moreover, some performers and performances complicate the very notion of woman as a term of study, which necessarily complicates any feminist ideology predicated on the existence of the category. Transsexual performer Kate Bornstein's work, such as the provocatively titled *The Opposite Sex Is Neither*, fits uneasily into any notion of feminism, given that Bornstein was born biologically male and continues to reject easy binaries of gendered and sexed identity. Nonetheless, while a variety of queer performances and theories pepper this study, I acknowledge that the concerns of these two (often overlapping) camps can be quite different, and sometimes actively divergent.

Expanding beyond taxonomic approaches to identity, at its intersection with narrative we find that "few words are as resonant to contemporary feminists as 'voice,'" notes Susan Sniader Lanser.[45] Lanser describes the affinities between a feminist notion of voice as the seat of authority and the narratological approach to voice as a component of narrative poetics. "In linking social identity and narrative form," she asserts, "I am postulating that the authority of a given voice of text is produced from a conjunction of social and rhetorical properties."[46] In the context of life writing, these properties are magnified by the implication of the real attached to the narrative voice; from both a narrative and a feminist perspective, the voice's claim to truth value also represents a claim to authority. When literalized by the stage, this claim to truth value is enhanced by the notion of performance (despite Derridean objections) through the existence of the performer's body in the presence of the audience. That is, when narrative voice is made live through embodied performance, the audience is offered a doubled claim to authenticity and authority. Therefore, we can see that staged life writing offers feminists a compelling conduit to bringing women's voices—often silenced ones—into the realm of authority, a claim I will examine more closely throughout the book. This effect is noted, for example, in criticism that cites autobiographical performance as presenting an authentic speaking subject, or even when historical written texts serve as the basis for the reconstruction of character in biography plays.

But as I've suggested, voice gains much of its enhanced power in performance from its connection to the body, which in the case of feminist theater and performance is contested concomitantly with the gendered identity with which it is often conflated. Butler's extension of her constructionist theory to corporeality in *Bodies That Matter*, suggests that the way the body is perceived is a direct product of the linguistic formations used to describe it and that everything from race to sex is subject to these corporeal constructions. While the truth value of voice enhances the rhetorical impact of a performance, the truth value of the body complicates it, and does so differently in different forms. Biography, for example, uses the body of the actress as what Elin Diamond (following Walter Benjamin) in *Unmaking Mimesis* calls a "dialectical image," a physical embodiment that uproots the body of the biographical object and the body of the actress from their historically specific places and creates a dialectic of historical narrative: a marker of the long history of women's oppression in this one performing body.[47] But the form runs into problems when audience members want to collapse the identity of the performer too neatly with the identity of the biographical subject. Such an interpretive move assumes that women's identities are easily interchangeable and therefore reinforces a notion of a uniform women's identity rooted in the sexed body. While Brechtian alienation tactics are widely used to defuse this tendency, the actress's body remains at an interpretive nexus of both radical and conservative reading practices. Meanwhile, autobiographical performance leverages the bodies of its authors into pointed critiques of self-construction, As Susan Bennett argues when she links the body to "the signification of identity, not primarily the identity that the writer constructs for him- or herself as the autobiographical project, but the identity that is a production of the body's exteriority."[48] So we can see that the contested relationship between the performer's body and the body of the performed subject, whether alive or dead, selfsame or other, gives rise to a range of theoretical binds that various performers solve in various ways.

In addition to the problem of performing the body of the subject of life writing, there remains the problem of objectification that both women's performance and women's life writing face. Because the male gaze is potentially a factor in each form of women's life writing in performance, feminist playwrights and performers have developed a range of tactics to disrupt, subvert, and outright critique the tendency to turn the performing female body into an object of visual pleasure. Accordingly, we see a range of tactics used to accomplish this, from the overt deconstructions of the female body as sexualized object in the autobiographical work of Orlan, Annie Sprinkle, and Karen Finley to the approach found in many biographical plays of splitting the subject between the biographical figure and a biographer who helps the audience contextualize the act of witnessing a life.

This impulse to bring the audience into the process of life writing suggests to a large degree the emphasis that many of these plays and performances place on the notion of community. While *community* is not a narratological term, inquiries into the nature of community in feminist performances necessarily turn to theories of readership for background. Notions of implied readers who are generated at the moment of writing are transformed into real audiences in the moment of performance, which complicates any textual study of feminist drama. Nonetheless, we consistently see how these performances rely on individual lives (in the cases of biography and autobiography) as lightning rods for the constitution of community among audiences and how they leverage the collective lives of women in plays like De Angelis's *Playhouse Creatures* to acknowledge the social fabric of experience, model community practices onstage for their audience offstage, and ultimately attempt to create community among their audiences for the purposes of encouraging collective action. Charlotte Canning writes, for example, that

> performance created by groups [developed into] the representation of a collective autobiography intersecting with the individual autobiography of the spectators. In solo performance it usually meant the creation of a collective autobiography through the convergence of the performer's autobiography with the spectator's in the moment of performance. All these performance forms work to foreground the idea that one's autobiography is not one's alone, but is part of a larger narrative about the experience of women in a particular culture. Thus, an autobiographical performance is not only the story of

one woman's "life," but also the story of the construction of "a woman" in that culture.[49]

While the notion of community must be examined closely for both its potentials and its foreclosures, it remains a potent site of strength for feminist performers, even as it represents a conceptual lynchpin in creating the reality effects of these performances, serving to validate the presence of the speaking body, to verify the narrative as history, and in doing so to effect uptake of the performative construction of identity.

Finally, we come to history, the linkage of a narrative past to our sense of the real. Specifically, in these performances, history is linked to the body through experience. As Bennett writes:

> The body archives a history that may or may not be part of the performance narrative, explicitly or implicitly; it also enacts that history irrespective of the other constituents of performance and irrespective of the autobiographer's intentions for it. The live, performing body renders the script three-dimensional, but it itself has been scripted, as it were, prior to its subject matter. Its very physicality— indeed, its liveness—is an account of all experiences leading to the present moment, the archive of a life lived.[50]

Bennett's argument, which both invokes and challenges the role of the body as verification of both a narrative history and the identity it constructs, refers specifically to autobiographical performance, but it also invokes the degree to which women's bodies are essentialized as scripted through their sameness, a scripting that plays out and is complicated by other sorts of life writing in performance, through the objectified body of the Venus Hottentott in Suzan-Lori Parks's *Venus* or the body performances of Orlan.

Furthermore, it is perhaps commonplace to suggest that feminist artists typically enact revisionist histories as a way of reclaiming their positions in the annals of human history. However, when these feminist performances are rooted in the lives of real people, the label "revisionist history" can be used in more positive terms than it is in the popular media. Because the term *revisionist* often implies an element of fictionalization— a convenient fabrication for the purposes of hawking a specific political agenda—alternative histories are often written off as indulgent and suspect. Reviews of De Angelis's *Playhouse Creatures*, for example, suggested that her history was exaggerated for rhetorical purposes and therefore used this critique to discount the merit of the performance.[51] But when the voices and central events of those histories are historically verifiable (as they are in the case of *Playhouse Creatures*), and are understood by the audience as such, they shore up the validity of the revisions and help to create a narrative of critique that underscores not only the abuses that these feminist life stories chronicle but also the silencing operations that have kept women out of power for so long. In feminist biographies in particular, where the subjects are scattered throughout both recent and distant history, this notion of verifiability becomes exceedingly important. It would be inaccurate to suggest that revisionist tactics are uniform across the spectrum of feminist performances. Some performances take greater license with the details of historical fact than others, while others (especially oral histories) deemphasize the details themselves in favor of concentrating on the metadiscourse surrounding events.

Because one of the goals of this study is taxonomic, the body of the study is divided into two parts, one on each of the primary modes of staged feminist life writing. Part I examines feminist autobiographical performance as a site at which to play out variations in public identity construction and presentation as a political act. Part II examines more traditional plays that take a central historical persona as their biographical subject, positing that these plays scrutinize the political investments of the biographical act through performance, even as they enact such biography. In part I, chapter 1, "Performative Lives, Performed Selves: Autobiography in Feminist Performance," examines the critical tradition that embraces performative identities in performance and posits that because they apply unreliable or self-contradicting narratives to these real-time, physically present performances, feminist performance artists such as Kate Bornstein and Bobby Baker perform the self to reveal selfhood as performative. Chapter 2, "Autobiography and the Rhetoric of the Embodied Self," argues that many feminist performers often rely on a more discrete connection between personal experience and live performance. Artists like Holly Hughes, Terry Galloway, and Karen Finley use the efficacy of their own self histories and the presence of their performing bodies to establish a reliance on the appearance of an essential connection between body and identity, suggesting the rhetorical limitations of performativity to a feminist performance praxis. Finally, given the emphasis on the performing body of the author in performance art, chapter 3, "The Autobiographical Play and the Death of the Playwright: Sarah

Kane's *4.48 Psychosis*," moves the discussion to a more traditional ac-
tor/playwright dynamic of the written play, where an actor's presence
stands in for the absent playwright. Taking Sarah Kane's final play, *4.48
Psychosis*, performed posthumously after the playwright's suicide, as its
subject, this chapter argues against the growing critical consensus to read
the play as universal, noting instead the importance of taking the particular critical and experiential issues of the play as central to reception of
women's life writing, particularly writing inflected with rage and despair.

In part II, chapter 4, "Staging Women's Lives, Staging Feminist Performances," provides an overview of biography plays by feminist playwrights, arguing that these plays in performance propose a new model of
biographical inquiry that doesn't merely seek to recover the life of exemplary women but rather to reclaim, through the performing body of the
live actress, the radical gender performances of those women. In chapter
5, "A Life in the (Meta)Theater: Writing/Rehearsing/Acting Out," I consider three biographical plays—Hélène Cixous's *Portrait of Dora*, April De
Angelis's *Playhouse Creatures*, and Maria Irene Fornes's *The Summer in
Gossensass*—that weigh the comparative values of various modes of representation for recovering and reenacting radical gender performances.
Taken together, these plays suggest the struggle feminist playwrights engage in when choosing whether and how to represent historical women's
lives onstage, and the degree to which modes of representation can ethi-
cally and effectively recover women's lives for political purposes. Chapter 6, "Performing Race and the Object of Biography," moves the discussion into performances of race and ethnicity, arguing that such plays are
chiefly concerned with the status of their biographical subject as an object
of the exoticizing desiring gaze—of her contemporaries, the biographer,
and the audience itself. By comparing Suzan-Lori Parks's consideration of
African identity within the context of European spectatorship in *Venus*
against the transborder journeys of the Russian Jew Isabelle Eberhardt in
Timberlake Wertenbaker's *New Anatomies*, this chapter suggests the degree to which biographical performances struggle against the very racialized and sexualized objectifications they seek to undermine, even as they
propose models of theatrical inquiry to mitigate those objectifying viewing practices.

Playing at Lives concludes by focusing first on the central question of
how life narratives pose a link between the historical body and the performing body, examining the range of ways that the performing body presents a dialectical image of history on the feminist stage. By considering

the importance that these plays place on the presence and power of the speaking subject, I argue that they represent the political problems inherent in theories that question the status of the author. In each of these forms, the tangled relationship among the experience of the subject of life writing, the voice of the author, and the body of the performer alternately expands and collapses notions of presence, identity, and authorship that apply not only to feminist performance but to literatures and lives far beyond this category. Indeed, as identity politics has given way in the last decade to an urgent global politics following September 11 and the U.S. invasion of Iraq, feminist playwrights have shifted their attention to a broader notion of feminist epistemology. Closing with a consideration of Judith Thompson's *Palace of the End*, this study concludes by considering how staging women's lives advances not only specifically feminist political goals but broadly humanist ones as well.

PART I : AUTOBIOGRAPHY

THE BODY AND SELF IN PERFORMANCE

CHAPTER 1 : Performative Lives, Performed Selves

AUTOBIOGRAPHY IN
FEMINIST PERFORMANCE

If any art form, theatrical or otherwise, might be said to be the proving grounds for a performative approach to identity, performance art is the obvious first choice. Although performance art itself is a nebulous genre—a loosely bound set of artistic practices that assembles the art object from the actions of the live performing body—the binding focus on the performer's body as the art itself already underscores some idea that the identity of that body is, like the artist's canvas or the empty stage, an available space on which to make meaning. Performance art, as RoseLee Goldberg has demonstrated, has a long and rich history that cuts across the twentieth century but was embraced by feminist artists and performers at the peak of second-wave feminism in the 1960s and 1970s and rolled into the lesbian-feminist heyday of the 1980s and 1990s at venues like the WOW Café and P.S. 122. Examples of feminist and lesbian-feminist performance art span a broad range of practices, from the photographic parodies of Cindy Sherman, the art-world installations of Eleanor Antin, and the Fluxus-inspired work of Carolee Schneeman to the more recent theater-oriented work of Split Britches, Holly Hughes, Terry Galloway, and many others.

Performance art scholar RoseLee Goldberg documents this rise and explicitly connects autobiographical performance to the surge of feminist politics: "[C]oinciding with the powerful Women's Movement throughout Europe and the United States, [autobiographical performance] allowed many women performers to deal with issues that had been rela-

tively little explored by their male counterparts."[1] That an already established tradition of avant-garde performance took this autodiegetic turn
with the resurgence of feminism suggests the affinity between this narrative form and feminist ideology. Deirdre Heddon, too, notes this historical convergence, observing that "though the use of autobiography pre-
dates the second-wave feminist movement, it was in the early 1970s that
the political potential of autobiographical performance was harnessed for
the first time."[2]

While both Goldberg and Heddon call explicit attention to the convergence of form and politics in autobiographical feminist performance,
we can locate a range of explanations for this convergence, some of
which, as I have already noted, contradict and countermand one another.
Certainly while these performers clearly work on the fringes of what we
might call drama, blurring generic boundaries of traditional theatrical
practice, they are also blurring the boundaries of the roles and identities
that are associated with the category "woman." Given that these performers—many of whom in conceiving the narratives for their own performances are also playwrights—implicitly and explicitly narrate their
own pasts, we must consider their stories within the frames of both their
narrative and performance dimensions. In doing so, we can begin to understand a number of specific appeals that life narratives offer to feminist
performance. Specifically, these artists bring particular power to their life
stories by incorporating their bodies as an element of their narratives both
as rhetorical evidence of truth value and simultaneously as a constructible semiotic sign system. At the same time, because they apply unreliable or self-contradicting narratives to these real-time, physically present performances, they call into question the stability of their own
gendered identities, thus prodding the seemingly stable concepts that
they hope to complicate and explode. Indeed, when we take these concepts together, we might argue specifically that such feminist performance artists perform the self to reveal selfhood as performative, even as
they rely on the truth claims of selfhood to ground their critiques.

In the three chapters that follow, I will trace the ways in which autobiographical feminist performance, criticism of that performance, and
theories of the performed self revolve around questions of authenticity,
agency, and presence—how performances variously rely on or deconstruct the notion of an authentic acting agent that can be said to be inherent and resident in the performing body. In this chapter in particular, I
will tell a story about the development of a theoretical practice of perfor-

mativity that grew on the stages of feminist performance art, just as those theories were being developed and advanced in the pages of academic prose. This is a story about artists working on the margins of the professional theater and art worlds, seeking out resistant expressions of gender, sex, and sexuality while struggling against the epistemological and ontological binds posed by notions of an unmediated performance, the traps of essentialist logic, a performing body compromised by voyeurism, and the very impossibility of reliable reference through performance. And, for a time at least, this artistic and political struggle seems to come to rest on an emerging set of ideas about the historically contingent, discursively constructed, performative subject. The argument is a historical one and a formal one, suggesting that these performers were part of a very particular moment in the history of gender culture and performance and at the same time were forcing us as scholars of form to reimagine the possibilities and tenabilities of the self in performance.

Performing the Self: The Feminist and Queer Performance Boom

In their introduction to *O Solo Homo*, their 1998 collection of queer performance art pieces, David Román and Holly Hughes note a boom in queer performance art, even as funding streams were drying up at a disheartening rate. The same boom can be said to be true of feminist drama and performance (indeed, many of the pieces in both that volume and this study might be said to fit into both categories). Second-wave feminism from the late 1960s into the 1980s found female artists locating forums for performance in unprecedented numbers.[3] At the height of this period in feminist performance in the late 1970s and early 1980s, Goldberg notes, performance art also took a turn toward theater. As it became more popular, " 'new performance' was given the licence to acquire polish, structure and narrative."[4] Even with such developments, the autobiographical turn remained in place for many of these performances: since many of these performers explicitly use their own bodies in space to create art, establishing the self as a component of their performances, even while in most conventional drama, that body is often used to depict a character, a fictive other who inhabits the body of the performer for a time.

Such performances through the 1980s begat a critical attention to the self in performance that took shape in the decade that followed. In his

1996 essay "Performing the Self," Marvin Carlson invokes Eric Bentley's simple "A impersonates B while C looks on" only to revise it as "A impersonates A while C looks on," suggesting at once an equation of actor and character but simultaneously indicating a similar sort of otherness in the term impersonates.[5] Just over a year earlier, John Brockway Schmor is a bit more specific, depicting what he calls "confessional performance" as a form

> in which the performer uses often intimately autobiographical text, chance improvisation and ritual to deconstruct or at least deflect traditional notions of identity and social reality. This form emphasizes almost exclusively the actual unmediated event in an inversion of traditional illusionist principles of theatre. Following Brecht, autobiographical performance art breaks theatrical illusion . . . but unlike Brechtian theatre, such works disrupt even the illusion of the "real" event by problematizing the identity of the performing self.[6]

Schmor's definition at once evokes the real that, however contested, is at the center of life writing and at the same time recognizes the degree to which that real is always up for debate, for reexamination. What we can say is this: the performer not only claims to be essentially the same as the character but is believed to be so both in the dramatic world and outside the dramatic frame. The identity of the character must referentially indicate the identity of the author/performer, even if it often problematizes it: "A impersonates A (or A', a public or stage self) while C looks on." Here, the tenuous, imbricated relationship between self-as-actor and self-as-character becomes a specific site of theatrical play, calling into question the nature of identity and the ability of feminist performers to manipulate notions of identity once thought to be stable.

In the years that have followed, autobiographical performance has become a well-traveled subject; existing scholarship has already at least touched on the appeal of autobiography to feminist writers, the authority offered by the suggestion of presentness made by autobiographical performance, the ways in which the body-as-text and the life-as-construction in tandem reveal the performativity of everyday identity, and the community-building functions of performed autobiographical narrative. These subjects not only help establish the rhetorical power of autobiographical feminist performance but also indicate potential areas of inquiry for other genres of life writing.[7] I am particularly interested, though, in the precise intersection between live performance and life narrative, what makes it so compelling for feminist rhetoric and politics, and what theoretical implications verifiable performing bodies have for constructed narratives of self. What we might seek here is the speaking subject onstage, as well as the agency to speak in public as a vehicle to determine (whether negatively or positively) an identity that the performer chooses to claim.

How that identity is constituted and constructed, however, has historically depended on the critical framework, the cultural moment, and the performance in question. On the one hand, even the earliest live performances of women's life narratives at once make political the personal, fulfilling the charge of that tried-and-true second-wave feminist slogan. Autobiographical narratives grant women the power to write their own stories. And by bringing the self to the stage, autobiographical performers assert themselves as politically viable speaking subjects. Yet because performance makes an object of the performer's body even as autobiography asserts her as the speaking subject, this simplistic notion of live presence as unassailable subjectivity goes inevitably awry. Instead, we see performers undermining their own assumed presence and apparent subjectivity, both by revealing the very constructability of the female body—as performers like Orlan and Kate Bornstein do—and by deconstructing the notion of the life narrative—as performers like Carmelita Tropicana and Bobby Baker do.

Heddon traces this earlier, second-wave-feminist line of thinking— one that tends to essentialize the self to the performing body—and links it explicitly to its political moment.

> The translation of personal—or autobiographical—material into live performance was inarguably tied to consciousness-raising activities which focused analysis specifically on women's experiences (under the banner of "the personal is political"). . . . If subjects of the "everyday" were not normally the matter of politics, neither were they the typical matter of contemporary art of theatre, and the entry of the explicitly personal into the aesthetic should itself be considered a political gesture. . . . Consciousness-raising generated self-consciousness on the part of women which allowed an articulation of specifically female (everyday) experiences in art.[8]

Underlying this political consciousness-raising is a theoretical conception of the self as specifically and inextricably linked to the live performing body. That is, the draw of autodiegesis here depends on the degree to which it emphasizes the speaking voice of the woman, the literalization of the vocal metaphor that makes performance even more potent. Writing in 1988, on the cusp of the performative turn in theory and criticism (indeed, in the same volume in which Judith Butler's early "Performative Acts and Gender Constitution" appears), Jeanie Forte argues, "Women's performance art has a particular disruptive potential because it poses *an actual woman* as speaking subject, throwing that position into process, into doubt, opposing the traditional conception of the single, unified (male) subject."[9] She goes on to connect the power of the speaking woman to the idea of the woman's body. According to Forte, presenting the female body as a subject instead of an object of the male gaze "clashes in dissonance with its patriarchal text, challenging the very fabric of representation by refusing that text."[10] Forte not only recognizes the power of the speaking subject to define the actual woman but she also highlights the political importance of speech's ability to do so. The presence of the woman as speaker, woman as agent, woman as presence (as opposed to Lacanian notions of absence) situates feminist autoperformance at a particular political nexus of power that has until recently completely excluded women from speaking. Similarly, Catherine Elwes summarizes this position when she writes, "Performance is about the 'real-life' presence of the artist. She takes on no roles but her own. She is author, subject, activator, director and designer. When a woman speaks within the performance tradition, she is understood to be conveying her own perceptions, her own fantasies, and her own analyses."[11] In this context, when interpreted as the unmediated presence of the woman as speaking subject, it is no wonder that autobiographical performance has been touted as a powerful tool for feminists.

Deconstructing the Unmediated Body as Object

Of course these assumptions, susceptible to charges of second-wave essentialism, draw some naive conclusions about the very possibility of an unmediated performance, conclusions that themselves have problematic implications. Foremost, by privileging the woman's body as a defining characteristic of women's agency, these performances tread dangerously close to an array of essentialist traps. To connect the female body to women's agency to speak in a new way may allow women access to a public space—and in the 1960s and 1970s this access was scarce. But as the relative success of feminist ideology in the 1970s has made women's roles more complex (and more varied), the use of the female body as a conduit to women's speech has itself become limiting. The assumption that "women's speech" is a category separate from male speech and connected exclusively to the female body still sets female speech off in its own corner, allowing that speech to be circumscribed, regulated, and ultimately marginalized once more.

Moreover, despite Forte's assertion that when assigned the subject position the woman's body disrupts the male symbolic order, the audience of autobiographical performance is still liable to objectify the performer—a symptom of both women's performance and autobiographical narrative. Brownley and Kimmich assert, for example, that "reading an autobiography is an act of voyeurism," while any female performer knows the consequences of the objectifying gaze: accounts of Karen Finley's career, for example, contain more than one anecdote about drunken frat boys heckling a naked woman smeared with chocolate.[12] That much of feminist performance of the last forty years has relied on what Rebecca Schneider terms "the explicit body" underscores the body not only as a site of feminist resistance but also as a potential object of the male gaze, especially if viewed as the unmediated, coherent signifier of the self.

And while Elwes's statement about the presence of the self may suggest the potency of performance, it also represents a somewhat naive position on the truth claims that can be reliably forged by the narrative form of autobiography. Following Hayden White's historiographic notion of the narrativity of history, and onward to poststructuralist readings of autobiography by Paul John Eakin and Timothy Dow Adams, the notion of life writing as the sign of authenticity is contested at best, and possibly downright misleading.[13] So while early feminist performance artists relied on personal experience specifically, and women's experience broadly, narratives of this experience are sometimes no more than representations, and therefore subject to a slipperiness of signification that defies authenticity.[14] Furthermore, Sidonie Smith notes, "As it promotes a literary theory of reflectionism and transparency, the celebration of a reified 'experience' paradoxically obscures the influence of determining structures."[15] As such, the very notion of personal experience that seemed initially to undergird the exigencies of feminist performance not only proves to be faulty as an authentic portrayal of women's selfhood but covertly supports the very "determining structures" that mask the operations of power in traditional male autobiographies like those of Saint Augustine

and Benjamin Franklin. For these reasons, the appeal of feminist autobiographical performance as a tactic to establish the woman as publicly acknowledged speaking subject seems easily undermined, despite what
was, through much of second-wave feminism, a desperate need to establish exactly that. These are the epistemological binds that cohered in particular around the Culture Wars of the 1980s and 1990s: the problems of
unmediated performance, gender essentialism, spectatorial (and govern-
mental) voyeurism, and the very impossibility of reliable reference.

Recognizing these theoretical obstacles to the notion of the embodied
performer as unmediated speaking subject, artists in the late 1970s
through the 1990s began to deploy more overtly deconstructive techniques to work against these obstacles, working in symbiosis with deconstructive theories of gender that were being formulated at roughly the
same time. Perhaps foremost among these tactics is the notion of the constructible woman's body. That is, if the notion of the woman's body as a
discrete sign plays into a dangerous essentialism, even as autobiographical performance allows for objectifying viewing tactics, then it follows
that feminist performers could effectively use Brechtian deconstructive
tactics to disrupt not only the essentialized body but also the male gaze.
Indeed, some of these tactics extend back to the earliest iterations of feminist performance, and while many of them are not autobiographical per
se—they enact women's experience in the present instead of narrating
past experiences—they reveal much about the construction of the self
through the performed body. Lisa Tickner, for example, emphasizes the
theme of corporeal transformation in works such as Eleanor Antin's photographic documentation of "a ten pound weight loss over 36 days in 144
photographs of her naked body in a piece called *Carving: An Intentional
Sculpture.*"[16] With the notion of intention already embedded in the piece's
title, Antin links body together with self and explicitly calls attention to
both the status of woman's body as art object and the violence inherent in
the act of "carving" that constructed the weight loss. Antin is "intention-
ally" constructing the body to underscore the violence associated with
idealized images of women, and in doing so lodging a critique against
(among other things) the apparent attractiveness that a ten-pound weight
loss would purportedly bring.

Feminist performance has a long history of using such tactics to expose how much cultural notions of beauty inflect the discourse surrounding women's bodies. Furthermore, they begin to reveal the way in which
these notions forge a stylization of the female body that constitutes the

very concept of gender itself, as Judith Butler has persuasively shown.[17] Valie Export, herself a performance artist, notes, "What was being fore-grounded in particular in my work is the social construction of the body, the body as a carrier of signs, and with it the social construction of the subject in performance."[18] Rachel Rosenthal's 1980 *Bonsoir, Dr. Schon!* offered up the same tactics, as when the performer undressed and had her assistant mark her "bad spots" with tape.[19] By acknowledging those parts of her body that do not conform to patriarchal notions of beauty or wom-anliness, and displaying them anyway, Rosenthal would flaunt her body *as text* in a direct response to the objectification of her body. By revealing her body to be a textual signifier, Rosenthal's self-critical move works to disrupt the male gaze that might make the same notations silently. Instead, the performance embraced these flaws and, like Antin, critiqued the processes that provoke such self-criticism as a common practice.

Similarly, in *Post-Porn Modernist* (1990), Annie Sprinkle famously created a denaturalized text out of her body by trafficking in the image of the prostitute as cultural signifier. In the oft-discussed scene, entitled "Public Cervix Announcement," Sprinkle would invite audience members to the stage to examine her cervix with a flashlight and a speculum. And while some professed "porn aficionados" brought zoom lens cameras to fetishize Sprinkle's open vagina, Rebecca Schneider reads this as the most fascinating aspect of the performance's cultural critique: "All of us at The Kitchen who chose to look stood in line for the theatrical 'moment' when, at the site of the cervix, the name of art would slap against the name of porn across the stage within the stage, the proscenium of the prostitute's body."[20] Here, Schneider explicitly acknowledges the degree to which Sprinkle foregrounds the constructed nature of the prostitute's body as an image of both economic and physical desire. In contextualizing her own identity as a prostitute within the space of "art" and "performance," Sprinkle overtly calls attention to both the image of the prostitute in art's history and the degree to which that image is shaped by a constructed set of stylized gestures that can be parodied as easily as they can be invoked in earnest. So in these performances, we clearly see a shift away from an essentialist presentation of the self/body dynamic, conceiving of the body as a deconstructive text that allows artists to use autoperformance as a forum for critique, foregrounding the abstract discourse of gender against the very real material bodies that discourse affects.

While Antin, Rosenthal, and Sprinkle reveal the degree to which the female body is subject to discursive construction, French artist Orlan

spent her career literalizing the process by constructing and reconstructing her body most explicitly in a series of nine surgical "interventions"
from 1990 to 1993. While her first stagings of cosmetic surgery (primarily
liposuction) as performance art were less about the end product of her
transformed body as art object than about the surgery itself, they did produce "relics," as Tanya Augsburg notes, little jars of her suctioned fat that
the artist then sold to call attention to the female body as commodity.[21] In
subsequent performances, parts of the final series of surgeries, entitled
The Reincarnation of Saint Orlan, the artist underwent a set of videotaped
surgeries, appropriating physical features of various women in famous
works of Western art in an implicit critique of the history of standards of
beauty, even as the results defy "the current supermodel ideals of
beauty."[22] Augsburg also calls Orlan's performances self-conscious blur-
rings of the subject/object distinction that seems to mark much of feminist performance art in this period, and I think it is important to note that
this corporeal self-construction also represents the artist co-opting herself
as object in order to establish her subjectivity. In essence, Orlan manipu-
lates her body as an object of the gaze to at once reveal how that body is
already subject to discourse and to demonstrate some measure of control
over that discourse by constructing the body's outward appearance to
make specific and pointed critiques about the status of women's bodies as
objects in general.

While Orlan's work—both the surgical performances and the photographic exhibitions she still does—complicates the discursive conventions surrounding women's bodies, transsexual performer and activist
Kate (née Al) Bornstein, pushes further to deeply undermine the naturalized categories of gender, sex, and sexuality. Her performance piece *The
Opposite Sex Is Neither* suggests the degree to which corporeal construction taps into more abstract notions of identity. While the piece is largely
made up of character monologues, its autobiographical elements and
Bornstein's own gender identity make her work particularly fertile
ground for examining the degree to which both sexual and gender identity are social constructions. Indeed, it is difficult to call Bornstein a feminist, since after taking on the physical sex traits of a female, she insists that
she is no longer female: "I went from male to female in this world, (and
then to neither, but that's another story entirely)" she asserts.[23] Nonetheless, her transsexual performances force her audiences to reconsider the
dissonances in her identity, revealing the fissures in the social discourse
that surrounds both gender and sex identity categories. While her body is

at least the simulacra of femaleness (photos reveal her to be, in true drag style, more female than female), her genetic composition still maintains the Y chromosome, and her life history contains, Tiresias-like, both male and female experiences—a notion that underscores how deeply dependent conceptions of identity still depend on gender categories. Given that the social discourse has no neatly marked category for her, her identity confounds the very existence of such categories, even as social codes like naming and dress tend toward performances of femaleness. Performers like Bornstein and Orlan, then, seem to be using the self in performance as a way to pick apart the notion of the body as signifier of identity, a notion that girded much earlier feminist performance art.

Still, we mustn't confuse such explicit body performance with autobiographical narrative per se. Bornstein does use some autobiographical text to provide context for the self-constructed body she puts on display. But in writing about Orlan, Augsburg asserts, "If we are to take Orlan's own statements about her life and work seriously, we need to first consider her art in relation to her autobiography."[24] Such a statement reveals the importance of the self-created life narrative in understanding the larger point of Orlan's body art, but its structured dialectic between art and autobiography also suggests to a certain degree that the creation of that life narrative is not central to Orlan's work. In fact, the distinction between embodied art and life narrative in the cases of both performers begins to refute the claims of the unmediated presence of the self asserted by Elwes and Forte. As their work in the 1990s seems to suggest, if the constructed bodies of Orlan and Bornstein, mediated by surgical and videographic technology, can be said to be artwork unto themselves, and the life narratives are merely the context, then the status of the body becomes unreliable as an essential signal of presence and subjectivity.

And yet, even as these performances seek to deconstruct gendered norms and binaries, we might also suggest the ways in which they depend on these binaries to make meaning. Orlan's embodied performances, even as they unmake the "feminine," do so on the very grounds of the "female." That is, she may subvert the shape that gendered codes might take on, but she does so by relying on a received correlation between sex and gender. Bornstein's case is more complicated, especially once her work began to assert transgendered identity as distinct from either male or female, and yet her public persona continues to take on the surface elements of femaleness, and even a hyperfeminity. And while she might be taking seriously Butler's call to insistently and persistently make gender itself a site for radical performative play, to do so continues to traffic in the language of a bifurcated system of gendered norms. In fact, even as political rhetoric, these performances remain bound by the codes that govern bodies as sexed, even under technological intervention. Given that these particular bodies become objects for public consumption, we can also see that feminist performers might find this distancing and denaturalizing effect to be desirable in establishing an autonomous female subject. And yet this distanced subject remains potent in part because of its femaleness (as site of political critique), and marginalized for the same reason (as frivolous, unserious, hysterical), a point that the most radically deconstructive performances run up against continuously.

The Performativity of Self

To suggest an untroubled binary between body and narrative that posits the body as constructible and the life narrative as somehow more discrete, more authentic, is similarly problematic. Linda S. Kauffman calls artists such as Schneeman, Sprinkle, and Orlan "cut-ups," not only because they often deploy humor as a denaturalizing tactic but also because they "examine the vicissitudes of psychic life, particularly the drives that lead men to turn the female body into fetish, icon or cut-out."[25] Similarly, Amelia Jones links the deconstructed body to a deconstruction of psychic life by suggesting, "Body art splinters rather than coheres the self; far from assuming some presocial coherence of the self, body art enacts narcissism as contingency."[26] And, indeed, if assertions of the constructible body reveal the contingency of the self that the body might be said to "contain," then the discourse of autobiography, with its now well-established emphasis on the notion of the life narrative as mediated and to some degree necessarily fictional, ups the ante even further.

"Body art," as Jones calls it, does indeed invoke the fragmentary subject through constructions of the body, but its interrogation of the self does not necessarily indicate the narrativizing of a life history that autobiography does. When these narrative lives are performed, though, they similarly, and perhaps more significantly, reveal the contingent status of the speaking subject. Surveying the range of performances that explore alternate and fantasy identities, Marvin Carlson asserts, "It would thus be very difficult to construct a clear line between the mimetic characters of traditional drama and the authentic 'alternate identities' of autobiographical performance."[27] That the boundary between these forms is blurred underscores the necessarily fictional component expressed most clearly at the outer edges of what we might call autobiographical by performers like Whoopi Goldberg or even Carmelita Tropicana. Indeed, Carmelita Tropicana is the stage name of Alina Troyano, though it is a persona by which she has been known offstage as well.

This blurring of constructed persona and "real life" extends quite thoroughly to her performance. In the introduction to the published text of her 1993 piece *Milk of Amnesia—Leche de Amnesia,* Tropicana writes, "In *Milk* I combined the campy stylized satire with a more personal autobiographical style. In this solo, I was able to let my schizophrenia surface, turning it into art."[28] This casual reference to schizophrenia at once taps into the notion of the fragmented subject. More important, the intermingling of "stylized satire," art of overt, even extreme artifice, and autobiography, which is presumed to be real, indicates the degree to which Tropicana's art plays with her own identity in order to problematize the very nature of that identity. We might note that she even refers to her more "authentic" source of material as "a more personal autobiographical *style,*" slyly pointing out the degree to which even the personal is stylized, just like her satire. In the piece itself, Tropicana moves from persona to persona (including ones named "Carmelita" and "Writer"), detailing her amnesia, a forgetting of her Cuban identity through American assimilation, and her recovery of that identity through the exploration of these many personas. Cultural identity here is connected to memory, and through Tropicana's process of remembering, when her amnesia has been eradicated, there is still no discrete identity to be claimed. "After so many years in America, I can drink two kinds of milk. The sweet condensed milk of Cuba and the grade-A, pasteurized homo kind from America," she tells us.[29] A unified national self is impossible to recover, if, indeed, it ever existed at all.

Locating an authentic self in this piece is equally fruitless. It certainly is not Pingalito Betancourt, "the Cuban Antonio Banderas,"[30] who welcomes us to the show. We might, however, consider the characters of Writer and Carmelita. Both seem to narrate the same life, but they speak in markedly distinct voices. Writer's is a methodical, date-oriented voice that narrates events in a straightforward fashion; Carmelita's is a more figurative, reflective, out-of-time voice, one that suggests a real fragmentation of selves. The end of the piece further problematizes this divide, since the character of Carmelita's final lines is notated thus: "(STEPPING

OUT OF CARMELITA CHARACTER AND ADDRESSING THE AUDIENCE.) I agree with Pedro Luis, and I want to leave you with a song by him called 'Todos Por lo Mismo,' a song that says it best . . . (THE TAPE PLAYS SEVERAL CHORUSES AS CARMELITA EXITS)."[31] There is a curious calculus of identities here, since, while the character speaking has stepped out of the central role and is therefore not Carmelita, it is also not Writer, the persona equated in the introduction with autobiographical voice. Yet we are clearly meant to assume that the persona that remains is some sort of authentic self, since stepping out of character is typically interpreted as stepping back into the "real world." Curiously, the stage directions note that it is Carmelita who exits, reminding us that the identity "Carmelita" functions in real life as well. Furthermore, if these words are spoken in yet another voice, that of Alina Troyano, who is never named in the piece, then we might find the notion of "authentic self" problematic, even empty, since this voice says nothing of its own, except to agree with another person altogether, and to play us his song. When this last voice speaks, the one we might otherwise assume to be the *most* authentic, have the *most* authority to establish identity, it actually seems almost *without* identity. As Chon Noriega writes in the introduction to Tropicana's collected works, *I, Carmelita Tropicana,* this multiplicity is central to her work.

> [The title] declares "I, Carmelita Tropicana," with an almost Cartesian certitude. But its two homonyms point in another direction, revealing the reaction of others to the self proclaimed identity. The first homonym registers shock, exasperation, or sexual pleasure as an interpersonal expression ("Aiiiy, Carmelita Tropicana"); the second conjures up the flip side of identity, the act of being seen and identified, the surveillance imperative that emerges alongside the lioberal notion of identity in the modern era ("Eye Carmelita Tropicana"). Identity is no simple matter here: What the self proclaims, another both authenticates and challenges by the very fact of a response.[32]

Therefore, identity in Tropicana's performance, be it Cuban, American, Carmelita, Writer, or Alina Troyano, is connected to reception—which is slippery, unpredictable, and out of the performer's control. It is connected as well to memory, which is always suspect, always compromised, always being created in an act of recovery, and revealing not a unified self, but fragmentation, multiplicity. "For Troyano," Noriega writes, "that 'multi' [of competing cultural systems] is language itself, but it is a lan-

guage that is always imprecise, especially when working between national cultures, political frameworks, or sexual orientations. Multi, multi,
multi."[33] For many feminist artists, this notion of fragmented identity is
part of a larger critique of the illusion of the coherent (straight, white,
male) subject as authority in classical autobiography; by revealing identity slippage, these performers argue that the authority of the individual
subject is contingent, even illusory. As Sidonie Smith writes, "Autobiographical narration begins with amnesia, and once begun, the fragmentary nature of subjectivity intrudes. After all, the narrator is both the same
and not the same as the autobiographer, and the narrator is both the same
and not the same as the subject of narration."[34] And in the case of *Milk of
Amnesia,* where the fragmentary subject not only intrudes but dominates,
the autobiographer, narrator, and narrated subject all appear as separate
personae, each alternately taking on roles that are the same and not the
same as the others.

Similarly, Bornstein, in the introduction to her partially autobiographical piece *Virtually Yours,* plays with the notion of the performer's
bio (which she points out is actually an autobiography written in the third
person). She muses, "Artists complain that 'my audiences don't know the
real me!' Good Lord, what on earth is the real me? The boy or man I used
to be? The woman I was briefly? Is the real me the ex-Scientology cult
member? Ex-IBM Salesman? Is the real me one of the several personas I
use when I do phone sex to pay the utility bills?"[35] After meditating on the
ease with which she could claim multiple identities, and, indeed, the absurdity of the theatrical bio as a way of establishing a coherent public
identity (and therefore a basis for public authority), Bornstein considers
the following one of the nine bios she offers.

> KATE BORNSTEIN has called over fifty-five geographical locations
> "home." Identitywise, she has transitioned from boy to man, from
> man to woman, from woman to lesbian, from lesbian to artist, from
> artist to sex worker, and it's taken her nearly fifty years of living to
> discover that she's actually more comfortable transitioning than she
> is in arriving at some resting place called an identity.[36]

The performance that follows remains true to this movement from persona to persona. Bornstein opens speaking as Allie (we recall that her
given name as a male was Al), a solo performer who receives calls from
Jayne (Wenger, Bornstein's lover and director of *Virtually Yours*) and Mark

Russell, proprietor of New York's famous performance art venue, P.S. 122. While we are to seemingly take this persona as autobiographical, it seems (as the introduction suggests) that this is no more the "real Kate" than is any of the five video-game avatars she takes on throughout the show as ways of confronting her fears. Ultimately, as she considers whether or not to leave her lover (who himself was going through a female-to-male transformation, Jayne to Daniel), she moves through these personas to come to the following question, asked by her video game: "Once the game is over and the players have left the field? Who am I?"[37] That this question remains unresolved by Bornstein's performance points to the degree to which the self claimed by Bornstein is as malleable as her sexed body, or, for that matter, any sexed body.

If such feminist autobiographical performances of the 1990s sought to establish both that the body is constructible and that selfhood is equally constructible, then the logical conclusions seemed to assert that the female body cannot be limited to the simple set of roles that patriarchal authority prescribes, nor is patriarchal authority itself any less a construction. Claire MacDonald, writing about British performance artist Bobby Baker, affirms this notion, describing the self in performance as a series of "assumed identities." In Baker's *Drawing on a Mother's Experience* (1988), the artist uses monologues from her life as a mother, and the material that comes from that life, to create a canvas. As the artist tells stories, she uses the items found in those stories—beer, milk, treacle—to "draw," after which she wraps herself into the canvas, making the work of art disappear. This performance of art (the canvas) alongside the performance of a mother's autobiography (the narrated monologues that accompany the production of the canvas's contents) signals, as MacDonald notes, a movement back and forth between two identities even as it shows the collapse of the work of art and the artist into one. She writes, "I read Bobby Baker's work as angry and subversive, using fractured notions of self to work across the divide between self as artist and self as mother. The divisions are signaled in her text and implied, of course, in her title *Drawing on a Mother's Experience*."[38] Even more than Orlan's surgical interventions on the status of the gendered body, which remain primarily limited to the corporeal self, this movement from role to role—and the refutation that this movement offers to the notion of an interior self "inside" the body—insinuates the concept of identity as unstable. Heddon describes Baker's presentation of self in similar terms.

Confronted by Bobby Baker playing Bobby Baker, I have no idea who
Bobby Baker is. It would be more accurate, then to refer to the identities constructed in her work, since there is no single cohesive subject
being represented. The contradictions and ambiguities are crucially
important devices in undercutting the inhabited stereotypical representations and suggesting the inherent complexity of subjectivity, of
"being" a person. If autobiography enables the production of subjectivity, then Baker uses this strategically to construct a "self" that is
multiple, complex and perhaps ultimately unknowable.[39]

Indeed, these readings of Baker's performance suggest that the autobiographical life, like the very notion of gender, is performative. Just as in the
late 1980s and early 1990s, Judith Butler argues that gender does not preexist the set of actions that constitutes it, and Sidonie Smith argues soon
afterward that a coherent identity does not preexist the self-produced
narrative that orders it: "Narrative performativity constitutes identity.
That is, the interiority or self that is said to be prior to the autobiographical expression or reflection is an *effect* of autobiographical storytelling."[40]
In short, the identity, or internal self (or in the cases of many performers,
multiple selves, public and private), that we might say is being outwardly
expressed in an autobiographical performance is actually being created
by that performance. That Smith made this argument in 1995 seems to
suggest not only a theoretical/philosophical truism about autobiography;
it also suggests the historicity of this argument. Indeed fifteen years later,
autobiography studies (as I will explore more in the next chapter) is beginning to seek out some notion of the essential connection between the
narrating body and the narrated self through cognitive narrative theory,
as well as through theories of disability. And yet, in the mid-1990s, artists
and theorists seemed to be speaking in very similar terms. For example, in
her introduction to *Milk of Amnesia—Leche de Amnesia*, Carmelita Tropicana echoes the same sort of impulse as does Smith to blur the lines between life and performance by asking, "Could it be true that artists don't
suffer from broken hearts, we just get material?"[41] Her question, more
complex than it initially appears, implicitly asks whether life itself *is* material, whether the making of experience into narrative actually creates
the self—or the selves—who experiences it. Artists like Baker, who moves
from role to role, or Tropicana and Bornstein, who move from persona to
persona, or Laurie Anderson, whose *Stories from the Nerve Bible* relies on
self-contradicting narratives of self, overtly call into question the very na-

ture of identity, thereby problematizing the seemingly stable categories they perform and hope to explode: woman, mother, citizen, outsider, lesbian, artist. In short, these artists perform the self to suggest selfhood as performative. And in doing so they are capitalizing on, at the very least, the political value of theories of performativity (if not necessarily a specific truth value to those theories themselves), in order to destabilize the roles that have historically discouraged women from making art, and implicitly and explicitly refute the idea that art making is outside a woman's domain.

Exemplary of the sorts of performances that capitalize on the rhetorical potential of such constructionist theories of gendered identity, Bobby Baker's *Kitchen Show: One Dozen Kitchen Actions Made Public* (1991) asserts the performativity of female social codes and autobiography as an expression of those codes. Her show is constructed as thirteen individual units (a Baker's dozen, of course), each of which contains three elements: an autobiographical monologue; an action, listed in the program; and a mark, some way of literally marking her performing body as a way of remembering the experience she narrates. Take, for example action No. 3 where Baker illustrates the anger and frustration of her homemaker's life by throwing a pear against a cupboard door. That monologue and action are then marked with *"Mark No. 3:* To put a pear in the top of my overall— all ready for the next occasion."[42] This series of monologues, thus contextualized, argue for the autobiographical performance as completely performative. By phrasing her mark of each monologue as an action, Baker explicitly turns our understanding of her performance (and therefore her identity) into a verb rather than a noun or object. "Throwing a ripe pear against a cupboard door" is an action constituted by language,[43] a stylized act that itself takes a step toward narrating Baker's experience and ultimately constituting her identity as a woman capable of experiencing rage (which for Carolyn Heilbrun is a hallmark of feminist autobiography). Moreover, the constructed body of autoperformance is implicated in the mark that follows each action. Heddon writes, "Baker's performance manages to bring to the surface—often literally—what is so often invisible or denied (because it is felt inappropriate to the 'role')."[44] In this way, Baker's corporeal identity is publicly constructed and presented through the actions she performs and the monologues she utters. The pear in her overall is a pointer to the action of throwing, which itself, through narration, produces an artifact of Baker's anger. Therefore, Baker's corporeal identity is a trace, a memory of those performative and uttered iterations that constitute the self.

Baker's performance also foregrounds the notion of performativity in its content, as well as its structure. For instance, she consistently emphasizes the concept of repetition in her piece. Lesley Ferris notes the ritualistic quality of Baker's work, the way that each unit binds her body to the actions she performs, and through this ritual, "The kitchen space becomes a site for sharing, telling, demonstrating and enacting her fantasies of chaos and violence. The kitchen is the space where we serve our guests, but it is also a daily battlefield of onerous tasks and repetitive activity."[45] The affinity of Baker's performance with ritual and her choice to reproduce the most repetitive tasks of homemaking foreground repetition as a component of domestic identity. In another monologue, Baker reflects on a freshly opened tub of margarine and remarks, "I've said it before and I'll say it again—it's moments like this that make it all worthwhile." The emphasis on repetition ("I've said it before and I'll say it again") signals to the audience that she *has* said this before, every time she opens a new tub of margarine in front of an audience. The return to this domestic moment in performance after performance underscores how homemakers themselves return to the same tasks in their proscribed roles as women in the home.

Baker's emphasis on the repetitive nature of homemaking further taps into the performative nature of the self, especially in its most proscribed gender roles. Repetition is, for Judith Butler, a crucial component in the performativity of gender. Among her simplest iterations of her theory of gender performativity is that gender is "an identity instituted through a *stylized repetition of acts*."[46] That is, through the continuous and compulsory performance of a range of specific activities and gestures, gender is constituted and becomes a system of control. In Baker's performance, such repetition signals not only the degree to which women's roles in the home are performative constructions but also the degree to which cultural norms insist that these constructions be reified over and over again by demanding their repetition: serving tea, cleaning, and cooking must be repeated daily for the woman to be a "good" homemaker. And yet, as Butler later iterates in "Imitation and Gender Insubordination," "It is precisely the repetition of that play that establishes as well [as the power exerted through gender and sexuality categories] the *instability* of the very category that it constitutes."[47] Therefore, by underscoring the repetitive nature of the activities she chooses to perform, Baker's performance constitutes a specific gendered identity while simultaneously destabilizing that identity by calling public attention to the very performativity of its operations within the space of performance.

Finally, in action No. 13, Baker stands on a cake plate to display the marks of her performance on her body. These marks are not subtle: She is drenched with water and has a spoon in her hair, a plastic trash bag draped over her shoulders, cutlery hanging around her neck, and dishtowels affixed to her shoes. She remarks, "I stand with one foot on the cake stand and revolve around slowly so that all the marks can be noted and remembered. It's the image they make all together that matters most." Her identity as homemaker is now put on display, coherent when viewed all together but made up of a series of stylized actions, exactly as Butler defines gender: *Kitchen Show* is thirteen stylized gestures—actions with corporeal marks accompanied by self-narration—that place Baker within the domestic sphere most commonly associated with women (i.e., female gender). Taken together, these bodied marks, the actions that they point to, and the narration that these actions engender encompass the entirety of her show; what we may call her entire identity as revealed in this autobiographical performance. By breaking her gender roles down in this way, and pointing in her final tableau to the way they *seem* to make up a complete, unified portrait of femininity, Baker methodically deconstructs these roles as distinctly and repetitively performative. In short, Baker not only moves fluidly between her identities as homemaker and artist but she also reveals the performative nature of both identity categories.

When performance artists present the self in this way, they reveal the performative, constructed nature of gender in order to critique the very idea of gender identity, and they do so both by undermining the body as a coherent, meaningful entity and by undermining the notion of a unified subjectivity that can speak in the moment. We will recall, however, that the presence of the woman's body as speaking subject is precisely what 1970s feminist artists claimed as the political power in autobiographical performance. While these conflicting ideas potentially represent a problem for these various feminist ideologies, arguments abound that work to reconcile them. We must first recognize, however, that what remains after all of the discourse of the sexed and gendered body and all of the discourse of multiple, fragmented identities is exposed is precisely and only the *agency to construct those identities and participate in the discourse.* Again speaking of Baker, MacDonald asserts, "In all performance art the artist is always present *as* agent but to allow for a range of readings the subjectivity of the artist must always be left open to question, fluid, ambiguous and unsettled."[48] The performances discussed here call into question all of the mechanisms by means of which women are circumscribed into specific biological, cosmetic, or social roles, precisely because these are the mechanisms that deny women's agency. So the performance of the constructable female body (sex and gender) and the fluid feminist self is at least a two-front operation. It both refutes boundaries placed on female identity and further asserts the ability of a woman to construct her own identity, her own life, and to control both her own body and *to some degree* society's perception of that body.

Indeed, much of the impetus of this agency to construct the self in the moment of performance derives from the ability to self-name. While many performers certainly use their given names in autobiographical performance (the "real" name is indeed a signifier of authenticity), the ability to control the discourse of the self can be revealed with direct attention to the naming of the performer herself. For example, while Bobby Baker does use her real name, she calls attention to the gendered aspect of that name at the beginning of her performances by saying "I'm Bobby Baker. Once a long time ago someone expected to see a man, so I want you to know that this is me."[49] Baker's introduction illuminates the power of naming: by calling attention to her gender-ambiguous name, she is able to foreground the role gender construction will play in the rest of the show. For others, though, naming is part of the act of self-definition. Carmelita Tropicana's chosen name taps into the stylized camp persona that she uses on- and offstage. Kate Bornstein's name signifies to some degree the notion of transformation that she embraces, but her choice to take "Allie" as the autobiographical character name signifies the fluidity that she ultimately seeks to promote, standing as it does on the brink between "Al Bornstein," her given name, and "Alice Silverman," her character's name. Orlan has similarly called attention to the act of naming as a significant component of the performance of subjectivity, claiming for some period of time that she would "ask an advertising agency to change her name and then will go to court to have her name changed legally."[50] In making naming a part of her art of self-transformation, calling attention to the commodification of the self by involving an ad agency, and implicating the juridical status of the subject by seeking to make the name change a legally binding performance, Orlan's claims tapped into the notion of self-naming as productive of the subject's status as such, and of the performer's agency to construct the discourse of the self that naming entails.

But if identity cannot be said to preexist narration, can any notion of the performer's agency preexist narration either? Butler's notions of subjectivity suggest that even the subject cannot be said to preexist the act. Similarly, Foucault argues that the individual becomes a subject (as it operates within systems of power) at the moment of confession, just as Smith argues that subjectivity appears through the act of self-narration. And the notion of agency in self-performance also raises the specter of the intention, as we consider how to interpret the self in performance when the embodied author is present to speak for her text, an issue I will take up in the following chapter. In short, it is perhaps too easy to say that agency remains the essential component of selfhood as revealed in performance. For after all, if women's autobiographical performance is a direct refutation of those forces that seek to co-opt women's agency, can it not be said that until those forces are themselves deconstructed, women's agency is as tenuous as the subject that might be said to claim it?

In that sense, the performance of self-narration not only constitutes identity, but it also constitutes the very agency that might be said to shape that identity. Therefore when a feminist performer such as Bobby Baker performs the role of homemaker in *Kitchen Show,* a role that is often perceived as one without agency, one that serves patriarchy, she is not only critiquing perceptions of the domestic sphere and revealing "homemaker" to be a construction that she creates in her performance, she is also moving the role into a position of agency by making it a site of insistent play. It is this excess of signification that both produces the subject in real time and provides the critique of the same notions of identity that have historically worked to make the speaking female subject an oxymoron.[51] Moreover, the self that is constituted by performed narrative disappears as narration passes, leaving only traces (marks no. 1–13 in Baker's case), and according to Peggy Phelan, "The after-effect of disappearance is the experience of subjectivity itself."[52] It is precisely this disappearance, this performativity of autoperformance, this slippery subject fluidly moving from identity to identity across time and space, that makes such explicit self-narration not only powerful but impossible to contain.

To suggest that the performance of self constitutes the agency necessary to perform the self may seem tautological (see "Introduction"). But we must remember that agency and intention are not precisely the same things; agency here has a public component. The autobiographer becomes a public agent by bringing the heretofore private experience of selfhood to the stage. This dissolve of the public/private barrier—a barrier that Kate Bornstein, for example, openly denigrates—represents the entrance of the performer into agency, identity, and ultimately power. There is a radical notion at work in this moment of self-proclamation: it is the achievement of presence through the declaration of presence. The self appears in real time because it is precisely *the self* that the performer chooses to construct in real time. That self may be fragmentary, multiple, and assumed or it may appear to be unmediated, aligned with an essential notion of the sign "woman" precisely because the artist chooses that self-definition. Therefore, the single linear narrative of Linda Montano's *The Story of My Life* is just as radical as Carmelita Tropicana's avowedly "schizophrenic" self-construction, and Carolee Scheeman's work (sometimes interpreted as essentialist) is no less performative than Bornstein's, precisely because all of these performances choose to perform the self (and its past) in real time, in the presence of an audience.

The Performative Self and the Performative Community

While the performer's choice to perform in public is specifically a self-constitutive move, its constitutive power radiates outward as well, linking the discursive self with a discursively constituted audience as well, creating within the category "audience" an implicit sense of community. Certainly, a step toward community is forged under the material conditions of the theater, in which audience members choose, of their own volition, to arrive at a theatrical space for the purpose of witnessing a performance. And yet this alone does little to create the sort of community that might be united by a call for social change—in this case, a change in the ways that gender is perceived and treated in Western postmodern culture. The moment of performance, however, also brings the audience together in more rhetorically significant ways, since it places the audience within the realm of the performer's experience. Such experience is precisely the source of the performer's autobiographical narrative, which itself is the site at which the performer's agency is constituted and her rhetoric generated. Since the performance of identity is also the narration of past experience, the audience makes an assumption (based on the assumption of the truth claims crucial to the label "autobiography") that the experience itself continues from the past of the narrative into the present of the performance. This extrapolated continuation of the author's narrated past into the performed present places the audience within the experience of the performer, and thus within the unnarrated part of her life. Charlotte Canning goes so far as to suggest that this effect creates a collective subjectivity in the context of what she terms "contiguous autobiography." She writes:

> In solo performance [a collective sense of subjectivity] usually meant the creation of a collective autobiography through the convergence of the performer's autobiography with the spectator's in the moment of performance. All these performance forms work to foreground the idea that one's autobiography is not one's alone, but is part of a larger narrative about the experience of women in a particular culture. Thus, an autobiographical performance is not only the story of one woman's "life," but also the story of the construction of "a woman" in that culture.[53]

Performer Holly Hughes offers a less theoretically inclined version of this idea, but one more concrete. In the introduction to her *Clit Notes: A Sapphic Sampler,* she writes, "This part of the script isn't finished. My role in the Culture War is still very much a work in progress, a story I'm telling as I'm living it. But the point is, it needs to be performed in front of an audience. If I'm ever going to be able to write this wrong, I'll need your help."[54] As such, the audience is transformed into a feminist community—one marked as much by its ideological commonality as its fragmented identities—existing together within the performer's experience in the present and joining her in her ideological fight.

Since I have suggested that, following the performative turn in autobiographical solo performance, the performer's life narrative is rarely presented as coherent, unified, unmediated, nor even precisely "present" as a coherent whole (nor can we say its ontological status coheres in any similar way), it becomes impossible to claim that the audience can be constituted as a coherent community when brought within the presence of that performer. Instead, what links the performer to each audience member as a member of a community is the discursive formation of narrative and rhetoric that makes up the feminist performance itself. It is the common entrance into the rhetorically charged and politically contested performance—as action and utterance—that constitutes the formation of

community. Indeed, Bornstein's *Virtually Yours* has the performer enter-
ing the "video game" wherein she constitutes and reconstitutes her identity by playing out various fears through various personas. The moment
in which the "Virtual Audience" appears (or rather, the moment when the
house lights are raised) is the moment in which Bornstein enters into the
game, and therefore into the narrative exploration of her and her part-
ner's transsexual identities. The audience makes the performance, and
the performance makes Bornstein's identity. "Of course I want an audience," she says, "I'm a performer."[55] Tim Miller and David Román write
about the importance of queer performance not as a primarily didactic
tool but as a tool for creating community, an observation we can also apply to feminist performance (especially since many of the performers discussed here would self-identify as both queer and feminist). Miller and
Román argue that "Once gathered into this space, spectators, artists and
technicians enact, even if only temporarily, community."[56] As the performer's narrative creates a discursive lightning rod around which community develops, each player in the ritual—from technician down to
spectator, is performing that community.

   Similarly, Jill Dolan, in describing what she calls the "utopian performative," identifies performance as an impetus for a notion of community
that serves as the lynchpin for social change. She explains, "Audiences are
compelled to gather with others, to see people reconsider and change the
world outside the theater, from its macro to its micro arrangements. Perhaps part of the desire to attend the theater and performance is to reach
for something better, for new ideas about how to be and how to be with
each other."[57] For Dolan, the development of community within the space
of the performance event gives live theater a potential for a specific type
of social change, here "how to be with each other." She goes on to describe
three feminist performers—Holly Hughes, Peggy Shaw, and Deb Margolin—as their performances created utopian performatives during a fall
2000 performance series in Austin, Texas. She defines *performance* in this
context as "an address to an audience that converts strangers into community" and describes moments in each performance that flesh that definition out.[58] In Peggy Shaw's performance of *The Menopausal Gentleman*,
for example, Dolan describes a moment when Shaw "leaves the space
marked off for performance to approach the audience, to mingle freely,
empathizing, greeting, allowing for moments of identification, curiosity,
desire, even love to extend through the audience."[59] In this moment,
which Dolan describes as "intersubjective," Shaw's performance brings

the audience members together as part of *her community,* constructing them as part of her experience, and therefore as a group of people more closely bound to her and to one another than when they entered, and therefore more prepared, as Dolan puts it, to "change the world outside the theatre."[60]

But it is the discourse of the life narrative in these performances, the need to simultaneously interact with a performer's life even as we objectify it, that generates the discourse of community. While written life narratives let the audience share in the author's life experience, performance of life narratives creates an even richer exchange, since not only does an audience member experience something with the playwright/performer but she also shares it with other audience members, while the performer herself shares in the audience members' experience just as they share in hers. The shared community, however, excites both rhetorical possibilities and political anxieties. Román and Miller note that these audiences:

> Bring to the theatrical occasion a specific social paradox. On the one hand, the support of many lesbian and gay audiences for community-based theatre results from the desire to be in a crowd of other lesbian and gay people. This desire rests on the comforts of identity politics and easily adapts to the primacy of sexuality in identity construction. And yet, on the other hand, many spectators also attend community-based events in order to defy the politics of sameness.[61]

Indeed, this paradox is just as evident (though in a somewhat different way) for feminist audiences and performers. Although the desire for community among ideologically sympathetic women (and men to a lesser degree) brings these communities together by posing the feminist life narrative as a site for identification and as a common experience for both audience and performer, the move to subvert essentialism (an essentialism that might be propped up by the cultural feminist emphasis on community as a uniquely female value) is perhaps even more powerful when connected to female bodies as opposed to queer practices.

As such, we see feminist performances that toggle back and forth between a general critique of the larger category "woman" and a reliance on the particulars of the individual life. Bobby Baker's *Kitchen Show,* for example draws on the common experiences of being a housewife and mother as a way of critiquing the proscribed gender roles of women, even as she celebrates the work that women do in these roles. Thus, she creates a commonality among her viewers, a sense of solidarity based on the similarity of their experiences, even as she demands that they recognize that those experiences derive from socially constructed assignments.

Conclusion

In the formulation of life writing in performance that I laid out in the Introduction, this conception of audience community—as a construction constituted by performance—is a lynchpin in the truth effect of life writing in performance. But typically, this effect tends to uphold the illusion of a coherent essential self, an identity framed by a true historical narrative of the discrete body and voice of the performer, verified by the participating audience. But when performers begin to break down one element or another of this chain of signification, as was frequently the case in the deconstructive feminist performances of the 1980s and 1990s, then the illusion of coherence tends to tumble with it. Different performers have worked in different ways to deconstruct the specifically gendered elements of identity. Carmelita Tropicana works through a deconstructed sense of personal and cultural history, while Kate Bornstein undercuts the coherence of the body as a marker of binary identity categories. Meanwhile, Bobby Baker works at destabilizing the very identities of womanhood that she herself inhabits. If anything, though, the construction of audience through performance tends to remain the most reliable component of this chain. Certainly, as a rhetorical system, a deconstructive performance of self requires an audience as much as does as essentialist performance, precisely because such performances are political even more than they are experimental.

This fact alone underscores to a large degree how such performances work, and why they functioned so effectively as theatrical laboratories for theories of performativity. Because as formal experiments they not only provide safe spaces in which to test the ontologies of self in public, the very possibility of testing those ontologies bears political and rhetorical weight. Inasmuch as the performative self in performance makes "the 'sex' of gender into a site of insistent political play" as Butler prescribes, it is doing so within the confines of an audience whose own identities are tied into the performance as members of the audience community has lasting effects. If, as Canning suggests, the contiguous autobiography of a woman transforms into a collective subjectivity of "Woman," then we might suppose that an autobiographical performance that destabilizes that category for the performer may do so for the audience as well. Such performances then become important not for the sameness that they acknowledge across the space from the stage to the audience but rather for its insistence on bridging difference.

In this way, feminist performances of performativity work as both experiments in self and experiments in the rhetorical and political value of such public experimentation itself. For upward of three decades, feminist performance artists (and I explicitly include lesbian and other queer performers in this category) have used the stage as a space in which to deconstruct stable boundaries of gendered, sexed, and sexualized identities by calling attention to the very fact that these identities are constructed in performance. In doing so, they work to destabilize the rhetorical system that maps self, body, voice, narrative, and history onto one another as a coherent whole, and make the audience complicit in this deconstructive political act, a complicity that they might have otherwise used in service of upholding a more traditional rhetorical system of self-performance. So for artists as diverse as Bobby Baker, Kate Bornstein, Orlan, and Carmelita Tropicana, the notion of performativity—as expressed by Judith Butler and those work around her—is useful precisely because of the opportunities and possibilities it affords as a political tool, one for dismantling gendered and sexed structures of power.

CHAPTER 2 : Autobiography and the Rhetoric of the Embodied Self

While over the last two decades, theories of performativity dominated the academic discourse of gender (and to a lesser extent that of theatrical performance), feminist performers have been reluctant to embrace the concept quite so thoroughly. In the previous chapter, we have seen the ways in which performance artists have used the concept of performativity to establish gender, sex, and sexuality as constructions of discourse. Yet these uses were never uniform and were frequently posited as rhetorical tactics as much as definitive ontologies of gender, sex, and selfhood. That is, performativity frequently served these artists as a *persuasive* tactic, one that worked in its historical moment to begin to dismantle the tangled web of obstacles to power. But at the same time, many performers and playwrights—indeed sometimes the very same performers and playwrights—held on to a notion that the body established an anchor point for body, experience, and identity. This preference for presence, for the body as a marker of a preexisting identity in the here and now, has its roots in the beginnings of feminist autobiographical performance, but it, too, has been marshaled in rhetorical service of a more theoretically sophisticated sense of the female body in performance, both in cases where the gendered body's presence as a historical marker carries discursive political weight and in cases where the experience of the disabled body demands acknowledgment of the relationship among history, self, and society.

There is, of course, a long-documented tension between *essentialist accounts* of the female body in performance as rooted in a deeply embodied experience and expression of the self, and *performative accounts* of the body as a mere surface on which social discourses of gender, sex, and identity are inscribed and contested. Radical versions of each of these accounts suggest that an essentialist (or a cultural-feminist, second-wave, or biologistic) view is incommensurable with a performative (or deconstructive, materialist, or constructionist) view. I would argue that both approaches have an ontological basis, and I will work from the premise that some at least primal notion of identity can be located in the corporeal body, even as the body itself, as well as a more advanced sense of identity, is subject to the flows of cultural discourse. That is, the performer's body is both an anchor for and constraint on the many possible iterations of selfhood that are always imbricated with the material body, that are always constructable and contestable within a massively complex matrix of discourse and power. Moreover, I maintain that as a laboratory for the political impact of these competing ontologies of the gendered self, feminist autobiographical performance has consistently implemented both approaches in such a way as to exploit the political potential of each position. While the previous chapter argued for the political uses of a performative approach to gendered identity, here I want to establish the continuing role of the body as an origin point for female and feminist identities in performance. And across a history of feminist autobiographical performance, we can trace four trends in both theory and praxis: one, that an insistence on the embodiedness of the female performer relies on an essentialist underpinning, even when that performer is deconstructing other more insidious essentialisms; two, that the consistent deployment of an embodied feminist self in performance across the last fifty years (and perhaps even longer) amounts to a historical feminist aesthetic of performance; three, that even in highly deconstructive performances, the body of the performer remains an archive of her historical experience in ways that may exceed her intentions as a performer; and four, that the female body, and indeed, perhaps, even the underpinnings of our biological humanness, form the basis for a mutuality on which the establishment of a politicized feminist community in the theater depends.

While this chapter locates and examines the tendency of feminist autobiographical performance to deploy essentialist tactics (or even a full-fledged aesthetics of essentialism), I am less interested in arguing for or against the logic of the body as an essential marker of selfhood and more in exploring the conditions and functions of its use. Therefore, in what follows, I want to concentrate on three moments in a history of feminist autobiographical performance, each of which tended to use the body as an *essential* marker of identity for related but conflicting rhetorical purposes. In the 1960s and 1970s, performers such as Linda Montano, Yvonne Rainier, and Carolee Schneeman invoked the embodied autobiography as a form of *écriture feminine,* French philosopher Hélène Cixous's notion of an explicitly female writing that derives from the woman's body. And while this idea and approach to performance fell out of critical favor alongside second-wave feminism, there remained the kernel of this idea: that a woman's embodied experience is crucial, if not central, to her identity and political voice. Then, in the 1980s and 1990s, during the heyday of the WOW Café, the wake of the Culture Wars, and the NEA Four case, Karen Finley and Holly Hughes, both plaintiffs in that Supreme Court case, relied on that notion as they sought to reanimate their experiences in performance. And finally, more recently, as activist performances of disability have found their way onto a more prominent place on the stage, an even more trenchant critique of pure constructionist notions of the body has suggested the limits of performativity as an effective stance, even as a clearer theoretical base for disability activism has emerged. In response to the medicalized transformation of the disabled body into metaphor, feminist and queer performers such as Susan Miller and Terry Galloway worked to establish the body as a site of presence beyond not only metaphor but even language itself. That each of these three moments in a history of feminist performance depends on an essentialized notion of the relationship of the female body to the self should not discount their sophistication either as politicized works of art or as effective feminist texts. Indeed, I follow Diana Fuss in asking, "If this text is essentialist, *what motivates its deployment?*"[1]

Second Wave: The Personal Body in Public Performance

From the height of second-wave feminism in the mid- to late twentieth century, autobiography as a narrative category has historically carried a strong appeal to feminist practitioners, onstage as well as in print. Frequently, feminist literary critics have discussed women's autobiographical texts within the context of their absence from a canon of autobiographical writing. These critics, frequently writing in the 1970s and 1980s, decried the degree to which the very category of autobiography had often been defined by male narratives like those of Saint Augustine and Benjamin Franklin, even as women's narratives from the same time periods presented a viable countertradition that had been thoroughly excluded from inquiry. Bella Brodzki and Celeste Schenck write that "the (masculine) tradition of autobiography beginning with Augustine had taken as its first premise the mirroring capacity of the autobiographer: *his* universality, *his* representativeness, *his* role as a spokesman for the community."[2] Such critics identify a logic inherent to this tradition, suggesting that the exemplary male recounts his life as a way of shoring up his public influence at the end of his life, as a way of determining his own legacy. Embedded in this notion are the ideas that autobiography signifies public impact and the author has some measure of control over that public impact.

It is no wonder, then, that these critics viewed the decided absence of women's narratives from earlier conceptions of the autobiographical canon as evidence of a lack of access to women's autonomous textual production. The underlying assumption was simply that through autobiography, a woman writer could more effectively control the presentation of her identity and experience within the public sphere, a position that pushed against a long history of women's circumscription within male narratives of dominance. The logic of this position rests on the notion that some measure of authority can be derived directly from the personal voice of autobiography, the first-person narration of the self as protagonist. This is a line of thought that derives directly from Hélène Cixous, whose landmark 1976 essay "The Laugh of the Medusa" asserted, "Woman must write her self: must write about women and bring women to writing, from which they have been driven away as violently as their bodies."[3] From this vantage point, the power to narrate the self into existence assumes an authority to exert control over how the self is perceived, how it is to be accepted into the discourse of women's experience in general, and how "woman must put herself into the text—as into the world and into history," even if the self and its reception are always to some degree inherently unreliable.[4] Susan S. Lanser notes that the personal voice does not retain the same sort of authority that the omniscient authorial voice might, and that "a female personal narrator risks the reader's resistance if the act of telling, the story she tells or the self she constructs through telling it transgresses the limits of the acceptably feminine."[5] But when the goal was *precisely* to transgress those norms of femininity, to break down the barriers that silence women's voices, then to speak in the first person, to speak as the self, represented at the very least the opportunity to exceed the restrictions traditionally placed on women.

Beyond simply the power to speak the self, autobiography also offered feminist writers and performers the opportunity to bring personal experience into the public sphere, even if that opportunity was itself already circumscribed within specific gendered codes of textuality. Carolyn G. Heilbrun notes, for example, the scorn typically associated with "confessional" narratives,[6] while Holly Hughes acknowledges that "memoirs and solo performances are frequently dismissed by critics as 'self-indulgent' and artless, as though there were no art involved in rescuing images and metaphors from the flotsam and jetsam of daily life."[7] The assumption of artlessness that the general public seems to attach to women's autobiographies (as well as those of other marginalized identities) suggests the degree to which the male tradition had reserved the *art* of autobiographical narrative for themselves, at the same time as they refused to accord the same status to the life narratives of othered identities. Since these performances are hardly artless, but instead intelligently constructed and forcefully argued, when we read them as such, we must then understand autobiography as opportunity: the introduction of the personal into the public sphere politicizes women's experience and forces the dominant discourse to acknowledge women's lives as legitimate sources of art and argument. Indeed, Marvin Carlson connects the power of the personal narrative to the shift toward narrative performance that was brought about through feminist performance.

> Clearly a major impetus for the shift from image to word was the work of feminist performers who beginning in the early 1970s offered an [sic] powerful alternative performance orientation that was deeply involved in social and political concerns and, thus, in textuality and narrativity. Personal experience was central to this work, and much of it was specifically autobiographical, such as Linda Montano's *The Story of My Life,* in which Montano walked uphill on a treadmill for three hours while reciting her autobiography into an amplification system or Yvonne Rainer's autobiographical performance *This is the Story of a Woman Who . . . ,* which she later made into a film.[8]

Heilbrun chooses the same time frame, with the 1973 publication of May Sarton's *Journal of Solitude,* as the watershed for feminist autobiography, "because Sarton deliberately retold the record of her anger. And above all other prohibitions, what has been forbidden women is anger, together with the open admission of the desire for power and control of one's life."[9] What Heilbrun's observation about Sarton and Carlson's claims about Montano and Rainer recognize is that the ability to assert narrative control over the personal material of one's life, often through expressions of rage, is a potent political statement that even today (as I suggest in the next chapter on Sarah Kane) runs against conventional views of the place of women in society. Furthermore, I would argue that while the later performative turn of the 1980s and 1990s would cast this view as somewhat naive, it is clear that during second-wave feminism this was a necessary step to enacting power in broader arenas and making more sophisticated claims about women's identity.

Of course while the narrative aspects of autobiography made that form appealing, the translation of narrative into performance enhanced that appeal, particularly for feminist critics of autobiographical performance in the years that preceded the appearance of more deeply constructionist theories of gender. Specifically, while autodiegesis was seen as emphasizing the speaking voice of women, the metaphor of the voice (as I have suggested) becomes more powerful when it becomes literalized on the space of the stage, marking not only visibility but also presence. I return to the words of Jeanie Forte, who argues, "Women's performance art has a particular disruptive potential because it poses an actual woman as speaking subject, throwing that position into process, into doubt, opposing the traditional conception of the single, unified (male) subject."[10] In revisiting these words in the context of the rhetoric of the present body, we can hear quite clearly the echoes of Cixous, who writes, "Women must write through their bodies, they must invent the impregnable language that will wreck the partitions, classes, and rhetorics, regulations and codes."[11] We can return again to Forte, who similarly presents the female body as writing subject (instead of as the written-upon object) which "clashes in dissonance with its patriarchal text, challenging the very fabric of representation by refusing that text."[12] Forte not only identifies the power of the speaking subject to define the actual woman, she also highlights the political importance of speech's ability to do so. We find in these two texts an attention to the combined potency of subjectivity, body, and language, and the challenge that both authors assert through the female body as speaker, as agent, and as presence which despite different aims (writing and performance) nonetheless allow us to imagine feminist autoperformance at a particular political nexus of power.

To illustrate the claims of the second-wave moment in a history of the essentialist impulse in women's performance, we might look to Carolee Schneeman's *Interior Scroll* (1975), which made explicit this marriage of autobiographical narrative, voice, and the body as subject. By verbally recounting an apparently autodiegetic text, which she reads from a scroll she unravels from her vagina, Schneeman collapses the notion of voice and body into one narrational identity. She reads:

> I met a happy man
> a structuralist filmmaker
> —but don't call me that,
> it's something else I do—
> he said we are fond of you
> you are charming
> but don't ask us
> to look at your films
> we cannot
> there are certain films
> we cannot look at
> the personal clutter
> the persistence of feelings
> the hand-touch sensibility
> the diaristic indulgence
> the painterly mess
> the dense gestalt
> the primitive techniques . . .[13]

Here Schneeman collapses into one performance the "personal clutter" and "diaristic indulgence" of autobiographical narrative (while critiquing the male filmmaker's resistance to it), along with the written text of auto-biography, the explicit image of her own female body, and the disruptive potential of her own female speech. Schneeman's piece crystallized the second-wave appeal of "presentness"—here understood as a confluence of voice and body in performance that signals the self—that early feminist autobiography deployed. Her performance positioned her as a woman who spoke in what cultural feminists understood to be female ways (personal, diaristic, emotionally grounded) through the uniquely female aspects of her body. Furthermore, she used this feminist lexicon to lampoon the structuralist filmmaker, a figure of male empowerment. Certainly, this performance can be read as an expression of Cixous's *ecriture feminine*, in which "by writing her self, woman will return to the body which has been more than confiscated from her. . . . Your body must be heard."[14] In doing so, Schneeman sought to disrupt patriarchal authority over women's bodies and social positions through the explicit performance of her female body, a stance that is itself rooted in a philosophical conflation of the self who makes political art with the body through which the art is made.

In this and other examples of what we might call the early stages of feminist autobiographical performance, we see a very particular approach to the political situation of women. Performances like Schneeman's would seem to support the assertion that women's emotions are valid material; that women must be accepted as present, embodied, speaking subjects; and that we must emphasize the femininity of the woman's body (e.g., Schneeman "giving birth" to her text). But even as Schneeman's performance suggests (in its literalization of much of Cixous's text) a deep essentialism, readings of its impulses suggest countervailing interpretations. Linda Kaufman, for example, notes, "In an interesting reversal, Schneeman locates thought inside the *body* rather than equating thought with *mind;* what 'comes out' are more signifiers than can ever be categorized and labeled."[15] Kauffman's resistance to reading Schneeman as deploying essentialism derives as much from a legitimate reading of the linguistic instabilities of Schneeman's performance as from a then current knee-jerk reaction against any essentialism. As Diana Fuss notes, "Few others words [*sic*] in the vocabulary of contemporary critical theory are so persistently maligned, so little interrogated, and so predictably summoned as a term of infallible critique."[16]

That critique has prevailed over the past two decades, consistent with the performative turn both in gender studies and, more specifically, in feminist studies of performance. Yet poststructuralist critics of gender and performance have been loathe to simply dismiss earlier performances like Montano's, Ranier's, and Schneeman's because these performers represent a crucial and radical intervention of female artists into histories of both art and performance. Therefore, these critics have sought to recuperate performances that might be discarded as *merely essentialist* by reading them as in fact already deploying sophisticated materialist arguments about the female body in performance. Here I want to consider the work of two theorists: Rebecca Schneider, whose 1997 *The Explicit Body in Performance* remains the definitive statement on the embodied signification of feminist performance; and James Harding's 2010 *Cutting Performances*, which puts such feminist performances more directly into conversation with a political avant-garde by writing a specifically feminist historiography of the avant-garde. Schneider imagines performances of the explicit female body as replaying "the historical drama of history or race . . . across the body of the artists as stage."[17] By configuring the body as stage, Schneider argues, these artists implicitly acknowledge the constructable nature of the female body as sign, that by performing the female body as a stage, such performances reveal the body to be performative (a claim, in fact, that I made in the previous chapter about somewhat later performances). Harding also reads this move specifically as antiessentialist, noting that Schneider's theorization of these performances "avoids a naïve sense of immediacy and authenticity. There is no sense here of nakedness as essence."[18] Harding goes onto to further assert that *"The feminist discourse for avant-garde performance only begins when the curtain has fallen on the myth of immediacy."*[19] Schneider would seem to confirm such a reading, arguing that "Modern construction and inscription of the female body, and more insidiously the 'reality effects' occasioned by those inscriptions, ghost contemporary counter-constructions."[20] Taken together, such commentary would therefore seem to read performances like Schneeman's as "counter-constructions" and thus complicit with the constructionist position that Schneider herself espouses. Given the cultural climate of *Interior Scroll,* however (performed a year before the publication of "The Laugh of the Medusa"), I am not entirely sure that Schneider's reading, while compelling as an ontology, is not anachronistic as an understanding of that performance's rhetorical project.

I further want to caution against such an approach as itself binaristic, eliminating a *merely* essentialist reading of the self embodied in performance for a more sophisticated constructionist account of the self inscribed on the palimpsestic body that is always already constructed within the history of gendered discourse. Schneider continues by arguing:

> The degree to which the "real" is a ruse of performance does not alter the mechanism by which such ruses bring everyday realities into their effects. Put yet another way: while the "real" may always be performative, or constructed, that construction and its reconstruction and its re-reconstruction exist in a battlefield ghosted by that construction's historical effectivity—its reality effects.[21]

Such a reading of the performer's body in performance is typical of criticism of the past two decades, and not necessarily wrong for its typicality. But in asserting such an absoluteness to the performativity of the body in performance, Schneider undermines the degree to which Schneeman's performances and others like it deploy essentialism in much the way that Fuss suggests when she writes that "there is no sure way to bracket off and to contain essentialist maneuvers in anti-essentialist arguments."[22] Fuss, however, accounts for the reconciliation of these two terms, later elaborating that "the strength of the constuctionist position is its rigorous insistence on the production of social categories like 'the body' and its attention to systems of representation. But this strength is not built on the grounds of essentialism's demise, rather it works its power by strategically deferring the encounter with essence, displacing it, in this case, onto the concept of sociality."[23]

So to read Schneeman's performances as deploying the apparently essentialist "reality effects" that Schneider deplores might in fact be deferring that "encounter with essentialism" onto the social battleground of "historical effectivity." In fact, we might choose to read Schneeman as deploying *precisely* an essentialist, embodied notion of a physical, real, and immediate selfhood in performance, if for no other reason than that *in its own historical moment* such an essentialist approach served an important political function within even other radical traditions of the moment. Writing of Schneeman's chilly reception at the radical Dialectics of Liberation Congress in 1967, Harding describes a systematic sabotage of Schneeman's work at an event that was dedicated to entertaining and enabling the ideas of such intellectual and cultural radicals as R. D. Laing, Erving Goffman, Herbert Marcuse, and Stokely Carmichael. Noting the way in which Schneeman's feminist tactics stood in opposition to the theoretical climate of the event, Harding argues that "Schneeman's kinetic theatre, grounded as it was in the sensual social immediacy of performance, not only offered but *enacted* a radical political alternative to the critical methodology" of other male-dominated radical discourses (Harding 124). Here a "sensual social immediacy" seems to be exactly the kind of deferral of essence onto sociality that Fuss describes. That is, from later historical vantage points we might feel compelled to decry Schneeman's effective conflation of body, self, and, writing as naive essentialist tactics. But it seems crucial to acknowledge that within a historical context that was at once germinating the seeds of a constructionist framework through poststructuralist theory (a point that Goffman's presence particularly underscores) such frameworks held no place for feminist sensibilities and politics. In such a context, an insistence on "the real" of women's bodies as sites of discourse can be viewed as at once essentialist and rhetorically sophisticated, enacting a radical feminist aesthetics of embodied selfhood that confronted dominant cultural modes of female subjugation, as well as the embedded subjugation of women even in the radical circles that would later provide a language for another generation of feminist performances.

The Culture Wars: Histories of the Self as
Public Histories

The second-wave feminist environment that gave rise to artists like
Schneeman and Montano (as well as other feminist art world figures such
as Yves Klein, Marina Abramovich, and Eleanor Antin) was constructed
against a critical backdrop of Cixous's "The Laugh of the Medusa" and
the work of Luce Irigaray. This theoretical climate came under deep critique in the ensuing fifteen years, a shift that built up to Judith Butler's
first major articulations of gender performativity in 1990 with *Gender
Trouble,* as well as Fuss's attempt in 1988 to recuperate essentialism as a
grounds for feminist inquiry. In the United States in particular, as the previous chapter illustrates, feminist autobiographical performance over
that period did indeed seem to anticipate that shift—the explicit body
performances of Schneeman gave way to more deeply deconstructive
performances that flourished in spaces like the WOW Café and P.S. 122.
Here the work of Carmelita Tropicana, Holly Hughes, Kate Bornstein,
Robbie McCauley, Terry Galloway, Split Britches (including Peggy Shaw,
Lois Weaver, and Deb Margolin), and Karen Finley, among others, drew
variously on the explicitly embodied tradition of the previous generation,
while more playfully and parodically deconstructing the constitutive discourses of the female body and women's gender roles. And so, just as second-wave, female-body-driven performances were being more fully theorized in the 1980s, a critical confluence—the politics of the Culture Wars,
new materialist performances of a radically queer-bodied aesthetic, and
the performative turn in theories of gender—seemed to insinuate that any
reading of these performances (if not the performances themselves) that
invoked essentialist tactics were at best naive and at worst counterproductive to a progressive politics of gender and sexuality.

Even as the boom in feminist autobiographical performance in the
1980s and 1990s seemed to assert gender as performative and explored
the political potential of such an assertion, many such performances at the
same time continued to deploy any number of essentialist tactics. These
tactics may not have involved a conflation of the particular body with the
sign "woman," but they did tend to depend on a rhetorical conflation of
the particular body with an experiencing, living "self." Indeed, because
many artists did seek to exploit the "now" of the performative moment
(even if implicitly acknowledging what Harding calls "the myth of im-

mediacy") as producing the *sense* of a nexus of self, political agency, and community, we must also consider the presentness of performance against the history of both women's bodies (both in daily life and in explicit performance) and the history of the individual self that we might say is constructed in performance.

I have already suggested that the extension of the narrative of the performer's past into the moment of performance is a key element in establishing the authority of the self and in performing community, but we cannot be uncritical of the personal history that might seem to provide this continuity. When feminist theories of life writing critique the unified conceptions of self that are presented by traditional autobiographies, part of the basis for that critique is the way in which such an unproblematized notion of identity claims access to authority on the truth and objectivity of the narrative it presents. As such, much feminist autobiography (and, indeed, much of the feminist life writing that this project explores) seeks to reveal history to be a construct while at the same time bringing alternative feminist histories based on the performers' own lived experiences, their own performative pasts, to light.

Such a position seems in part to rest on a contradiction: that while deconstructive performances like those of the 1980s and 1990s seek to thoroughly unsettle stable notions of identity, their very reliance on autobiography as a narrative tactic appears to reaffirm the notion of self-identity as a preexisting site of agency and subjectivity. Such a reaffirmation of the a priori subject is a notion that Butler has persistently refuted, but such performances instead seem to invoke Fuss's claim that "The deconstruction of identity, then, is not necessarily a disavowal of identity."[24] To that end, David Román, writing of queer autobiography, notes that "autobiography is perhaps the most immediately understood form of . . . self-representation, and it is also often part of a larger collective and ongoing process of revisionist history."[25] Román here acknowledges two crucial components of the project of autobiographical performance as history. Foremost, in the notion of revisionism, we see a notion of history as an overly simplified, male-centered history-textbook historiography, which, through its claims to objectivity, is decidedly oppressive in its exclusionary tactics.[26] Female artists (along with a host of other marginalized positionalities) have spent much of their politicized energy on a process of countering the myths and filling in the silences of history, and autobiographical narrative in the 1980s and 1990s in particular sought to achieve these goals in several ways. First, an emphasis on the constructability of the self destabilized the narrated history of the self, and second, by positing alternative perspectives on the lived past and then destabilizing even this "other side of the story," these performances called into question the nature of historical representation more broadly. This is the nature of Sue-Ellen Case's 1988 call for a feminist history of theater, up through Harding's feminist historiography of the avant-garde in 2010, and, we could argue, implicit in much of the referential nature of feminist performance in between.

The second important component of Román's description involves the interaction of the ideas of self-representation and collectivity. Certainly these performances represent one type of response to the faux-objective, univocal, patriarchal presentation of history as a linear narrative of white male progress. Yet it would seem paradoxical that the problematic dominant history would be best countered by performances featuring similarly univocal narratives. Instead, part of the solution to this issue can be found in what Román and Hughes identify as the boom in such *individuated, overtly politicized,* self-representation. That is, given that much of the boom in solo autobiographical performance from the 1970s onward has been overtly feminist, overtly queer, or in many cases both, we can see that these individual monologic performances are significant both as solo pieces of self-representation and as part of a collective of voices that challenge the uniformity of a patriarchal norm. And even though the NEA Four scandal still found artists such as Karen Finley and Holly Hughes referred to as "nonmainstream," the fact that such performances were able to garner so much public and critical attention over that period speaks to the degree to which those voices were able to generate a powerful collective response to traditional patriarchal histories. In short, the collective personal histories of those performers together narrate an experience of living in at the end of the twentieth century that countered much of the official histories found in textbooks available at that moment in history.

Moreover, during this period in a history of feminist autobiographical performance, the collective response of multiple individual voices was accompanied by a deconstructionist stance toward history. Given that the first order of business for many performers was to specifically critique historical representations and narratives of women's lives, performers unsurprisingly took historical narrative as contested territory. In performances like *My Father and the Wars, Indian Blood,* and *Sally's Rape,* for example, performer Robbie McCauley overlays her family stories with narratives of her own life to assert a broader narrative of history that decenters white male experience and instead recenters an African American experience that is decidedly racinated and gendered. History in her performances is always contested and always under negotiation in such a way that accepted American histories are displaced and decentered. Similarly, Schneider compellingly illustrates that such critique of history through the self in performance seems to have taken place in part as a concerted deconstruction of a history of representations of women. For example, Orlan's series of performances, *The Reincarnation of Saint Orlan*, is not merely a deconstruction of contemporary standards of beauty. Rather, by choosing to emulate body parts of specific works of art from across the Western canon, Orlan connects these standards (which have been relentlessly applied to the artist's body by the general public and critics alike) to a long pattern of women's oppression through the enforcement of beauty standards. Similarly, Schneider reads Annie Sprinkle's performances of *Post-Porn Modernist* as a general take on the obsession of modernist artists such as Pablo Picasso and James Joyce with the figure of the prostitute, and a specific take on images of artists Gustav Courbet (*Origin of the World*) and Marcel Duchamp (*Etant Donnés: La chute d'eau; la gaz d'éclairage*). How does the artist revise this trope of modernist art? "Sprinkle's body, unlike Duchamp's *Etant Donnés* and Courbet's *Origin*, bears a head and a gaze which complicates the seeming identity between view point and vanishing point."[27]

Given the degree to which such large arcs of history have come under such intense scrutiny, it follows that, like self-identity, self-histories must be subject to the deconstructive pressure of performance. The relationship between self-representation and collective revision must therefore come through the same mediation of constructedness and essentialism that I argue many feminist performances undertake. That is, while we may say that feminist performances often seek to present an individual personal history as an expression of an a priori self, we remember that these personal histories are themselves often presented as fragmented, plural, and even collective in their own right. The proliferation of individual autobiographies is one remedy for an objectively presented, univocal history of a dominant culture, but such performances rely on lived experience and personal history, notions that still depend on an essentialized conflation of public performing body with individual, interior self, a deferral of essence into sociality. If we insist on the performative constitution of the public self that coheres only in the moment of performance, can we simultaneously insist on the existence of a coherent self that inhabits these narratives of the past?

Similarly, if these performances posit the self as constituted through a performed narrative, it certainly must seem true that the history in which this notion of self is couched is similarly constituted and emplotted by its own utterance. In this sense of history—as historiographic discourse—we return to the performative notion of autobiographical performance explored in the previous chapter. Like public histories, and performative identities, histories of the self in these performances are often posed as equally performative: the self becomes "the self" in the context of a narration of past events as coherent, causal, and orderly. Past experiences are narrated as a collection of prior performances of self, some within the public sphere and others in private. This simultaneous play between the performance of past experience and the performance of present self seems to be the crux of the theoretical debate, as well as a central issue for the same performers who narrate the selves that they construct onstage.

As narrators of self-histories, the performers of such life narratives exemplify Sidonie Smith's claim that "the narrator is both the same and not the same as the autobiographer, and the narrator is both the same and not the same as the subject of narration."[28] If as Smith suggests, author, narrator, and autobiographical subject are both the same and not the same, we must think of their identities as imbricated, overlapping but not perfectly congruent. The self who performs simultaneously *composes,* is *composed by,* and is *composed of* the performance of self and the history of self onstage, that is, (1) the performer as agent composes that narration, constructing the self through the narration of past experience; (2) the performer's self-identity is also composed by that narration, inasmuch as the self is constituted by the performative utterance of self through narration; and finally, (3) the self, as it encompasses the entirety of past experiences, memories and self constituting performances, is partially composed of (although not entirely so) the narration itself, an experience that falls into the body of material from which the performer herself can draw. In this way, therefore, we can say that Bobby Baker's performances feature Baker as an agent who narrates, a performative narration that helps constitute Baker's identity as homemaker (one she reveals to be overdetermined), and a body of experiences as a homemaker and artist that both find their way into the narrative and include the performance of that narrative.

During this boom in autobiographical performance, then, it was not uncommon to see performers presenting their own selfhood as a collection of constitutive performances and experiences that led up to and included the moment of performance. All of life was a constitutive performance under such a theoretical framework, and staging such narratives could only be imagined as highlighting this truth. Certainly, however, we can say that the self in many ways exceeds the boundaries of the narrative self-history, just as we must acknowledge that the narrative includes and exceeds both the self and truth of past experience. This appears to be true of all autobiography, both text and performance. And so frequently performers played on the hyperdiscursive nature of performance art to focus audiences on life narratives, life histories, and public histories as sites of political contestation. Exploring these tactics, Sidonie Smith enumerates the ways in which feminist autobiographers in print have constructed "truth" while exceeding the boundaries of experience in this way. The first is through mimicry of traditional masculine autobiography, a tactic that adds menace by usurping traditional form and that functions primarily in several print autobiographies that Smith examines.[29] The second tactic is masquerade, which puts "into textual play an over-identification with the 'feminine,'" the sort that we see in play in Bobby Baker's work, from *Drawing on a Mother's Experience* through *Kitchen Show* and up to more recent performances of hyperfeminine roles. Smith calls her third tactic "I-lying," a strategy in which the narrator stretches the truth of the self far enough to call into question the efficacy of the self, as is the case for both Carmelita Tropicana and Kate Bornstein.

These approaches to autobiographical narration are deeply complicit in a constructionist project, and it is no surprise that many of the most compelling theoretical components of this conjecture come from postmodern accounts of historiography, as well as narrative theories of avowedly referential, nonfictional literature. And yet positing an unstable, constructionist relationship of such narratives to the real depends primarily on an assumption that such narratives are first and foremost discursive rather than material. And to make such a assertion, there must exist an underlying claim that the material body must have no a priori relationship with the experiencing self other than as a surface for inscription. And yet autobiographical *performance* (as opposed to the printed texts that Smith most directly analyzes) depends as much on a performance of the *embodied* self as it does on a narration of past experience of the body, precisely that component of identity that might be said to pre-exist, or at least exists beyond the boundaries of the constitutive act of autodiegesis. So while the feminist autobiographical tactics identified by Smith underscore how performance highlights the slippage between author and narrator, and between narrator and subject, we must also recognize that a great deal of the appeal of autobiographical performance lies not only in the slippage that complicates and deconstructs notions of gender but also in the sameness that separates autobiography from fiction, the referentiality of narration to reality, and the role that the performing body plays in shoring up that referentiality.

In print autobiographies, the overlap between the performing agent and the performed subject is always tenuous, unstable, and therefore unreliable, as accounts from de Man up through Smith rightly assert.[30] Yet in performance, we can locate (if not precisely map) this overlap within the performing body, the source and sign of the truth claims of autobiographical performance. If, say, Carmelita Tropicana's body represents the conjunction of the author (Alina Troyano), narrator (Carmelita and a host of other voices), and subject (Carmelita herself), it does so because in performance her body becomes an authenticating sign of her autobiography. The autobiography can lay claim to truth value because each of these personages shares a performing body. Through this performing body, then, autobiographical performance establishes a referentiality that eludes written autobiography, even as performance is subject to the same machinations of constructability. The performing body, then, verifies the narrated past of experience. Through narration, the performer implicitly says, "Trust me, I know. I was there," and through performance she is able to bolster that claim by further saying, "And I am here to tell you about it." Susan Bennett articulates this formulation in her essay "3D A/B." She writes:

> The body archives a history that may or may not be part of the performance narrative, explicitly or implicitly; it also enacts that history irrespective of the other constituents of performance and irrespective of the autobiographer's intentions for it. The live, performing body renders the script three-dimensional but it has itself been scripted, as it were, prior to its subject matter. Its very physicality— indeed its liveness—is an account of all experiences leading up to the present moment, the archive of a life lived.[31]

Autobiographical performance, then, is both presence and represence, presentation and representation, all brought together under the auspices of the performing body. Therefore, performed self-histories offer an appeal that textual autobiography cannot, since the very corporeality serves as a sign that resists potential falsification of the narrative itself. Indeed, although much of feminist autobiographical performance seeks to undermine notions of essentialism that tie identity to the female body, such performance relies on that very essentialism: that the performer's narration is essentially *hers*. When Susan Miller, in *My Left Breast*, ends her performance of her story of surviving breast cancer by unbuttoning her blouse to reveal her scar, she verifies through her performing body itself the veracity of her narrative. If, say, Holly Hughes were to perform Susan Miller's piece, its truth value, and therefore its rhetorical value, would function differently.

This fact underscores the tension inherent in feminist performances created in the constructionist climate of the Culture Wars. On the one hand, such performed narratives worked persistently to undermine the politicized essentialism that so frequently circumscribes women as subjects. Yet on the other hand, in doing so the performer relied on her (sexed) body to authenticate her narrative of experience, exemplifying the impossibility that Fuss identifies of separating out "essentialist maneuvers in anti-essentialist arguments."[32] Autobiographical performance reveals itself to be as composed of constructed text—as I determined earlier in the antiessentialist performances of Baker, Tropicana, and Bornstein— as are the histories of representation that they seek to deconstruct. Yet they implicitly claim primacy over those histories through the very presence of the performing bodies that stand in front of the audience as self-empowered agents. Their claims to referentiality appear to be more reliable precisely because the corporeal body to which the narrative refers is present, cannot be falsified, and serves as a verifiable trace of the narrative it claims to have experienced.

To examine this tension between essentialist tactics and antiessentialist narratives, I will turn to two performances from the front lines of the Culture Wars that both critique the process of heteropatriarchal history making as false and establish self-histories as reliable alternatives to official ones. In 1990, both Karen Finley and Holly Hughes moved from their small but significant place in the world of avant-garde performance into the much more prominent national spotlight as two of the four artists who came to be known as the NEA Four, artists whose National Endowment for the Arts grants were rescinded on the basis of a perceived violation of decency. In the now familiar narrative, the four artists sued the NEA and the courts found in their favor, both in the original suit and in appeal. However, in 1998, the Clinton administration appealed that case to the U.S. Supreme Court, which found by a vote of eight to one that the NEA could indeed restrict funds on the basis of decency.

At the time of the ruling, Finley was in performance of a piece entitled *The Return of the Chocolate-Smeared Woman,* at once a deconstruction of her earlier piece, *We Keep Our Victims Ready,* and a pointed diatribe against the titillating sexualization of art by Senator Jesse Helms, who led the attacks against the artists.[33] Finley's self-narrative, which also included pieces from earlier performances, contained one particular monologue that echoed sentiments she first expressed on the steps of the Supreme Court the day of the initial hearing.

> I've come to realize that I've been in an eight-year, sexually abusive relationship with Jesse Helms. Jesse is intensely, passionately out of control in his sexual need to dominate me. And I've had enough. The sexual relationship began on the Senate floor, when he eroticized my career, my work, my livelihood. He could never see me as a person doing my job.[34]

In the memoir in which this monologue is published,[35] Finley goes on to suggest that Helms's treatment of her was sexual harassment, and that the performance of *Return* was a way to end that relationship, "to get out of the role of the victim once and for all."[36]

Finley's camped-up account of the case's history in the performance (itself a version of Smith's "I-lying") and the public feud between herself and Helms runs counter to what we might call the "accepted history," which includes on the one extreme narratives that paint Helms as a family values champion and Finley as a filthy avant-garde deviant, and on the other, Finley as an embattled artist facing off against a vicious, self-serving politico. Sympathetic to Finley or not, these accepted accounts of the NEA Four case elide the sexualized nature of the proceedings, an element that Finley's performance emphasizes. Finley's first use of this line of argument followed closely on the heels of the public hearings on Supreme Court justice Clarence Thomas's harassment of Anita Hill. Indeed, by choosing sexual harassment as her metaphor, Finley in many ways underscored the performativity of her self-history. That is, a component of sexual harassment law suggests that an offense does not need to follow the typical quid pro quo of the most identifiable cases; the mere creation of a sexually hostile work environment is grounds enough for prosecution. Moreover, the potential victim determines whether an envi-

ronment is hostile or not. While actual court cases have been variously effective in granting women the voice to effectively determine whether
their environment is hostile or not, the definition of the offense is itself linguistically performative: "I call it hostile, therefore it must be sexual harassment." By calling out Helms's eroticization of her career, work and
livelihood through the linguistic performative of accusation, Finley performed his sexual harassment of her as a way of moving out of the victim
position. And by creating a personal history that tapped into the performative, she could underscore the degree to which the official history of
the NEA Four case is a construct built by those in power: the Supreme
Court and Congress.

Nonetheless, even as Finley's performance deconstructed the history-
making operations of Helms and company, she relied on the veracity of
her own account to achieve rhetorical value. And here her performing
body became key as the authenticating sign. Given that the NEA controversy focused on Finley's *We Keep Our Victims Ready*, her choice to reper-
form sections of that piece tied her performance in the present to her past
performances, performances that themselves were components of the
past she narrated in *Return*. In doing so, she reified the referential nature
of her piece, tying this self-constituting performance to a past performance that itself played a (perhaps overbalanced) part in constituting her
public identity. Furthermore, given that what Finley did with her body in
performance was precisely the point of contention in the Supreme Court
case, her title (with its emphasis on the bodily acts she performs), and indeed the performance itself, established Finley's performing body as a
site of authority. Because she was performing her own past, and doing so
with her own body, her performance claimed agency to counternarrate
the official history, one that in this case is crucial, since few of her as-
sailants ever witnessed her performances.

Moreover, Finley's work in *The Return of the Chocolate-Smeared Woman*
brings full circle a sense of the deep entanglements of essentialist and
antiessentialist strategies within feminist performance (particularly feminist avant-garde performance). Most of Finley's performances can be read
as deeply and complexly constructionist in their approach to the female
body as stage, as site of discourse, and as materially performative. And
yet, despite this, such performances as *Constant State of Desire* and *We Keep
Our Victims Ready* persistently cited a history of avant-garde feminist performance, from the Dadaist Baroness Elsa von Freytag-Loringhoven in
the early moments of the twentieth century through Carolee Schneeman

as well as figures of the fine arts world like Marina Abramovich and Yves Klein. While each of these predecessors might be said to possess varying ideological and aesthetic aims, together they help us construct a feminist history that (as Harding convincingly acknowledges) is predicated on a sense of collage as discursively constructable, but also on the persistent presence of the body as *both* signifying text *and* experiencing self. Indeed, we might go so far as to say that the history of the various experiencing selves of these performers and artists radically amplifies the discursive critique of their art, effectively transporting essentialism as an *ontology* of the woman's body in performance into a historical feminist *aesthetics of essentialism* (the very idea containing the contradiction of bodied essence and artistic construction) through the woman's body in performance. Within this framework, Finley's character-driven performances of *We Keep Our Victims Ready* and *Constant State of Desire* already represented the reinvocation of a feminist aesthetics that balanced the essentialized body with the discursive body. But in *Return*, Finley further complicated the essentialist/performative tension by transforming a character monologue from *We Keep Our Victims Ready* into a public presentation of *herself* as the chocolate-smeared woman.

At no moment was this tension more explicit than on the evening that the Supreme Court's decision came down. Finley interrupted her show to hold a press conference. In her memoir recounting the event, she notes, "I wanted to turn the bad news into performance on my turf."[37] News stories the following day reported both moments from the rehearsed performance, including the famous offer to lick chocolate off her body, and Finley's extemporaneous responses to the ruling ("'unhappy' and 'very disappointed'") and the effects of the trial on her ongoing life: "that she had been the object of stalking and death threats, and that her marriage had dissolved under the pressure."[38] The press conference offered Finley an opportunity to respond to the ruling in a way not permitted by American legal culture and at the same time constituted her body as a site of performance; after the press conference, the show went on.

Holly Hughes's 2000 performance of *Preaching to the Perverted* similarly offers an alternative history of the trial, and more pointedly of the patriarchal, heteronormative institutions that were in control of that history making, in both senses of the word. Hughes's performance was, in its conception and execution, a deconstructive take on history making, identity making, and the relationship of art to public discourse. While Finley's performance revisited the already staged acts that were under contestation, Hughes's narrative directly tells the experience of the Supreme Court hearing of *The National Endowment for the Arts v. Finley et al.*, highlighting the patriarchal interests and control mechanisms of that institution while simultaneously working to reclaim authority over her own identity out of the one that the courts, the government, and the media had constructed for her. And while Hughes's performance does not deconstruct the female body in the same way that many other autobiographical feminist performances do, *Preaching to the Perverted* certainly stands as an example of the potential of materialist, deconstructive autobiographical performance for feminist artists, serving as a site at which to reconstruct her own identity within the space of transgressive performance, foregrounding her voice as an alternative to the silencing impulses of the American political system—a system her performance methodically reveals to be patriarchal and Eurocentric. And yet, despite the degree to which Hughes's performance explored the rhetorical political potential of performativity, hers, like Finley's, still relies on the truth claims of autobiography that are tied to the rhetorical effects of conflating her present speaking body with a past self of historical experience.

As a deconstructive piece, Hughes's performance hit a number of important notes. In perhaps less expected ways, the piece calls attention to the idea of the female body as stage, to paraphrase Schneider's work. Yet here Hughes chose *not* to expose her body to critique in the way that Finley's performances have, or even in the ways Hughes herself was accused of doing. Richard Meyer observes of the postcard used to advertise *Preaching to the Perverted:*

> The postcard offers a wide-eyed Hughes holding an American flag at chest level. The flag drops, garment-like, in front of her body. Although Hughes appears at first glance to be naked beneath the flag, she is in fact wearing a black bra and panties, undergarments that become increasingly noticeable the more one looks at the image . . . In the postcard for *Preaching to the Perverted,* Hughes revisits the image of her naked body on stage but on terms that reveal that image to be a misrecognition by others, a mistaken perception of sexual exposure.[39]

Similarly, in the performance itself, Hughes donned a simple white shirt and black pants, while the performance itself acknowledges the degree to which she (like Finley) has been sexualized by outside discourse. For example, a voice-over reads a newspaper article declaring that "these mediocre artists are in the enviable position of having every move watched with intense interest," while another, a man breathing heavily, says, "I've been watching you, Holly Hughes."[40]

The undermining of the (historically potent) feminist trope of the explicit body highlights the body as a contested site for writing identity, not unlike Bobby Baker's or other earlier deconstructive performances, and for the circumscription of identity that Hughes is more concerned with in this performance. In this particular case, though, Hughes's battle is even more public; the huge amount of "bad publicity" she receives constructs her as merely one of the NEA Four,[41] or, as she notes, "Karen Finley and the Three Homosexuals," or alternately "Karen Finley and the Three Non-Mainstream Artists."[42] This performance is for her a public reclamation of her own agency, her own imperative to self-construct within the public space of performance, and it is replayed against a constituent theme of silencing, in which Hughes's own narrative is truncated and suppressed until she is forced to remain silent during the Supreme Court hearings, as both posted warnings and Secret Service agents repeatedly remind her that *"there is absolutely no talking in the US Supreme Court!"*[43] This silencing of the performer's voice in court comes against Hughes's second theme that the entire process of *The National Endowment for the Arts v. Finley et al.* was theatricalized.[44] She focuses, for example, on the demand for tickets as if the hearing were a sold-out Broadway show; the disembodied voices describe her function in the case as her "part" (even without lines); as a performer, she recognizes conventions such as "quiet during the performance."[45] Just as Karen Finley theatricalized history making by interrupting her show to hold a press conference, *Preaching to the Perverted*'s voice-over reminds Hughes and her audience, "This is real theater, sister, big money, big production values, and there's a script and it's not yours."[46]

But there is nonetheless a rhetorical ambivalence to the overtly performative nature of the performance and its narrative. This script, and the way it is recorded in history, suggests both the limits to and potential of the power of Hughes's own self-history in performance. She focuses on and deconstructs the process of history making—the silencing process of the court proceedings, both the patriarchal and theatrical nature of the Supreme Court, the circumscription of the artist into various proscribed roles by the complicit media. In this way, she shows us that history is no less theatrical, no less performed, and no less a construct than what she is performing on the stage, only the U.S. government has more money, and more impressive production values.[47] Yet even though she reveals the status of the Supreme Court cases to be just as theatrical (and therefore just as constructed) as her own performance, she does not suggest that these are two equally valid versions of the event. Instead, her show, which includes both the past of the narrative and the present of the performance, works to establish rhetorical authority over the official accounts, and Hughes accomplishes this *through her own performing body,* the sign that verifies her experience and grants her narrative a rhetorical authority that her performance's disembodied voices, quoted hate mail, and excerpted newspaper articles all lack. By presenting a funny, eloquent narrative of her own history alongside her deconstruction of the court's narrative, Hughes begins the process of revising the official history of the incident. Even when it is deeply deconstructive, and not explicitly embodied, Hughes's performance still relies, then, on an essentialism of the speaker's embodied voice as guarantor of her identity as (at least) a historical archive of experience. This is an essentialism whose deconstruction goes back as far as Jacques Derrida's *Dissemination,*[48] and yet within the history of feminist autobiographical performance, even at its most performatively playful it remains the central rhetorical trope of the form and reveals the continued reliance on the body as guarantor of the implicit authority over the narrative. Even when (as in Finley's case) the performer uses tactics like Sidonie Smith's "I-lying," the claim of authority rests in the performing body to create such "I-lies." As such, a reliance on performed autobiography *at all* invokes the body in essential relation to the self it performs.

Twenty-first Century: Disability and the Return of Embodiment

While queer and feminist concerns dominated the critical response to the deconstructive autobiographical performance of the 1980s and 1990s, some solo performers were also creating compelling performances that interrogated disability and embodiedness along several similar lines of inquiry. For example, in her essay "3-D A/B," Susan Bennett analyzes the persistence of the physical self, and the preeminence of embodied identity in performance. In considering the work of monologist Spalding Gray, she notes the frequent, deliberate, and sustained reference to his physical well-being across his autobiographical performances. In particular, Bennett examines the piece *Gray's Anatomy*, which details the performer's degenerative eye condition and the medical travails that accompanied it. Of course, the status of the straight, white, male body as a subject is hardly contested, but as performances *of disability*, Gray's narratives refer directly back to his own embodied experience, a parallel that Bennett argues is equally salient for both male and female bodies as indexes of selfhood. The body stands, Bennett asserts, as a historical archive of lived experience, one that bears historical marks irrespective of intention.

Ric Knowles, in an essay that directly follows Bennett's in the volume *Theatre and AutoBiography,* largely argues that embodied performance (or what he calls "autobiology") is "a confrontation between the discursive 'I' as social and grammatical 'subject' and the *culturally produced and abjected body.*"[49] The performer he describes is Emily Taylor, whose show, *Bathroom,* details her experience with bulimia, including on the one hand instances of "graphic autobiographical moment[s] of self-alienation" and on the other "a moment of powerful bodily presence."[50] The performance, which, as Knowles describes it, ends with Taylor eating a large apple fritter onstage and then departing with the line "I have to go to the bathroom,"[51] depends on an ontological interplay between the unalienable connection of the performer's body (materially chewing, swallowing, and either vomiting or digesting that apple fritter) and her self (the identity constructed through the narrative of bulimia she has just performed). From this, the audience comes to understand the degree to which her sexed, gendered, consuming, and medicalized corporeality is subject to a contested set of cultural significations. This and dozens of other performances of disability, often by women, hinge on the body as archive of experience, locus of selfhood, and explicitly sexed site of inscription that is presented by these performers as an a priori condition of identity and social construction. In this way, it seems fitting that the growth of disability studies in the last decade should find performers and theorists seeking a balance between the body as biological determinant and selfhood and identity as social script.

This is not to say that performers of disability represent an uncritical return to essentialist approaches to embodiment: frequently it is quite the opposite. In her essay on the Austin, Texas, performance group *Actual Lives,* initiated by deaf performer Terry Galloway, participant and theorist Chris Anne Strickling writes, "We wanted to shape a materialist performance paradigm that would treat disability as a culturally constructed identity derived from a specific set of power relationships (wielded through pathologized medical and social discourses) and then use the body-in-performance to expose those power relationships and resist them to whatever extent possible."[52] In considering these two positions against one another, Susan G. Stocker notes the particular usefulness of a materialist/performative approach for feminist disability studies, writing, "Butler enables us to fend off moralities that would intrude upon us definitionally. That is, Butler's understanding of oppressive discursive power gives the disabled and our allies social and political resources for contesting moralities external to us that exclude and 'define' us in oppressive ways."[53]

Nowhere is this more apparent than in specific *Actual Lives* performances (themselves comprised of several individual pieces performed alternately by single or multiple performers). One thematic trend that Strickling notes is a persistent challenge to the cultural desexualization of the disabled body through the use of explicit sexual material. "This insistence," Strickling writes, "constitutes a militant resistance to the many ways that disabled people are desexualized."[54] She goes on to document multiple ways in which "sexual innuendo, flirting, and sexual jokes" are integral parts of both the performance's entertainment value and its cultural critique.[55] Similarly, writing on the ways in which crip and queer identities inform one another onstage, Carrie Sandahl argues, "Crip-queer artists redefine gender and sexuality by cripping and queering both. Here, too, it is clear how coming out as crip, even as it challenges queer performance traditions, draws its reference from those traditions, which confuse and rearticulate normative gender laws."[56] Further, she writes, "In addition to claiming sexuality by displaying their bodies on their own terms, these artists assert sexual agency by recounting their experiences."[57] Like Strickling, Sandahl also invokes the work of Terry Galloway, whose solo performance *Out All Night and Lost My Shoes* interrogates her experiences and identities as both deaf and lesbian. Writing about an episode during which Galloway recounts "her love affair with another adolescent girl at the Lion's Camp for cripples," Sandahl asserts that Galloway "transforms the invisibility of childhood sexuality, lesbianism, and disability from burden to advantage, a means of operating outside authority's gaze."[58]

But despite the urgency for disability theorists and activists to rewrite cultural narratives about disability through materialist interventions into prevailing social discourse, disability theory also focuses attention on the problem of pain itself as a specifically and ineluctably embodied materiality. Accordingly, such a notion offers an important pathway for theories of feminist or queer performances to theorize embodiment as well. Pain, in this conjecture, becomes the conceptual site where linguistically coded experience meets physical sensation, and it can be seen to perhaps undermine radical constructionist accounts of embodiment like Butler's.[59] While Butler (as well as her predecessor on this topic, Michel Foucault) argues persuasively for the challenge that the disabled body poses to normative culture, there is little said about the *experience* of that body, in part because pain as a physical experience has been long seen to complicate discursive conceptions of reality. In her landmark 1986 text, *The Body in Pain,* Elaine Scarry asserts, "Physical pain does not simply resist language, but actively destroys it, bringing about an immediate reversion to a state anterior to language, to the sounds and cries a human being makes before language is learned." She goes on to explain that "physical pain—unlike any other state of consciousness—has no referential content. It is not of or for anything. It is precisely because it takes no object that it, more than any other phenomenon, resists objectification in language."[60] Tobin Siebers puts this very observation into conversation with the constructionist model of identity:

> Physical pain is highly unpredictable and raw as reality. It pits the mind against the body in ways that make the opposition between thought and body in current body theory seem trivial. It offers few resources for resisting ideological constructions. . . . Pain is not a friend to humanity. It is not a secret resource for political change. It is not a well of delight for the individual. Theories that encourage these interpretations are not only unrealistic about pain; they contribute to the ideology of ability, marginalizing people with disabilities and making their stories of suffering and victimization both politically impotent and difficult to believe.[61]

Thus, disability theory, activism, and performance stage the same tension that we have found in feminist performances. Constructionists privilege language, discourse, and consciousness over the material body, while a body-centered approach maintains a sense of the real rooted in bodily experience.

If we choose to take a medical view on embodiedness and identity (an approach that we must acknowledge as tenuous within a poststructuralist feminist framework), we find that cognitive science on identity and pain suggests that this is neither a particularly simple issue nor one

that is clear-cut.[62] In terms of a biological basis for identity, we might look
to the work of Antonio R. Damasio, which complicates the duality of
mind and body that the terms of this debate might set up.[63] His work pos-
tulates a three-tiered model, in which the roots of identity, or "proto-iden-
tity," begin at the level of the most basic human processes, with the central nervous system regulating involuntary processes like body
temperature, breathing, and heart rate. These processes, he argues, all begin with an instinctual impulse toward stability, a sense of coherence from
moment to moment that ensures the body's survival. This drive toward
coherence and stability translates at the second level, which he calls "core
identity," to our cognitive sense of coherence simply in the acts of per-
ceiving and knowing the world around us. This "sense of knowing," as
Damasio puts it, depends on a fairly stable sense of self that distinguishes
the individual from the outside world. And it is the stable self that gives
rise to "meta-identity," the third-level consciousness that emerges into
language, watches itself, and creates the illusion of a purely mental selfhood. And yet, in Damasio's model, this narrative sense of self is in fact
crucial to normal human functioning. So identity in this model is both ineluctably embodied and simultaneously inextricable from language.

Cognitive theories of identity come together here with cognitive approaches to pain. The work of Patrick Wall focuses on the host of phe-
nomena in which the subjective experience of pain does not map reliably
onto physical circumstances: pain in phantom limbs, psychosomatic pain,
and several types of traumatic physical pain that does not set in until well
after the initial injury, when the victim has moved out of immediate danger.[64] These instances, he suggests, move the very experience of pain out
of the body and into the brain, suggesting that the brain processes stimuli
from the body and then instantaneously decides how to encode it. Indeed,
if the brain is structured like a language, as many cognitive theorists have
suggested, we might read this experience of pain through at least pro-
tolinguistic processes, even as it more firmly supports the idea of a more
fluid interchange from the material self through to the discursive self.
While Wall himself may not have been particularly interested in, or even
persuaded by, the idea, an interpretation that rectifies biological and discursive accounts is available.

Such a digression into the cognitive bases of embodiment, experience, and identity becomes important for theorizing possible ontologies
of the self-narrating performer, especially those who establish their own
selfhood through expressions of disabled embodiment. The interrelated-

ness of embodied and social senses of self and the degree to which pain itself might traverse this fluid path have led autobiography theorist Paul John Eakin to settle on two ideas: "that the autobiographical narrative might be tied to the well-being of the human organism" and that "the teller-effect . . . has the more immediate potential to illuminate our reading of autobiography."[65] In this form, the teller-effect is the self-aware feeling of identity that becomes the locus for a politicized contestation of the discursively constructed self, an effect that arises from Demasio's notion of metaidentity. In performances of disability, in particular, we can see precisely this effect through a self-conscious invocation of these fluid connections between the persona that narrates and the body that experiences. We can see it, in fact, in a range of performances: from installations by Marina Abramovich, in which her own physical discomfort becomes part of the art object; through the performances of Terry Galloway, who registers her invisible embodied disability through a range of physicalized performance tactics; as we will see below; to the surgical interventions of Orlan, whose experiencing body amplifies the critique of her constructed self by coupling it with the physical pain that her reconstructed body quite visibly archives.

Another way to imagine the presence of the body as imbricated with the constitution of the self in performance comes not from the body as an expression of the self but from the body as bearing the effects of the self in performance. It is certainly no stretch to imagine that the performer's body *feels* the effects of performance itself. Although this is certainly true for the labor of any actor, Philip Auslander suggests ways in which this effect might be augmented in solo autobiographical performance. Like Bennett, Auslander looks at the work of Spalding Gray, suggesting that his "autopathographic" monologues not only narrate the disabled body (which Bennett has shown itself archives his prenarrativized experience) but have a therapeutic effect on the anxiety that he experiences. "The fact that Gray is able to perform does not imply that he has recovered from the psychological afflictions he describes in some of his monologues," writes Auslander, "even when those monologues reach narrative closure. Gray does not perform because he feels better—he feels better when he performs."[66]

As much as Auslander may argue about the persistence of the physical body as archive and collateral beneficiary of autobiographical performance, the performing male body does not reliably inform us about the status of the woman's body in such performances. Feminist performers are less guaranteed the subject position over their own bodies than male performers are, and indeed, as much materialist feminist criticism has shown, the discursive status of the woman's body is by no means guaranteed by its materiality. Yet we might argue that the same vectors along which the male body comes to bear, as both archive and collateral of the self in performance, apply in different ways to the pain and threat of pain on women's bodies. Following her examination of Gray's performances, Susan Bennett turns to Karen Finley's *American Chestnut,* a performance that, as Bennett documents, "is an explicit territorialization of the (female) body."[67] In accounting for her own body during and after pregnancy, Finley's performance comments on the site of women's most insistent and intense essentialization in dominant culture: maternity. She narrates the pain of childbirth down to a broken tailbone. And, as Bennett asserts, "[T]he body in live performance can provide a critique of an assigned identity that assumes such submissive behavior [as suppressing the screams of childbirth] at the behest of social norms, the denial of pain as proof of an appropriately docile and indeed, female body. But it is also the case that the body in front of the audience is that one with the presumably healed tailbone."[68] Moreover, since Finley is known to travel to give performances with both her mother and her daughter, Bennett argues that it "makes a difference . . . that part of the archive that is Finley's performing body is a complex relationship of mothers and daughter, work and motherhood, giving birth and making art."[69] And so maternal pain, as a specifically female experience, archived in the specifically female body, becomes an essentialized, biologized expression of self-history through Finley's own archived experience at the same time as it becomes a site of contestation through her critique of the medical response to the pain of childbearing. And if that contestation isn't clear enough, it revisits Finley's body as the guarantor of performance: Bennett notes death threats attendant with Finley's performances and wonders, "[H]ow is it possible to ignore the reality of that threat to Finley's performing body?"[70]

Susan Stocker, in considering the links between feminist and disability critiques, quotes Iris Marion Young in arguing that "women in sexist society are physically handicapped,"[71] making a connection between the sources of oppression for both female and disabled bodies in a hierarchical society, as well as underscoring the embodiedness of an ethical response. She further argues that, despite the potential inherent in a materialist approach that imagines bodies as sites of discursive production, this approach has important limits: specifically, that in foregrounding critique and contestation, an approach advocated by Butler forecloses mutuality. Stocker opts instead for an approach that uses the paleoanthropological work of Maxine Sheets-Johnstone. For Sheets-Johnstone, Stocker argues, "Meaning is not contingent because it unfolds originally from this *structure* of the human body."[72] Stocker considers the biological imperatives of hominid existence as giving rise to precisely the sense of mutual care and concern that she sees absent and impossible in a Butlerian account. In doing so, she notes the specific limits of critique, arguing that "not only hegemonic definitions but disconnection hold oppression in place; and to counter it, we must allow for the conditions for the possibility of mutuality."[73]

She continues by arguing that "the *possibility* of mutuality, whose genetic history Sheets-Johnstone reconstructs, is also an essential resource for appropriate relation responses to disability. For this dimension of morality . . . is rooted not in oppositional power, but in mutuality and affirming connection."[74] In this sense, one can easily see the possibility of mutuality as a precondition for the sense of community that I argued in the previous chapter is performatively constituted in feminist autobiographical performances. Certainly, self-consciously Butlerian performativity in performance provides artists a platform for critique of established gender roles and for contestation of those roles and norms. Yet, as Jill Dolan shows, many artists also take recourse in the notion of intersubjectivity, the connection that a performer creates with her audience in performance. According to Stocker, intersubjectivity is a genetically coded, panhominid response and is the mechanism by means of which mutuality and community can be established.

Examples abound. Susan Miller in *My Left Breast*, after invoking her own corporeality by revealing her mastectomy scar, turns her narrative into a call for solidarity among women by saying, "I miss it, but I want to tell all the women in the changing booths that we are still beautiful, we are still powerful, we are still sexy, we are still here."[75] This final invocation of presence—"we are still here"—positions Miller as a part of her community, not as merely an exemplary member. And it is this dialectic between the particular autobiographical life and the life of the female performer as "Woman" that generates community in the moment of performance. This connects with the same sort of community building that Miller and Román identify in their essay "Preaching to the Converted" and that Holly Hughes seems to depend on in her performance of *Preaching to the Perverted*. As Richard Meyer points out, "Hughes' title (like her performance) also insists on the creative and political power of identifying with 'the perverted' and of directing one's art toward—or 'preaching to'—an avowedly queer audience."[76] If this community is in part discursively constituted as "the perverted" through the discourse of the performance, its constitution also depends on more physical, literal, and consciously staged connections. While Dolan describes Peggy Shaw, in *The Menopausal Gentleman,* moving out into the audience to create a connection, Hughes takes the tactic a step further, bringing audience members onstage to read the hate mail that she has received, transporting the audience into *her* lived experience. By making the audience literally experience what she has experienced, she forces them into her narrative, a rhetorically charged tactic that creates community out of empathy, out of a mutuality that seems to depend on a deeper humaneness that Stocker advocates as a desirable alternative to Butlerian critique and contestation.[77]

This shared experience provides autobiographical performance with an additional appeal for feminist practitioners: this drawing of the audience into a common discursive community, momentarily defined by a speaking subject who dares to construct her own identity amid a wave of hostile historical and social forces. Whether or not a performer may claim the priority of the embodied intersubjective self or the dominance of discourse over the body as a surface for cultural and performative inscription becomes largely irrelevant, inasmuch as many such performances rely on both vectors for imagining, expressing, and engaging identity in a culturally contested but community-oriented fashion.

To conclude, I will look more closely at Terry Galloway's *Out All Night and Lost My Shoes,* a performance piece that engages, in specific ways, storytelling and performance around both her disability and her sexuality, a narrative that in sum presents a fractured narrative self that nonetheless depends on both the biological conditions of existence and the precondition of mutuality. Hers is a performance that critiques cultural signification even as it depends on a sense of community. Galloway herself is a mainstay in lesbian feminist performance circles (she was a regular at WOW Café in the early 1980s), alternative theater (she was a founding member of *Esther's Follies* in the 1970s in Austin and more recently of *The Mickee Faust Club* in Florida), and disability performance (her workshops for performance and disability led to the creation of *Actual Lives* in Austin). *Out All Night* draws on all of these threads, and although it first appeared in the late 1980s and even then drew on material from earlier in her career, she has performed it for a wide variety of audiences in the two decades since its first appearance.[78]

That Galloway's solo work engages the deconstructive, performative tactics of other WOW Café performers is hardly surprising, given the interplay of performers and performances in that period. Galloway's "Jake Ratchett, Short Detective" certainly shares a critique of normative masculinity with the work of Split Britches, or with Holly Hughes's *Lady Dick*. Strickling links this and other character performances in *Out All Night* to what Jose Esteban Muñoz calls "disidentifications," which parody, critique, and reject dominant cultural positions, intertwining autobiographical narrative with fragmented character narratives, including a send-up of etiquette maven Amy Vanderbilt and "Sherrie Loose and Handchops," a hand puppet made out of a mop that parodies Shari Lewis and her hand puppet Lambchop.

Certainly, Galloway's approach to autobiographical narrative is sophisticated. Strickling, quoting from an interview with Galloway, writes that when Galloway "'narrates herself into existence' on the stage . . . she leaves behind any notion of the singularity of the self, and performs multiple 'selves.'"[79] And while certain autobiographical stories repeat themselves across Galloway's oeuvre—including not only performances but a memoir, *Mean Little deaf Queer,* and a forthcoming film about her recent cochlear implant surgery, *Rewired*—these are always acknowledged early and often *as stories*, couched within other stories told by her family about her, other family members, and the world. Galloway's is a world of stories, crafted for maximum effect. It would be naive to assume that the repetition of these stories across media somehow authorizes their veracity.[80] And yet also common across these narratives is the body that Galloway narrates, a body that is visibly, though performatively, female; that corresponds at least roughly to the descriptions of herself that she offers; and that through her voice, at least, bears traces of the deafness that she has experienced since she was young. Galloway herself links embodiedness and performance in complex ways and has said:

> I've always been vaguely ashamed of being what I am—deaf, queer, a woman. I was buckling under what I thought to be the scorn or indifference of the whole, wide world. Performing myself became a way of performing myself into being—performing a better self that wasn't ashamed, that had the real guts, the real courage to claim meaningfulness for myself as all those things the world hated—deaf, queer, a woman.[81]

We see in her approach to her performance both a discursive, materialist response—performing herself into being as a counterengagement to discursive scorn and indifference—and a response that engages the body that precedes the self.

Moreover, the stories that she tells in performance are frequently about her body and the ways in which her corporeal reality conditions her experience in the world. She tells stories of the Berlin doctors whose haphazard administration of prenatal antibiotics caused her disabilities and about her experiences in swimming competitions and talent shows at the Texas Lions Camp for Crippled Children, as well as her early erotic adventures there. At the center of her performance is a narrative of living in New York and experiencing the paranoia and anxiety occasioned there, the "state of galvanized psychosis,"[82] that brought her to the city's Gracie Square psychiatric hospital. These stories amalgamate the embodied and psychic, the material and the discursive. Her disability is not visible per se: there are no visible scars for Galloway to reveal to us. Strickling writes:

> Finally, and perhaps most importantly for my project, Galloway's disability is difficult to locate. In the moments of "identification-based performance" in which she performs herself as Terry Galloway, her deafness is integral. When she is performing disidentifications, as in Jake Ratchett, "Etiquette of Suicide," and Mr. Handchops, deafness is not clearly evident. She can choose when to perform deafness, at least on stage. This gives her a kind of performative or theatrical range not available to David Roche or to members of *Actual Lives*.[83]

As much as we might say, however, that her deafness can be performed, and is subject to a discursive contestation, her body archives these experiences nonetheless. And it matters that she wears her hair short to make visible the hearing aids that both mark and mitigate the disability whose existence she performs and performs against when she tells these stories.[84]

Galloway also suggests that her performances themselves are a process of making visible an embodied reality. She writes, "In *Out All Night* in particular, I use and abuse my body—fling it around, hit my hand with a hammer, burn my palm with a cigarette, shave my wrist with a cheese grater, prick it with a butcher knife, fall flat on my butt. I make myself a physical, sweating, transforming-before-your-very-eyes presence."[85] This is a presence that depends in part on performances of pain to establish the embodied relationship between the performing body and the narrating self, but they also have a political impetus. This presence, she suggests, counters the invisibility that comes with social attitudes toward physical and emotional disability, toward queerness, toward femininity. In this way, while we can see ways in which embodied disability becomes part of Galloway's performance of self, her bodied experiences as a woman and as queer are similarly parts of the rhetoric of the body onstage. Frequently, the narratives she offers in her memoir describe discrimination and dismissal based on prejudices that stem from both sexism and ablism. And the degree to which her own performances include narratives of sexuality echoes (or more accurately prefigures) the sexual overtones found in *Actual Lives*. This is all part of what she describes as a radical sensibility governing her work.

> To anyone bothering to look, mine is just a plain old white, female middle-aged body. It wouldn't at first glance seem to harbor the radical impulses that it does. . . . Because yes I have been arguing for a revolution of sensibility and yes in many ways I have—as so many thousands of others have—helped bring that revolution of sensibility into being. Feminism is a given these days. Queerness is well on its way. And disability is roaring at its heels.[86]

Finally, we must consider the ways in which Galloway's performances for audiences depend on intersubjectivity and mutuality. In *Out All Night*, we see storytelling posed as an activity that defines, and even constitutes, familial community. According to Strickling, "Galloway equates theatre (where people crowd into one room, stay up late, and create an occasion for listening to stories) with family, and thereby includes her audience in the category of 'family,' at least a momentary, temporally bounded, site-specific family (one type of family that many queers construct)."[87] We might equally call this effect a queering of family, a feminist community, or a disability-conditioned mutuality; we might call it a performative constitution of community, or a pan-hominid biological response. Either way, Galloway's solo and group performances, from *Out all Night* to *Actual Lives* and *Mickee Faust*, offer up narratives of embodied lives that serve specific goals for deconstructing and contesting identity categories while asserting the particulars of individual lives as evidence, all of which become part of a collective *political* experience of performers and audiences alike.

Stocker suggests that a genetic/biologistic approach that favors mutuality, and a constructionist/performative approach that favors contestation and critique, are basically mutually exclusive intellectual propositions. Therefore, because of the promise of mutuality to a feminist disability ethic, she advocates for latter. But as both this chapter and the previous one suggest, a sense of community that grows out of the performance of the self might be explained by *both approaches*, and accordingly might be said to be the work of both sets of ontological stakes. That is, the genetic impulse to mutuality may indeed serve as the precondition and mechanism for an intersubjectivity that is constituted in the moment of the performance, the constitutive "I perform myself" that accomplishes many effects at once: it writes the self onto the body; it constitutes the group of people in the theater as an audience; it gives an account of the self for the audience; and, in both depending on and invoking that sense of mutuality, perhaps resident in a common female identity, perhaps resident in a common human identity, it begins the process of building a feminist community in the theater. Through this community, built at once on essentialist and materialist mechanisms, but deeply embodied by performer and audience alike, the performance affirms the "I" of the performer in such a way as to validate the truth effects of autobiography and to potentially activate the audience toward future recognition of the woman's body as a site of struggle.

In conclusion, we must note that even as the broad web of autobiographical feminist performances (and feminist criticism of autobiographical performance) variously theorizes the body as source of identity, as site on which identity might be written, as archive of experience, as locus of contestation, or as platform for mutuality and intersubjectivity, the body remains central to this history. From Schneeman's *Interior Scroll* through the explicit performances of Karen Finley and the autobiographical investments of actuality in *Actual Lives,* an aesthetic emerges of women's bodies performing the self as an act *toward* agency, if not always an act *of* agency. As this aesthetic has developed over the past several decades, such performances continue to make use of the performance space as a lab for configuring women's bodies and narratives of women's lives as resources in the ongoing work of dismantling the hierarchical structures of power that circumscribe them.

CHAPTER 3 : The Autobiographical Play and the Death of the Playwright

SARAH KANE'S *4.48 PSYCHOSIS*

When Paula Vogel's play *How I Learned to Drive* opened in Washington, D.C., in the spring of 1999, the playwright celebrated a homecoming. Hailing from the same suburban Maryland town in which her play is set, Vogel had just won the Pulitzer Prize for the play; her longtime collaborator, Molly Smith, had just been named artistic director at Arena Stage; and Vogel herself had been named playwright in residence there. The company I was working with, The Theatre Conspiracy, had recently produced Vogel's *Desdemona: A Play about a Handkerchief*, and Arena was following *Drive* with Vogel's *Hot 'n' Throbbing*, and later her play *A Civil War Christmas*. The importance accorded to Vogel's identity as a local playwright was central to this publicity; her biography was readily available to any D.C. theatergoer who was interested. And yet despite the celebration of Vogel's life story, and despite the explicit invocation of the historical time and actual place of her own childhood in the narrative that *Drive* presents, critics were, and have remained, loathe to make connections between Vogel's play and her life. The closest reference one might find is *Washington Post* critic Lloyd Rose's connection of *Drive* to other "plays in which the writers try to forgive their families" such as Eugene O'Neill's *Long Day's Journey into Night* or Tennessee Williams's *The Glass Menagerie*.[1]

Certainly, Vogel's own disavowals of the play's autobiographical nature hold some weight here.[2] But why, we might ask, would a playwright who has already presented semiautobiographical work (in 1990s *The Baltimore Waltz*), write a play with a child protagonist, set in her own hometown in the era of her own childhood, if she were not interested in at least risking autobiographical readings? The denial of such a connection, while

admittedly equivocal, still suggests a critical reflex against the autobiographical reading of plays about women's traumas that is deeply conflicted, conditioned by equal parts poststructuralist theories of authorship
and a broader cultural squeamishness about representing women's rage.
Plays that risk such autobiographical identification abound, of course,
and they range from the overtly autobiographical, like Lisa Kron's *Well*,
Emily Mann's *Anulla: An Autobiography*, or Vanessa Redgrave's performance of Joan Didion's *The Year of Magical Thinking*, to more tenuous connections, like those to be found in *How I Learned to Drive* or Sarah Kane's
4.48 Psychosis, which serves as this chapter's test case. Certainly, theater's
collaborative nature helps undermine such connections between playwright and character, a point I discuss in the following chapter on biography plays: directors, designers, and actors all mediate the construction of
a character in such a way as to at least dilute an efficacious sense of present selfhood onstage. And yet I would suggest that there are ample and
important reasons to follow the impulse to interpret these performances
through the lens of autobiography, particularly in the case of women's
narratives of trauma, violence, and anger, even when critical orthodoxies
point us in precisely the opposite direction.

Among the most charged of such critical discussions around the
place of autobiographical readings of scripted plays we find Sarah Kane's
final play, *4.48 Psychosis*. Sarah Kane, as every biographical portrait of her
notes, burst onto the London theater scene in 1995 with her play *Blasted*,
which made the radical statement that a rape in a Leeds hotel room had
something to do with civil war in southeastern Europe. The play was controversial enough to be tabloid fodder, and so her similarly explosive fol-
low-up plays, including *Cleansed* in 1998, received publicity based as
much on their shocking subject matter as their formal innovation or rich
language, despite the fact that theater luminaries such as Caryl Churchill
and Harold Pinter declared themselves fans. When Kane committed suicide in 1999, she left behind *4.48 Psychosis*, a "play" with no stage directions, characters, or even much in the way of recognizable dialogue. It is a
fragmentary, poetic, often muddled and just as often brilliant piece of
writing. First produced by the Royal Court Theatre in June 2000, the play
received the unabashed critical success that her work (particularly her
earliest plays) rarely received in her lifetime.

Two critics who initially responded with outrage to Kane's first play,
the *Independent*'s Paul Taylor and the *Guardian*'s Michael Billington, each
praise *4.48 Psychosis*, and importantly, do so while describing the text as

"a suicide note."[3] Taylor, for example, writes that "if the play is a suicide note, it is an extraordinarily vital one," while Billington calls the play "a rare example of the writer recording the act she is about to perform." Unsurprisingly, perhaps, these early reviews follow the impulse to read the play autobiographically, as the phrase "suicide note" recurs across not just the theatrical reviews but also the academic criticism that attends the play. But while the early reviewers are quick to take the autobiographical path relatively uncritically, other writing on Kane has struggled against this impulse. In fact, much of the earliest criticism, often written by those who knew Kane personally, not only refutes but belittles this reading strategy, characterizing it as limited, literal minded, and a disservice to the work of the playwright herself. On the contrary, I would suggest that not only is it justifiable that we read this work as autobiography but in fact it is important to do so, just as it might be important to seek out autobiographical elements in other conventional drama by women playwrights. That is, *4.48 Psychosis* not only leaves plenty of clues that it is *about* the author but also gives readers insight into how we might imagine theatrical autobiography when the author is, literally and sadly, dead. For as theories of autobiography and theories of performance converge in the work of performance artists and other playwrights, we might do well here to disregard certain poststructuralist dogma and the exhortations of Kane's (primarily male) friends and family members and read this play not simply as one in which the author's identity is available in the text but as a staged autobiography—a textual performance of identity that is transformed in the space of theater.

Why We Should Perhaps Avoid Autobiographical Readings

Certainly, there are multiple reasons to avoid reading Sarah Kane's final play, and indeed any traditional drama, as autobiographical. Literary criticism has decried the intentional fallacy for decades, and with Roland Barthes's "The Death of the Author" and Michel Foucault's "What Is an Author?" theoretical accounts of authorship have been emphatic in removing the personage of the author from written texts.[4] Typically, in this poststructuralist paradigm, a living author is only ever another reader of a text, and interviews, journals, and commentary on a text issuing from the same author might at best be read in a playfully intertextual fashion.

In Kane's case, her death means that there are none of these postpublication (or postdiscovery) texts to bring to bear on the play in any case. Moreover, even if the work were avowedly autobiographical, theory is skeptical of making too quick conflations of the work and the life, as several previous chapters here have suggested. Paul de Man's "Autobiography as De-Facement," for example, is particularly emphatic on this point: "The interest of autobiography, then, is not that it reveals reliable self-knowledge—it does not—but that it demonstrates in a striking way the impossibility of closure and of totalization (that is the impossibility of coming into being) of all textual systems made up of tropological substitutions."[5] The inherent failure of autobiography, then, has been cast as endemic to all writing; the poststructuralist distrust of language and its ability to reliably represent reality understands such narrativization as inherently suspect, ultimately fallible, and therefore untenable as an expression of subjectivity.

In fact, as earlier chapters here suggest, even solo autobiographical performance that features the present body of the speaking performer can be read as unreliable autobiography, its subject coming into being only through speech acts that constitute it, rather than preexisting those speech acts. With dramatic texts performed by an actor other than the playwright, and commonly produced with a comparatively large number of collaborators, the notion of a single subjectivity emerging from the representation is even less tenable, as the "subject" of such a play is fragmented and dispersed over multiple identities, multiple bodies, multiple histories.

While critical and theoretical consensus pushes away from an autobiographical reading of any drama, the stakes for Kane's play are amplified, a scenario that plays out in a critical panic among those closest to Kane writing about her in the years immediately following her death. David Grieg, in his introduction to the playwright's *Complete Works*, urges readers "not to search for the author behind the words, but to freight the plays with our own presence."[6] Indeed, Kane's own brother and executor of her estate, Simon Kane, delayed the release of performance rights for *4.48 Psychosis* in the United States for fear that literal-minded Americans would only interpret it as autobiography. Because the play is "about suicidal despair . . . it is understandable that some people will interpret the play as a thinly veiled suicide note. [But . . .] this simplistic view does both the play and my sister's motivation for writing it an injustice."[7] In his book-length study of Kane's plays, Graham Saunders takes a similar, if more measured, stance. Saunders notes that "this last work was also the most clearly biographical and personally driven."[8] But he also echoes the caveat issued by Grieg and Simon Kane, warning that "thinking of *4.48 Psychosis* as little more than a suicide note also risks impoverishing the play: moreover such a commentary runs the risk of providing too reductive a reading, both of the play's content and its themes."[9]

There is a broader rationale to this injunction against reading the play as autobiography: Saunders cautions that "if *4.48 Psychosis* is to be seen exclusively in these terms, then the interpretation of suicide as an all encompassing theme could equally be applied to *all* Kane's work."[10] Similarly, Annabelle Singer addresses the autobiographical reception of *4.48 Psychosis* in light of the critical reception of her earlier plays, noting the frequent references made by theater critics to what they perceived must be Kane's mental illness, as though ascribing mental illness to the playwright allows critics to write off the challenges of the work.[11] This is no minor issue: the early reception of Kane's work, notably begun in Jack Tinker's *Daily Mail* review of *Blasted*, "The Disgusting Feast of Filth,"[12] was quick to ascribe Kane's disturbing vision to a diseased mental outlook. Singer goes so far as to suggest that *4.48 Psychosis* divides critics into "two camps: one saw her entire body of work in light of her suicide, the other mourned her death, but declined to even try to connect her death and her work."[13] These lines of thinking seem to contend that if we read *4.48 Psychosis* as autobiography, then it reveals Kane to be mentally ill, a designation that would, in effect, drain her previous work of its apparent efficacy, intelligence, and justified political critique. But there are certainly refutations available for such reactionary responses to Kane's work: we could identify the simple fallacious logic of the ad hominen attack, or invoke the collaborative nature of theater to ask such critics whether everyone associated with Kane's plays was equally deranged.

Nonetheless, author-based criticism can be and is used as a tool for ad hominem attacks, and while these are intellectually sloppy, they do invoke a long history of the circumscription of madness. One need look no further than Foucault's *Madness and Civilization* to find this line traced out. Foucault writes:

> In the serene world of mental illness, modern man no longer communicates with the madman: on one hand, the man of reason delegates the physician to madness, thereby authorizing a relation on through the abstract universality of disease; on the other, the man of

madness communicates with society only by the intermediary of an
equally abstract reason which is order, physical and moral constraint, the anonymous pressure of the group, the requirements of
conformity.[14]

He continues by asserting, "The language of psychiatry, which is a monologue of reason *about* madness, has been established only on the basis of
such a silence." Foucault's text, however, is not a recuperation of the language of "the man of madness" but "the archaeology of that silence."[15]
This confrontation of the language of madness and reason, what Foucault
calls the Reason-Madness nexus, "constitutes for Western culture one of
the dimensions of its originality; it already accompanies that culture long
before Hieronymus Bosch, and will follow it long after Nietzsche and Artaud."[16] It is no surprise, then, that we see *4.48 Psychosis*, in violent conversation with the language of psychiatry (and frequently connected to
the theatrical aesthetics of Artaud), placed under the critical erasure of a
diagnosis of mental illness.

The case is perhaps even more insidious because Kane is a woman
writing the language of madness and is therefore subject to an even more
insistent circumscription of unruly women's artistic production as hysteria. Shoshana Felman asks, "Is it by chance that hysteria (significantly derived as is well known, from the Greek word for 'uterus') was originally
conceived as an exclusively female complaint, as the lot and *prerogative* of
women?"[17] It is almost critical shorthand now to ask this question next to
Sandra Gilbert and Susan Gubar's analysis of the figure of the madwoman in the attic as a trope for female transgression.[18] And we might
similarly invoke Catherine R. Stimpson's analysis of the "violent yoking
of homosexuality and deviancy."[19] Given that Kane's work is not only
gendered but queer, the critical danger inherent in an autobiographical
reading is a perfect storm of cultural discipline against madness, against
women, and against homosexuality. And to connect Kane's final play
about suicide and mental illness to Kane's identity and personal history is
to therefore risk placing her entire oeuvre, indeed her entire life, under the
threat of erasure.

Nonetheless, while there are ample and urgent reasons to dismiss
reading this play as autobiographical, there are also rich and compelling
alternatives, the range of content and theme that Saunders and others
seek to highlight as they refute the autobiographical. The initial Royal
Court performance in 2000, for example, cast three actors to deliver the

unattributed and often undifferentiated language of the script, which (initial reviews of the play notwithstanding) might seem to subvert a purely autobiographical reading by calling attention to discrete acting bodies and discrete speaking voices. Certainly such a staging choice speaks to a more universalized notion of despair that can be expressed, experienced, and understood as deriving from a less specific set of experiences, and by casting one man and two women, the choice—which is reproduced in the larger portion of productions of this play—tends to degender the specific attributes of despair and rage that the play expresses. The play can also be read along formalist lines, representing an extension of the formal departicularizing of character and dialogue that the playwright began in her previous play, *Crave,* and which, as Saunders notes, reveals the influence of Kane's contemporary, Martin Crimp. Indeed, Grieg suggests that it is precisely "the play's open form [that] allows the audience to enter and recognize themselves within."[20] Saunders goes on to explore a number of themes that emerge through such a depersonalized strategy: metadiscourse on "the boundaries between reality, fantasy, and different mental states"; "the fragility of love"; "the search for self-hood"; and, of course, death.[21] Meanwhile, Annabelle Singer and Alicia Tycer each explore the play's handling of issues of psychiatric discourse, bodily mutilation, and the relationship between pain and art.

Through the play's critique of psychiatric discourse in particular, criticism has developed some of its most elegant readings. Ariel Watson reads the play among a group of "psychotherapy plays" that appeared in a relatively concentrated moment on the British stage, suggesting that "the hermeneutic structure of psychoanalysis and psychotherapeutic practice allows writers to reflect on the interpretive and judgemental [*sic*] processes of spectatorship as well as on the patient's anxiety about the performance of roles."[22] For Watson, who often writes persuasively about metatheatricality, the autobiography ends when the performance itself begins, a shift noted in the play's final lines—"It is myself I have never met, whose face is pasted on the underside of my mind / please open the curtains."[23] Suicide, in Watson's conjecture, "is the fulfillment of all expectations and the final assertion of free will. The end of the play, and of life, is the opening of the curtains, the beginning of performance."[24] Alicia Tycer's psychoanalytic reading of the play in performance hinges on the same assumption that the final line of the play signifies a move outward from the fractured subject of the play toward the witnessing audience through a process of "melancholic witnessing." She asserts:

Critics who define Sarah Kane's *4.48* as a text that is primarily autobiographical diminish the ability of readers and audience members
to enter into the play text and performances. *4.48* demands active involvement from its readers and audience members, encouraging
them to identify with depictions of loss and trauma that are not limited by Kane's personal narrative or their own. *4.48* fosters melancholic identifications in many ways, including its minimalist form,
the disorienting stage design of early productions, and its depiction
of characters that remain resolutely unresolved.[25]

By refocusing the performance not on mourning Kane as a specific absent
(and specifically absent) woman but on the process of melancholic witnessing undergone by the spectator, Tycer suggests that interpretation in
this play is radically open, a phenomenon that she argues is foreclosed by
autobiography.

Such a model that focuses on audience experience seems to have
grounded Claude Régy's French-language production, *4.48 Psychose,*
which featured Isabelle Huppert as the primary speaker and one other actor as interloper. Martin Harries notes this reduction of the typical cast
from three actors to two. Much criticism notes, as Harries does, that
"Kane's text includes a trio of positions: 'Victim. Perpetrator. Bystander.'
. . . In *4.48 Psychose* there are only two actors onstage. This 'théâtre' is a
drama that has cast the audience in one of Kane's roles. But we should not
assume too quickly that we know which position we occupy."[26] What
most of these readings and reviews argue is that an autobiographical understanding of Kane's play represents a kind of closure on the text, that an
open-ended reading of the play's many ambiguities is foreclosed by pin-
ning it to Kane's life, and more significantly, her death. The play's political critique might be similarly reduced to an apparently apolitical understanding of Kane's mental illness. And finally, they imagine that an
experiential approach to the audience's place in the play as a piece of theater is completely cut off because of the temporal closure that a fetishiza-
tion of a past act must necessarily represent. While these are central components for understanding Kane's play and acknowledging its depth and
richness, I want to argue that it is not only possible to retain these elements of the play alongside a reading of it as an expression of Kane's specific subjectivity but in fact placing it within the body of staged feminist
autobiography amplifies these concerns and connects the particulars of
Kane's life to the politics of her play, the ambivalences of its rich rumina-
tive capacity, and the identificatory valences of an audience's experience.

How We Can Read *4.48 Psychosis* as Autobiography

To consider how we might read the identity of the author of this play into the play's representation of subjectivity and selfhood, I want to turn briefly from the theatrical criticism that has thus far treated Kane's text most thoroughly. Instead, I want to think about Kane's authorship of this play through the theoretical lens of narratology, where thinking about the author as a figure in the text has a long and complex history. In his 1961 landmark book, *The Rhetoric of Fiction,* Wayne C. Booth first articulated the concept of the "implied author," the flesh and blood author's "official scribe" or "second self" as it appears in the norms, values, style, technique, and textual design of a given text or a given oeuvre.[27] The implied author "chooses, consciously or unconsciously, what we read; we infer him as an ideal, literary, created version of the real man; he is the sum of his own choices."[28] Although the concept has hardly been universally accepted, it has been defended on multiple lines, ranging from Seymour Chatman's reduction of the concept to only include the notion of the textual design available in the text itself, and only in the text itself,[29] to Susan S. Lanser's acknowledgment that, although the implied author remains essentially "incoherent" in a text, "some texts, some readers, and some settings [are] more likely to produce the sense of an author-as-persona."[30]

The implied author becomes useful as a concept here for any number of reasons. First of all, it delimits in some ways the notion of the life of the author as foreclosing the text, defining the author as it does, as an effect of reading or watching a play. Like Foucault's notion of the author-function, the implied author is always a textual construct, a product of discourse, around which inferences of intention, specters of agency, and other narratives, fictional and historical, cohere. And as narrative theorists, Booth included, have refined the concept, we find that many of the ways we account for the image of the author in the text already contain the slippages, incoherencies, ambiguities, and contradictions that all but the most radical deconstructions of authorship contain. And yet it is precisely through this figure of the playwright-in-the-text that I would assert that we can read Sarah Kane's actual suicide onto "Sarah Kane's" final play.[31]

Lanser, for example, in admitting the possibility of identifying the author-as-persona in a text, notes, "If we forego the need for coherence that has dominated our discussions of implied authorship, if we read textual surfaces instead of attempting to resolve them into a noncontradictory deep structure, we might figure the implied author not as a body but as the clothes the body wears."[32] Similarly, Booth, in one of his final defenses of the concept, argues:

> In every corner of our lives, whenever we speak or write, we imply a version of our character that we know is quite different from many other selves that are exhibited in our flesh-and-blood world. Sometimes the created versions of our selves are superior to the selves we live with day by day; sometimes they turn out to be lamentably inferior to the selves we present, or hope to present, on other occasions. A major challenge to all of us is thus to distinguish between beneficial and harmful masking. And that challenge is especially strong in literary criticism.[33]

Lanser's notion of the implied author as a kind of costume and Booth's notion of multiple selves as roles or performances seem to place an understanding of the author available through her text precisely in line with notions of performed selves that we find in the most deconstructive of autobiographical performances, where the persona of, say, Holly Hughes in performance must be taken to be both a character onstage and a referential signal of the life and experiences of Hughes offstage.

In this "bothness" of fictional construct and autobiographical reference, narratology offers audiences and critics of *4.48 Psychosis* a useful avenue for understanding the simultaneous presence and absence of Kane in and from her text. Lanser explores precisely this phenomenon when she examines first-person narratives that represent an ambiguous relationship between a fictional first-person narrator and the persona of the author. "Because autobiography and homodiegetic fiction deploy the same range of linguistic practices," Lanser writes, "the ontological status of most I-narratives cannot be proved by citing any part or even the whole of the text."[34] The typical response to this ontological ambiguity, as Lanser notes and Kane's academic readers have enacted, is to deny biographical reference and thus remove the author's persona from the text. This strategy, Lanser asserts, is as limiting and reductive as Kane's readers declare that wholly biographical readings are. Instead, she argues, "readers *routinely* 'vacillate' and 'oscillate' and even double the speaking voice against the logic of both structure and stricture."[35] If we acknowledge this, she continues, we can see "the complicated and transgressive ways in which the 'I' of the beholder—the 'I' the reader constructs according to what we might call his or her intelligence, in every sense of that term—is not always the singular 'I' of a fictional speaker but the 'I' of the author as well."[36] In short, Lanser's argument suggests that audience members watching Isabelle Huppert's performance of *4.48 Psychose* can hold in their minds the simultaneous presence (and meaningful absence) of Sarah Kane alongside Huppert's performance of the interchangeable and interacting roles of "Victim. Perpetrator. Bystander" in such a way that Harries argues includes even the audience itself. In this way, *4.48 Psychosis* is both autobiography and not autobiography, both particular to the life of Sarah Kane and simultaneously a collage of references, intertexts, personas, and sites of a broader identification.

When we come to read the implied author of Kane's text as equivocally attached to the personas of the text, as multiple, and as contradictory, a range of possibilities arises. Booth, for example, examines the complex case of Sylvia Plath, particularly in what was likely her final poem, "Edge." As the locus classicus of the literature of suicide, Plath's final work provides a significant precedent for how we might read Sarah Kane's last work. And in "Edge" Booth finds a range of contradictory implied authors: a deeply depressed woman, a furiously angry spouse, a masterful crafter of language, and an author pulling her readers "into a powerful confrontation with death!"[37] As a template for reading *4.48 Psychosis*, Booth's reading of Plath is instructive, because even as he enumerates the various performances of selfhood and authorship found in "Edge," he also enumerates his own responses as a conflicted and self-contradictory *reader* of Plath's poem, identifying the multiple "Booths" reading the poem: the poetry lover reveling in Plath's use of language and thematic richness, the reader informed of Plath's suicide, the critic preparing to write an article engaging Plath's poem, the distracted reader thinking of his other commitments, and the "lifetime moralizer [who] finds himself thinking not about the poem but about suicide."[38] So in Booth's own engagement of the multiple, contradictory, and equivocal attachments of Sylvia Plath to her poem "Edge," we find a model for the audience member sitting through *4.48 Psychosis* who can apply a biographical reading of Kane's life to the play at the same time as she performs the "melancholic witnessing" that Tycer argues is the audience's deepest ethical and experiential response.

Perhaps this is what Kane's agent and comanager of her literary estate, Mel Kenyon, means when he admits, "I pretend that [the play] isn't a suicide note but it is. It is both a suicide note and something much greater than that."[39] If we look to the text of the play itself, such a reading becomes both obvious and complicated. While there are close reading signals that tell us this might be autobiography, dwelling on them here simply to establish the possibility of such a reading seems beside the point; such an effort tells us little about Kane herself and virtually nothing about autobiography in the theater more generally. What we can see, however, are the sorts of cues that do signal the possibility of the narrativized self, and foremost among the signals of such an attachment is the persistence of first-person address that abounds.

> I am sad
> I feel that the future is hopeless and that things cannot improve
> I am bored and dissatisfied with everything
> I am a complete failure as a person[40]

And while these lines read like an "Are You Depressed?" self-help questionnaire, the questions gradually turn from the faceless to the particular.

> I am fat
> I cannot write
> I cannot love
> My brother is dying, my lover is dying, I am killing them both
> I am charging towards my death
> I am terrified of medication
> I cannot make love
> I cannot fuck
> I cannot be alone
> I cannot be with others
> My hips are too big
> I dislike my genitals[41]

Here, references to writing, her brother and lover, and eventually the details of her own body move us away from universal to the personal details of one woman's psyche. Of course first-person narration doesn't necessarily mandate an autobiographical reading, even if it is perhaps autobiography's most common narrative component. Of course, the other primary component of autobiographical narrative is the representation of a life history, and while it may be mere pedantry to detail where Kane's life overlaps with the narrative that we can piece together from this collage, enough references to life details exist that we can make at least make a tentative claim to its truth value. But the greatest truth claim that this play makes is in representing the interiority of the suicide, written by a woman who left behind the script after she hanged herself. To suggest that this represented thought process is somehow fictional seems to be an insistence on a more discrete divide between the mimetic and the mimed than autobiography ever presupposes.

My hesitance to indulge in the "mere pedantry" of seeking out the details of Kane's life in the text echoes the impulses of critics like Graham Saunders and others who eschew biographical readings of the play. And I agree with them on many points, particularly Saunders, when he calls out the diminishing effects of the term *suicide note,* for, as he rightly observes, "Suicide notes by their nature are brief, and only ever partly articulate what they want to say. One of the crucial things that must be stressed about Sarah Kane's last play is that it was not hastily written like a suicide note."[42] And I agree with Ariel Watson, who believes that Kane's "haunting prescience [in the play is] made all the more painful by the sense that the attention that the work has received has resulted from morbid curiosity rather than the substantial merits of the text."[43] But inasmuch as these readers express anxiety about the reception of *4.48 Psychosis,* they also reveal a misapprehension about what an autobiographical reading can and must open up about Kane's play. To invoke such a reading does not, as these readers assert, reduce or minimize the politics, philosophy, or experiential potency of the play—precisely the opposite. That, constrained by my limited knowledge of Sarah Kane as a person, I cannot make the most minute connections between the life and the text does not signal the weakness of such a connection but rather that reading the equivocal attachments of *4.48 Psychosis'* speakers to Sarah Kane as a living, breathing, queer, female subject in a heartbreaking world renders what is significant about her text even more so.

Why We Must Read *4.48 Psychosis* as Autobiographical

When readers of this play, like Grieg and Tycer, caution us against reading the play as autobiography, they not only misapprehend the possibilities of an autobiographical reading but they misunderstand the genre entirely. Their apparent sense of the genre as a purely factual documentation of a life ignores the degree to which autobiographical writers, particularly women writers, have opened up the genre by calling attention to its possibility of reference and of representing "the whole truth." Scholars of autobiography have long read works like Mary McCarthy's *Memoirs of a Catholic Girlhood* or Lauren Slater's *Lying* as troubling the assumptions of the form by calling attention to its epistemological claims. Timothy Dow Adams, for example, has written:

> Although the literal accuracy of an autobiography's words is not important, it is important that the writer chose to stray from what really happened. The complicated series of strategies behind an author's conscious and unconscious misrepresentations is not beside the point. We often discover that whether or not an autobiography rings true is as important as whether or not it is true. And although it is certainly impossible ever to ascertain the whole truth of a life and pointless to attempt to identify every minute factual error in a personal narrative, in between is a fertile field for analysis.[44]

Thinking, then, of the strategies that Kane uses in this autobiographical play forces us to consider it as a rhetorical text, one that oscillates among personal truth, nonfictional collage, and fictional creation. And in this oscillation, we can connect it to a host of other women's autobiographical texts that deploy these strategies, for, as Sidonie Smith recognizes, "Contestatory 'truth' also arises from a recognition that the autobiographer is entangled in competing, even contradictory regimes of truth."[45] That Kane's response to the medical discourse of psychiatry is not merely a "suicide note," with its implications of haste, narcissism, and disease, but rather a complex and sophisticated contestation of the truth of her selfhood places her text specifically within the realm of women's autobiographical production.

Indeed, far from embodying a collection of marginal, insignificant, inward-gazing, purely private narratives, the body of women's autobiographical plays and performances over the past several decades instead reveals that both the form and the reading strategies it requires constitute a deeply intellectual, theoretically sophisticated, and politically potent enterprise. By placing Kane's text within that corpus, we find not only that her work enriches our sense of how the playwright's selfhood and experience find their way to the stage but also that the range of interpretive practices that artists like Carolee Schneeman, Orlan, Holly Hughes, and Terry Galloway demand opens up Kane's text even further to connect her portrait of suicidal despair not just to a universal sense of melancholic witnessing but also to the specific and particular political and personal rage that resonates across the genre of performed autobiography. That is, to understand *4.48 Psychosis* as a specific kind of subject construction offers far more to the play—its understanding of identity fragmentation, its critique of medical discourse, its approach to the discursive maneuvers that circumscribe queer women's bodies, its expression of the anger that women are still punished for expressing, and the critical mechanisms it provides for reading suicide in literature generally, as well as autobiographical suicide literature specifically. All of these become particularized and therefore politicized when we choose to read the play not as a universal portrait of pain but as the representation of *this* woman's subjectivity, *this* woman's anger, and the theatricalized corporeal violence that results.

When we look at the critical impulse to ignore these particularities, we cannot help but see the resonances of Barthes's "The Death of the Author" and its manifesto against the authorial fallacy in favor instead of the primacy of the text, the intertext, even the reader. But while Barthes generally proposes to elide the specific historical identity of the *auteur* in order to replace it with the anonymous language worker, the *scriptor*, that worker's maleness is never up for debate. When Barthes writes, "Succeeding the Author, the scriptor no longer bears within *him* passions, humors, feelings, impressions," he first of all acknowledges the gender of the scriptor as male (indeed, the original French offers him no other choice).[46] Barthes seeks to accord the scriptor the same status that he sees accorded to the reader: "without history, biography, psychology."[47] But when we view this theoretical desire—one that has historically been cited with far less subtlety than it is accorded in Barthes's other work—to elide the author within the field of staged feminist life writing, we find that women become the collateral damage of such de(con)structive impulses. When we take away Sarah Kane's "history, biography, psychology" we elide precisely that which has been denied her as a woman across history. While Barthes's desire to kill off the author does nothing to disrupt the status of men's contributions to a history of subjectivity, women's contributions to that history are still by no means well established in the popular imagination, and much of what *is* established comes from precisely this source: what we know from women writers and their texts. To elide the specter of the body of the author (even in that body's conspicuous absence) is to prevent women generally, and Kane specifically, from writing themselves back into history. To read this text equivocally, as both not-autobiography and autobiography, engages precisely the kinds of transgressive, subversive reading strategies that Kane's work has always demanded. Under this approach, then, we must hear Lanser when she argues that "the beholder has a queer and shifty eye, attaching and detaching by turns, and doing so *despite* the 'fact' that all fictional voices are fictions or that the 'I' can technically represent only one speaking entity."[48]

Indeed, the fragmented multiplicity of the self of this play becomes a charged site of interpretation. Saunders suggests that the line "It is myself I have never met, whose face is pasted on the underside of my mind,"[49] signals "the search for self-hood."[50] This is a theme that he traces back to Kane's previous play, *Crave,* and one that manifests particularly in a thorough exploration of the duality and discontinuities of the body and the mind. Saunders notes in particular an episode in which the speaker is in dialogue with the therapeutic voice of the play, talking about the self-mutilating practice of cutting, in which the speaker declares that "it feels fucking amazing." Careful to suggest that the scene was likely inspired not by Kane's own self-mutilation but by "someone Kane knew," Saunders implicitly refutes the kind of simple biographical reading that he earlier rejected.[51] Yet this is precisely where an equivocal attachment, the I/Not I of the text comes into focus, for even as the play includes details that were not Kane's own, it embeds those details within a repeated concern for the embodied problems of selfhood. That is, the collage of voices and personas that *4.48 Psychosis* employs is entirely in keeping with the ways the play expresses selfhood as fragmented. Throughout the text, we hear lines like "I am deadlocked by the smooth psychiatric voice of reason which tells me there is an objective reality in which my body and mind are one,"[52] "My mind is the subject of these bewildered fragments,"[53] "Body and soul can never be married,"[54] "Do you think it's possible for a person to be born into the wrong body?,"[55] and "Here am I / and there is my body."[56] The persistence of this theme across the text ties to a range of feminist autobiographical texts not only in its response to the "smooth psychiatric voice of reason" but also to the alternative expression of the self that is deeply fragmented, and rooted in a feminist response to Lacanian analysis. Indeed, this fragmentation of selfhood and the radical refusal of coherence expressed by the play become both the hallmark of Lanser's understanding of the implied author and her suggestion of the transgressive potential of reading the "I" of this play as equivocally attached simultaneously both to Sarah Kane and to multiple fictional and nonfictional personas.

The stakes for such a reading become clearer when expressions of a fragmented selfhood are placed in conflict with the medicalized language of psychiatry, a critique widely acknowledged in other criticism on the play.[57] We find this conflict throughout the text, embodied in passages like the following.

> Sanity is found at the centre of convulsion, where madness
> is scorched from the bisected soul.
> I know myself.
> I see myself.
> My life is caught in a web of reason
> Spun by my doctor to augment the sane.[58]

It is not difficult to hear echoes of Foucault as he writes that "the language of psychiatry . . . is a monologue of reason about madness." And we might read *4.48 Psychosis* as a countermonologue, one that can—through the expression of the fragmented self, also contain dialogue between madness and reason, careening between order (as in scenes that stage therapeutic exchanges) and disorder (as in the undecipherable fields of numerals that appear). In the this passage, for example, the expressions of self-knowledge and self-recognition are expressed as convulsion and bisection rather than coherence, which is instead posed as a "web of reason" that serves the interests of the social order represented by "the sane." The antagonistic relationship between doctor and patient here and elsewhere is not simply the speaker's reticence to submit to the doctor's healing regime but rather a determined stance, one that implicitly critiques the power relations inherent in the relationship, complete with the coercion and restriction of pharmaceutical remedies.

Doctors in particular come under this scrutiny as agents of a certain kind of social order.

> Inscrutable doctors, sensible doctors, way-out doctors, doctors you'd think were fucking patients if you weren't shown proof otherwise, ask the same questions, put words in my mouth, offer chemical cures for congenital anguish and cover each other's arses until I want to scream for you, the only doctor who ever touched me voluntarily, who looked me in the eye, who laughed at my gallows humor spoken in the voice of the newly-dug grave, who took the piss when I shaved my head, who lied and said it was nice to see me. Who lied. And said it was nice to see me. I trusted you, I loved you, and it's not losing you that hurts me, but your bare-faced fucking falsehoods that masquerade as medical notes.[59]

That all doctors here, even the betrayer, are linked by medical discourse, and by covering "each other's arses" suggests the way the play poses psychiatry as a kind of power matrix, self-sustaining and defending, but one that ultimately seems bent on containing the subject of madness. The critique of doctors, then, stands in for a more abstract theme of constraint—social and medical—and freedom, which suicide seems to offer. One darkly humorous line expresses this tension: "I dreamt I went to the doctor's and she gave me eight minutes to live. I'd been sitting in the fucking waiting room half an hour."[60] This is precisely the "gallows humor spoken in the voice of the newly-dug grave" that the speaker describes, and the scripted silence that follows from the scene's assumed interlocutor seems to lead the speaker to a capitulation: "Ok. Let's do it, let's do the drugs, let's do the chemical lobotomy, let's shut down the higher function of my brain."[61] The silence here is obviously a response to the humor of the previous line, one that an audience will experience first as laughter and then, as the interlocutor's staged silence continues, as an explicit denial of laughter, which we must take as a kind of medical refusal to engage the speaker as a person. This refusal then seems to coerce the speaker away from her own "voice of the newly-dug grave" to the medical alternative of "chemical lobotomy." That denial of humanity, the cold medicalized gaze of psychiatry, becomes, for the speaker, as perhaps for Kane, the only alternative to suicide, and one that stands in opposition to the bisected, fragmented selfhood that she recognizes as her own. The alternative with which the speaker is left at the end of the play is stark, as she says, "Nowhere left to turn / an ineffectual moral spasm / the only alternative to murder."[62] To read these lines as fictional I believe minimizes the serious critique that the play offers up. As an expression of Kane's own narrative—of mental anguish, of the struggle to reconcile a sense of fragmented identity with the drive to psychiatric coherence, of betrayal and coercion by doctors generally and by specific doctors particularly, by the real sense that no alternatives exist between suicide and "the ineffectual moral spasm" that is offered by a regime of medicalized reason, of the logic of *her own suicide*—this play becomes something that demands witnessing not as an abstraction of despair but as a material human loss. This is not merely a hypothetical death predicated on a hypothetical experience of psychiatry's response to depression. Kane's play is instead, and must be understood as, the narrative of a real death that through language forces its audiences to understand the stakes of its own critique, and its own anger.

Of course we well know the social proscriptions against women's anger. Carolyn Heilbrun, writing about women's autobiographies, asserts that "above all other prohibitions, what has been forbidden to women is anger, together with the open admission of the desire for power and control over one's life (which inevitably means accepting some degree of power and control over other lives)."[63] Anger, then, becomes the expression that exceeds the boundaries of social control, prohibited by women's gender codes and enforced by medical controls against madness. So when the speaker expresses anger (as she does often and forcefully), we must read it not as a symptom of madness but rather as a pointed, violent response against the regimes of truth that would otherwise seek to repress her rage. We can see this effect in a segment that parodies the language of the medical chart. Tucked into lines of medical narration of treatment, complete with symptoms, diagnosis, and pharmaceutical treatments, the "chart" reads, "Mood: Fucking angry. / Affect: very angry."[64] Other segments include tirades of rage, populated amply with "fuck yous," which serve as linguistic markers of an anger that seems to exceed not just the bounds of the therapeutic session but of language itself. Another scene seems to be a one-sided dialogue, perhaps with a lover or a doctor (even the doctor for whom the speaker earlier expressed love). The speaker asks questions, but is met only with silence; she ends with:

> Fuck you. Fuck you. Fuck you for rejecting me by never being there, fuck you for making me feel shit about myself, fuck you for bleeding the fucking love and life out of me, fuck my father for fucking up my life for good and fuck my mother for not leaving him, but most of all, fuck you God for making me love a person who does not exist, FUCK YOU FUCK YOU FUCK YOU.[65]

That the speaker presses at the boundaries of language as she struggles to express anger here, and that anger ends dialogues as in this scene, underscores the degree to which the combination of madness and rage, and a woman's madness and rage in particular, becomes the site of resistance, even as it struggles to achieve a kind of agency. When Heilbrun links anger and agency as prohibited women's expressions, she provides a key to Kane's text, which artfully deploys language at the same time that it exceeds the limits of language. This fact seems to answer Shoshana Felman's call to respond to the hysterical "phallacy": "The challenge facing the woman today is nothing less than to 're-invent' language, to *re-learn how to speak:* to speak not only against, but outside the specular phallogocentric structure, to establish a discourse the status of which would no longer be defined by the phallacy of masculine meaning."[66]

We must therefore read *4.48 Psychosis* as a struggle to establish the agency of the self by "speaking both as *mad* and as *not mad.*"[67] And the struggle for agency is apparent throughout, as when the speaker says, "I know what I'm doing / all too well."[68] In another section in which the speaker enumerates her desires, she lists "to be free from social restrictions / to resist coercion and constriction / to be independent and act according to desire."[69] This freedom from constriction also comes with a sense that agency entails responsibility, an ethical argument that runs beneath the text and butts up against multiple iterations of the line "It's not your fault." In one specific therapeutic exchange, the therapist's voice intones, "It's not your fault. You're ill."[70] This expression can easily be read as a seduction of psychiatry to rescind agency, to offer up control of the self to the regimes of medicine. But the voice here rejects that palliative.

> ———No. I'm depressed. Depression is anger. It's what you did,
> who was there and who you're blaming.
> ——— And who are you blaming?
> ——— Myself.[71]

This last line raises the most troubling ethical issue of the play, and one that hinges on the reading of the play as autobiographical—the relationship of suicide to agency. Indeed, the play sometimes sets up suicide as an ethical imperative, that this is "Not a life that I could countenance,"[72] that when given the last choice between "an ineffectual moral spasm" and suicide, that there is no "sane" choice. Many critics have noted the connection of Kane's text to Martin Crimp's play *Attempts on Her Life,* specifically one scene in which the protean central figure, Anne (elsewhere Annie, Anushka, and Anny), is an artist who makes art installations out of the materials and documents of her own suicide attempts.[73] While the art critics who discuss the work in Crimp's play are clearly parodies, and one suspects that performance artists like Orlan or Marina Abramovich are referenced in the art under discussion, the specter of a suicide artist represented in this scene by Anne is one that remains deeply unsettling under the sophisticated veneer of the other speakers' language of art criticism. Reading *4.48 Psychosis* against this scene, Saunders calls attention to the satire itself of "the attempt to say something clever or profound about a work that tries to represent or comment upon intense human despair."[74] What Saunders does not address is the grisly possibility that less sympathetic accounts would raise the possibility that Kane's play is itself that kind of performance art.

To take this possibility seriously is deeply dangerous, and I am neither sufficiently rash nor sufficiently cavalier to say that Kane's suicide was itself merely an act of art that served as a companion to the text. But what this possibility raises is the interrelationship between the text and the act of suicide as acts of agency. To understand suicide as only an act of agency is itself overly simplistic, and Kane's division of "Victim. Perpetrator. Bystander" must be taken to signify the deeply divided self who inhabits all three roles in the act. Yet at the same time, we must take together the following premises: that the play is among other things a critique of the disempowering mechanisms of psychiatry, that the play represents a struggle to reconcile selfhood and madness through some sense of agency, and that the suicide that coincided with the play's completion is itself a tragic act of agency. Taken together, we must be left with the conclusion that at some level Kane's suicide is a performed act that makes meaning, even if that meaning-making process is hardly the entirety of the act itself. This last point is crucial, for I do not intend to say that Kane's death can be reduced to an artistic act. But to deny that it performs meaning in concert with the play she left behind is to deny Kane's own agency, both as a woman who suffered intensely and as an artist. It is under these conditions that we must read the play as both autobiography and not-autobiography, and we must read the suicide as art and not-art. To do so is not to reduce the work or the life to mere metonymies of one another but rather to recognize and honor the absolute risk inherent in delivering this script in concert with the taking of her own life.

If we do so, we might read Kane's final play as participating in what Ken Urban has characterized as her pursuit of an "ethics of catastrophe" wherein her work "emerges from calamity with the possibility that an ethics can exist between wounded bodies, that after devastation, good becomes possible."[75] Here, I would argue, to even begin to ascertain the possibility for good in a brutal world, we must overtly acknowledge the catastrophe that underscores it. Kane's theater is rife with wounded bodies and wounded psyches. The theater world was shocked and outraged at the brutality staged in plays like *Blasted* and *Cleansed*, works that externalized the kinds of violence done to bodies and selves. To understand *4.48 Psychosis* as an account of her own experiences that ended in 1999 with her death demands an even greater outrage against the social discourses that left her feeling she had no other choice, and it is through the play itself that we find a record of the process by which these discourses systematically robbed the self of choice. If there is an ethics of catastrophe, we can find in her theater "neither solutions nor redemption," as Urban expresses it.[76] But we must acknowledge the fullness of the catastrophe to see the possibility for good.

Ultimately, I would argue that performances of this play must somehow reflect on the importance of insisting on reading women's life writing as particular to the woman and not simply as a universal rumination on suicidal pain. While traditional drama leads us to expect bodies other than the playwright's on the stage, here that representational expectation is made strange—even queered in a representational fashion. The absence of Sarah Kane's body, therefore, is not a mere fact of the traditional relationship of playwriting to performance but rather a signifier, an absence with meaning. Her body—the body of the author—is no longer just circumstantially elsewhere but consequentially *not here*. Where the semiotics of authorship becomes more than a symbolic not-life—an act of submission of the text to forces that elide the author—but rather an act of death, the play requires and points out the agency of the author over her own body even as it refuses to indicate her instructions about the bodies of her actors.

Of course, this choice to read absence as agency, to refuse to read writing as not-life, but rather as active death (and by extension, as a sort of life writing in its final stage), must continually evoke in us as audience members and readers a kind of anxiety of criticism, one about intentional fallacies, and biographical criticism of the most dangerous kind. This is the anxiety that Grieg, Saunders, and Simon Kane express by pushing us to read *4.48 Psychosis* as universal. But to do so depoliticizes this work in an oeuvre of otherwise deeply politicized work and uses the absence of Kane's particular body to inadvertently erase the particular life that Kane's play writes—precisely because Kane's play writes the active erasing of the body. So no matter how we choose to approach the difficult ethical question of reading suicide as an act of self-determination, the decision on our part to universalize *4.48 Psychosis* makes that choice an impossibility because it refuses to link the writing to the body and voice of its author—self-determination is not a consideration precisely because we have elected not to read a specific self in question. Instead, agreeing to consider Kane's work as autobiography, even as that choice carries with it a kind of danger, lets the work itself answer that question, by speaking on behalf of the body whose death it narrates and whose absence it performs.

Conclusion: Risking Autobiography

At some level, we must also ask about the possibility of reading *as auto-biographical* a play that is not avowedly specifically an autobiography. Can the lessons of *4.48 Psychosis* apply to a play like *How I Learned to Drive*, where the playwright at once inserts cues to read biographically, even as she publicly denies the play's plot as autobiography? Can we read as meaningful the absence of the playwright onstage as something other than a Barthesian death-of-the-author, particularly in cases in which the flesh and blood author is still alive? Perhaps, but such a strategy always risks a great deal. And that risk tells us much about writing, performing, reading, and witnessing autobiography, particularly when trauma is at stake. I, for example, can never completely suspend my disbelief enough to accept that *4.48 Psychosis* is somehow a fictional rumination. To ignore the truth effects of that play seems to me to be a willful blindness, one that also asks us to turn a blind eye to the conditions that produced the play and the act that it narrates. Sarah Kane's entire body or work consisted of forcing audiences to look at things they did not want to see, and to risk audiences *not seeing* her own life at the center of the work is the risk of this particular text. In other cases, as perhaps in the case of a play like *How I Learned to Drive*, the playwright risks what audiences can see about the life in the work, and to completely erase the possibility of the traumas that underlie that work is to continue to elide the traumas themselves, like incest and the complexities of love and betrayal that incest occasions in the case of Vogel's play. To refuse to witness, to continue to turn a blind eye to the possible truths that undergird these plays' traumatic plots, must remain an ethically suspect move under the cover of critical orthodoxy.

I am not advocating that we suddenly return to a regime of biographical readings of every text or performance by every playwright or author, for the entirety of this book argues that we understand the deeply contingent construction of truths and selves in any performance and any text. But to acknowledge the constructedness of truths and selves is not to deny the possibility of the real, particularly when the witness of real historical trauma, or violence against bodies, selves, and whole categories of people, is at stake. I am advocating that we risk reading these texts not with the medically diagnostic gaze of pure criticism but with the "queer and shifty eye" that their equivocal attachments of selves to characters ask. This is precisely what is demanded by *4.48 Psychosis*, which at least provides us with a way to think about the absent body of the playwright (and therefore a necessary presence of some other performing body) as a component of a performed autobiography, one that assumes the fragmentary nature of identity, and in doing so utilizes the collaborative nature of theatrical production to literalize and express that fragmentation.

Paul Taylor's initial review of Kane's play in the *Independent* archly opens with the line "Nothing will interfere with your work like suicide."[77] It is a line delivered by a voice we must presume to be a doctor's or a therapist's, and it is met in the text with a scripted silence, an echo and a ghosting of the silence and absence attended by the playwright's death. We might easily find ourselves agreeing with that voice and shaking our heads sadly at the silence that Kane's suicide ultimately produced. And yet to view the death and the writing as diametrically opposed ignores the rest of the play. We honor the generosity and risk involved in constructing this play not through reading Kane's life as separate from it but rather by insistently reading Kane's fragmented, bisected, convulsive self, and "the voice from the newly-dug grave," back into the text.

PART II : BIOGRAPHY

STAGING WOMEN'S LIVES

CHAPTER 4 : Staging Women's Lives, Staging Feminist Performances

In the National Statuary Hall Collection in the U.S. Capitol, a visitor can stroll along a parade of great men, admiring the busts, standing figures, and horsed figures carved in Italian marble and other polished chunks of stone. The parade marches on in traditional style until it reaches the suffragists, a memorial to Lucretia Mott, Elizabeth Cady Stanton, and Susan B. Anthony. Immediately the visitor notices the stylistic and ideological incongruities of the suffragist memorial amid the phalanx of polished soldiers that surrounds it: Mott, Stanton, and Anthony are incompletely carved, their bodies rising from a partially formed, seven-ton slab of marble; rising behind them, taller than the three, is an unformed figure, the beginnings of a fourth feminist yet to be realized. I was introduced to the statue, a gift of the National Woman's Party, by a friend of mine, herself introduced to it by a friend who insists that every young feminist she knows take a photo in front of the statue as an image of her potential to become that as yet unformed fourth figure.

In a sense, this sculpture is an excellent metaphor for the biographical plays examined in this chapter, as well as the larger tradition of feminist life writing that has flourished over the last thirty years. Like these plays, the memorial is working to represent a life through a feminist framework. That is, feminists staging biographical plays face much the same parade of great men (Shakespeare's histories come to mind) as did Adelaide Johnson, the sculptor of this piece. Like the sculptor, feminist playwrights find the gendered tradition of biography (constructing a life into art) problematic in its ideology and insufficient in its capacity to adequately recover feminist lives without compromising their feminist politics.[1] Instead, in order to claim their places in the footlights of history, feminists must find a new way to represent their own. And they have: just as these suffragists are incompletely carved and overtly sculptural, many staged feminist biographies show the process of representing a life while they present the life itself; they show their subjects in communities and not as discrete entities; and they do so in a way that makes the lives of the past templates for the lives of the present and the future, all notions I'll discuss in this chapter. Like the memorial, staged feminist biographies respond to the imperative to place women in the pantheon of history, but in a very specific fashion. These plays as a group seek to avoid the gendered trappings of the biographical tradition by contextualizing and calling attention to the construction of their narratives and the performativity of the lives they narrate, and in doing so, they project the significance of their biographical subjects' lived performances into the present and the as yet unformed future.

There are also, however, significant differences between the sculpture in the Capitol Building and the feminist biographies that populate today's stage. One is simply quantity. As I noted in the introduction to this study, plays about real women proliferate, almost as common to feminist playwrights as autobiography has been for feminist performance artists. And yet little critical attention has been paid to the form, despite an interest in biographical work within theater historiography itself.[2] The narrow critical attention paid to this emergent category, which brings the same project to the stage that feminist theater historiographers have undertaken in their work, seems singularly odd given the explosion of texts and performances available to examine. It is precisely my project here to pay that attention, to examine feminist biographical drama as a category that speaks not only to feminist playwrights' stagings of subjectivity but also to their negotiations with history.

Nonetheless, Adelaide Johnson's sculptural feminist biography gives us an important analogy: in offering us that fourth unformed figure, she emphasizes not what Stanton, Mott, or Anthony *were* but rather what they *did*. In a more traditional biographical model, the artist might seek to recover and reclaim from history's oblivion a personage and the identity she staked out for herself; Lucretia Mott, Elizabeth Cady Stanton, and Susan B. Anthony might themselves be held up as role models. While this is certainly a feminist project—indeed, one that defined much second-wave feminist scholarship—it follows certain objective and objectifying conventions of the traditional male biography, which hold up the "great man" as an unattainable ideal. Yet while we might be tempted to think of Johnson's suffragists as exemplars, the prominence and distinctiveness of that fourth figure draw the eye and claim the viewer's attention. We come to realize that through the act of *becoming,* this fourth figure can claim a place through actions, or to put it more pointedly, through feminist cultural *performances.* Similarly, recent feminist biographical plays emphasize the real-life acts and transgressive gender performances of feminist and protofeminist women, a recovery facilitated by the very performativity of gender. These plays avoid merely holding up historical women as museum pieces removed by time from their audiences and choose instead to hold up their subjects as dynamic agents who, through accessible and repeatable acts, resisted or exploded traditional gender roles. In doing so, these plays offer audiences an accessible model of acting in the world. Working on the assumption that audience members can never *be* the same as the feminist subject of biographical inquiry, these plays posit that audience members can nevertheless *do* the same things that the biographical subject did, emphasizing real-life performances rather than merely the facts of existence. While certainly not every staged feminist biography of the last thirty years follows this model, the notion of the "reclaimed performance" highlights trends that we find across the mode: the historical performance as a site of feminist praxis for both biographical figure and actor, the metaperformance of biographical inquiry itself, and a replaying of the eliding processes of history that make such a reclamation possible and necessary. That is, by playing the lives they hope to unearth, feminist biography plays reclaim precisely that which *can be reclaimed*—the performances of their feminist subjects that feminist audiences can witness in the art-making space of the theater and replay as theatricalized performances in public and private spaces of their own.

Reclaiming Transgressive Performances

The second-wave project of reclamation that underscores feminist biographical plays finds its origins all across the historical discourses of feminism and drama: the recovery work of feminist critics from 1974's *Hidden from History* through current work on life writing in performance.[3] Sue-Ellen Case justifies the project succinctly: "I hoped to 'name' a few of the relatively invisible but pioneering women in traditional theatre, so that feminists can claim a heritage."[4] Even in "naming" the few, Case undertakes the beginnings of feminist biography for the stage, recovering women's voices throughout history, establishing a feminist theatrical tradition, and legitimizing current work. Of course, both feminist historical scholarship and feminist playwrights as far back as Megan Terry and Ann Jellicoe had been doing this both on the page and on the stage for years, even if criticism that marries these two prongs has been slow to develop.

Despite this imperative to enter the intersection of feminism, biography, and drama in order to enact this kind of recovery work, certain theoretical problems associated with the task persist. Perhaps the most obvious (and best documented) is the problem of representing the "real" that is inherent in any life writing project, a problem made even more acute by the mimetic embodiment of the actor so central to theater's representational vocabulary; that the actor's body is not the "real person" only exacerbates the issue. Evelyn J. Hinz argues that drama becomes an apt metaphor for the problems of theorizing life writing precisely because the two genres share the element of mimesis as a foundational concept.[5] Yet if drama solves problems for Hinz by providing a language with which to talk about textual biographies, when we actually turn those biographies *into drama* those problems are doubled: the theoretical and generic binds caused by mimesis are compounded by the representational and performative binds of mimesis. That is, the responsibility to narrativize reality is compounded when that responsibility is extended to embodiment, a demand that autobiographical performance satisfies in potent ways because actor and character at least are understood as occupying the same body. But when we add the tension between live, present bodies and a distant, absent historical event to the equation, too much rests on the tenuous suspension of disbelief. Both modernist critiques of objectivity and postmodern critiques of history as necessarily fictional come to bear on such plays. This double bind leads to what Ken Mitchell calls "a long and cantankerous relationship between history and story, and between biography and drama."[6]

Indeed, that many of these plays could be accused of doing "bad history" may be evidence of this double bind, and may also explain the lack of attention they have received. However, representational referentiality—specifically in the form of historical accuracy—is not always a primary concern for these plays. In fact, in the introduction to her 1991 *Delirium of Interpretations,* an "antibiography" of sculptor Camille Claudel commissioned by Theatre Cocteau in Basel, Switzerland, playwright Fiona Templeton explicitly states, "In this play I am not interested in who or what was or should be biographically correct" (i).[7] Instead she claims that her play is specifically about the interpretive problems of doing biography amid a range of contradictory representations of the biographical subject. Even more blatantly dismissive of the strictures of historical precision is Joan Schenkar's *Signs of Life,* based on the life of Alice James. In her author's note on the relationship of her narrative to its historical antecedents, Schenkar argues that "Art made from extreme situations can often find its 'facts' (i.e., the hinges upon which certain of its circumstances swing) in history," after which she goes on to explain the historical antecedents of characters and instances in her play, ranging from the biographical (the presence of Katherine Loring in Alice James's life, Henry James's burning of his sister's journals) to the inspirational (Dr. J. Marion Sims's Uterine Guillotine as the basis for her characterization of Dr. Sloper, himself a fictional creation from Henry James's *Washington Square*).[8] In this case, Schenkar makes all but explicit that history is put in service of the political underpinnings of her art. Of course, individual playwrights prioritize the recovery of history versus the interrogation of history making differently, and yet these concerns find themselves in tension with one another across the genre.

With postmodern historians espousing the necessary fictionality of history, and narrative theorists asserting the necessary truth value of fictional narratives, "good history" seems an impossible goal, a task that can only be undermined by its own necessary fictionality, lost in the blurred lines between fictional and historical discourses. However, we must not assume that the appeal of "real" historical narratives that lies at the center of these dramatic projects is simply a critique of the processes of writing history. Like much of what Linda Hutcheon has called "historiographic metafiction," these plays assume in their very exploration a deep sense of the stability of historical truth, that historical narratives are worth exploring, and that they must be excavated for specific political purposes. Eric Berlatsky has suggested the limitations of the extreme postmodernist position that might undermine the truth value of history, noting that "the historical real is a site of political contestation," especially given "the difficulty for socially and politically oppressed peoples to participate in their own coherent and stable identity formation and representation through memory in an age identified as postmodern."[9] To claim history uncritically, then, is to accept the historical narratives that have marginalized women, but to completely undermine the value of history for women is similarly problematic, disrupting, as Berlatsky suggests, "the central importance of both individual and collective memory in advancing the political interests of oppressed peoples, particularly in protecting a communality and shared identification from the effacing powers of 'official' or institutional history."[10]

Thus, feminist playwrights are responding to an imperative to recover lives, but they must also do more than uncritically locate a feminist tradition as a justification for the present. These plays must also establish how they differ from more far-flung historical revisionists. So we must examine how these plays establish the role of historical representation in trafficking in historical truth—in terms of both the past they excavate and the present they hope to illuminate. Narrative theorists such as Michael Riffaterre have noted on the one hand that all fictional narratives are rooted in truth simply by virtue of their plausibility within the rules of the known world.[11] If such a baseline for "truth" applies to fictional narratives, truth value only increases when their subject matter addresses a historical real (as perceived by the audience). The questions that remain involve drawing a line between what constitutes fictional discourse and what constitutes history, the answer to which may lie in Schenkar's claim that the "facts" of her play are "the hinges upon which certain of its circumstances swing," the historical real that Berlatsky notes is often crucial for oppressed and marginalized groups. Indeed, by characterizing the function of history in these plays as the hinges, she literalizes history's pivotal role in constructing the narrative and its politics, and in serving as the hub around which the functional elements of the drama (i.e., the political commentary, the polemic, the rhetoric, etc.) revolve. To extend her metaphor, we must acknowledge that a door may be decorated in many ways (coherent, plausible ways if the rules of fictional truth are to apply), but its service in the liminal path is that it opens, that it hinges on the frame that surrounds it. So, too, might these plays vary in their embellishments, but these essential facts, the "hinges" if you will, root them firmly to "the real." These moments in the text are those that fill out a plausible correspondence with the known facts of history; it is what separates them from purely speculative revision. This aspect of historical narrative grounds the contemporary rhetoric of the symbolic order in the verifiability of historical facts: it establishes that the real underpins these biographical narratives, shores up the metadiscursive explorations they undertake, and legitimates the political critique that they hope to bring into the present.

At a glance, these two apparent goals of staged feminist biography may appear to be in conflict: the appeal of cloaking oppositional polemic within the accepted discourses of history seems to come at the expense of both effective polemic and good history. But in fact, these goals can work in concert. For in utilizing history, feminist drama taps into more than just legitimacy by association. It also relies on some notion of historical verifiability—the provable correspondence between the facts, Schenkar's hinges on which her narrative hangs—to resist easy refutation. It is difficult to refute the argument that *Signs of Life* makes about women's history being silenced when Schenkar's note presents us with the fact that Henry James *did* burn his sister's "hysterical" journals.[12] Ultimately, the verifiability of historical narrative and its resistance to simple malleability make criticism of its historical accuracy seem more like mere pedantry—history forgives mistakes on the details to create better polemic and furthermore magnifies the urgency of these contemporary political analogues by pointing out how overdue change is and how deeply entrenched many of these issues really are. So issues of "correct history," while they offer room for close reading, don't change the plausibility of a narrative that hinges on several choice "facts" of the biographical narrative, certain key correspondences between the real and the representational that foreground the arguments made by these plays.

Indeed, we must remember that even the facts, as William Epstein reminds us, are culturally constructed and authorized within the processes of what he calls "biographical recognition."

> The availability of culturally authorized "facts" permits the recognition of poly-functional biographical subjects *only* in terms of their engagement in sanctioned discursive activities. This is how cultural institutions appropriate the "natural" and make it an instrument of what Barthes calls their "mythology." A "fact" then becomes, as Barthes suggests, a second-order sign in and through which culture asserts its "natural" authority. And biographical recognition serves as one way of reinforcing that cultural myth.[13]

Epstein's examination of the role of "fact" in biography suggests reasons why feminist biographies might be compelled both to pin their narrative to "facts," given the degree to which those facts are conflated with naturalized authority, and granted equal footing with the institutional mythologies that have served instead to install male lives as the dominant of lived experience. Further, the degree to which feminist polemic might otherwise be ascertained as something other than "factual" (e.g. "biased," "shrill," "radical," "deviant," and any number of other stereotypes assigned to women's rhetoric) has marked out its divergence from (and challenge to) "sanctioned discursive activities." But at the same time, this challenge to the sanctioned discourse also underscores an ambivalence to wholly claiming factuality as the warrant for this rhetoric, since these very mythologizing processes of male-dominated history are frequently the site of critique. And finally, Epstein's emphasis on biographical recognition returns us to reader, or audience, reception in establishing the effectiveness of these processes. So here, as in many feminist performances of life writing examined in this book, we find that the appearance of the reality effects of performance, even ones self-consciously founded on a deconstruction of historical fact, depends on some level of audience "uptake." The "happy performative," to return to Timothy Gould's unpacking of J. L. Austin's term, depends on the audience's acceptance of certain key historical facts *as facts* to validate the efficacy of the performance, but in doing so, these facts underpin the rhetorical effectiveness of the entire performative sign system of the play.[14]

The question remains as to who—or what—is being recovered and how this recovery takes place. Noting the exclusion of women from the canon, Susan Groag Bell and Marilyn Yalom also note how feminist scholars have "questioned the paradigm of 'singular' or 'exemplary' lives."[15] And Peggy Rosenthal, responding to the first biographies printed by the Feminist Press in the 1970s, identifies a discrepancy between the rhetoric of women as plural and generalized and the subject of the biographies as singular and particular.[16] "The reader that [these biographers] seem to want to inspire by these stories full of achievement," Rosenthal writes, "may very likely be inspired to wonder at these women but also to wonder about the inapplicability of their lives to her own."[17] Moreover, the implication inherent in the traditional model of presenting exemplary women's lives seems to be that only these few women were capable of doing great things; so by granting the exception, biographies of exemplary women confirm the rule that exemplary public behavior—and the notion of the biographical subject as monolithic museum piece—is the domain of men.

Jamie Pachino's *Theodora: An Unauthorized Biography* dramatizes this precise dilemma. In a dialogue between Theodora, the sensationalized wife of the Byzantine emperor Justinian, and her present-day female biographer, called simply "1990," Theodora presents this argument as an objection to her own "recovery."

> 1990: They talk about you because you were remarkable and strong
> and passionate and brave. And you lived at a time when
> women weren't allowed to do that.

Theodora: Women were *always* allowed to do that! Women have
    done things for hundreds and hundreds of years. Fought
    husbands and left them, brought children into the world
    illegitimately and raised them without shame. Fought battles
    and commanded empires. It's just that no one ever wrote it
    down.
1990: Then why did they write about you?
Theodora: Because I was Empress. Because if they made me
    "remarkable" and "unique" then *women* were not capable, only
    I was—*women* were not strong and powerful, or decisive and
    cruel and ravishingly beautiful, only *me*.[18]

Of course, the argument that Pachino's protagonist makes here is in part countered by the mere existence of her play, and the existence of many other staged biographies of women. But more significant here is the character's emphasis not on her own deeds but on the things that women have done throughout history—acts of competence and courage that defy the notion of the exemplary. This emphasis on the everyday acts of women over the identity of an exemplary figure (one whose history is found ultimately to be virtually impossible to recover accurately) suggests that the inaccessible pastness of the historical personage is an insufficient model for feminist audiences. Similarly, Rosenthal argues for a tactic that dramatizes "the connections between the inner and the public life, instead of reducing these connections to simple formulas," thus making them applicable to women in general.[19]

Some playwrights, like Pachino or Caryl Churchill in *Top Girls*, use their "biography" of remarkable figures to create a dialogue with women in the present. Still others place women within larger communities of women, or in search of such communities, like Pam Gems's title character in the second act of *Queen Christina*. What these tactics all seem to have in common is that they speak to the present by holding up the lives of their subjects as models to emulate rather than simply presenting historical personages to admire. Gems's 1977 *Queen Christina* is a classic example. Elaine Aston notes specifically that *Queen Christina* "takes a historical subject as a vehicle for contemporary feminist issues."[20] The play reads like a laundry list of late-1970s feminist concerns: reproductive choice, female access to power, sexual freedom, even clothing choice. Here, Gems is not simply doing the kind of revisionist history that is so often ascribed to plays like these, although most critics note the contrast between Gems's stooped, hideous central character and Greta Garbo's doe-eyed androgyne in the 1920s film, while further contrasts might be drawn against Strindberg's theatrical depiction of the queen. It is one thing to revise history. It is still another to use this recovered history as both a forum to advocate for social change and a site in which to model it in the present. And yet both statements represent simplified commonplaces in literary criticism. For when Christina argues for her own choice in having a child or shuns the bluestockings of Act II for their complete rejection of all men, Gems is not *just* speaking to her historical subject matter and she is not *just* making claims about and recommendations to her audience. Gems's character instead serves a *dual function,* representing a conversation across time that interrogates the past, informs the present, and builds a greater sense of urgency and outrage, thus invoking a stronger call to action in the present. This is true for most of the texts in this category: they do the recovery work of history not just to revise history but to use a revised version of that history to speak to the present, deliberately implicating two historical moments to imply a long narrative of repression that spans them both.

Ultimately, interpretive strategies that focus less on the historical accuracy of the text, or even the physical resemblance of the actress to her historical referent, point us—by self-reflexivity, by stylized performances, by the necessarily fictionalized embodiment of the character by the actress—to the possibility of historical context as an interlocutor with the present. Elin Diamond, in *Unmaking Mimesis,* articulates this relationship clearly: "Thinking historically . . . does not mean . . . to recover the past 'the way it really was.'"[21] Citing Walter Benjamin, Diamond advocates reading feminist performance that evokes history as a "*dialectical* image, [which] doesn't stand for an absent real (woman, man, toaster, Chevy), nor is it internally harmonious. . . . The dialectical image is a montage construction of forgotten objects . . . that are 'blasted' out of history's continuum."[22] That is, the actress's body, a dialectical image, provides an analogue for what is historically relevant: not necessarily the historical body itself but *the transgressive performances it undertook.* Indeed, that body encompasses the performative dialectic that includes historical subject, authorial subjectivity, the collective of theater practitioners, and even the spectators who might similarly reenact such performance.

Again, Pam Gems's rogue queen serves as a salient example. "Central to her exposition of masculine and feminine identities," writes Elaine Aston, "is the *gestus* of the cross-dressed body." She argues that "Gems uses the device of the cross-dressed body towards a more subversive end . . . a 'misfit' body which invites us to question gender roles, identity and behavior."[23] Here, the body of the actress playing Christina, her physical mannerisms, and the clothes she wears all work together to produce this image for the audience. The body of the biographical subject, initial site of reclamation, is long gone; it can only be reclaimed *as history*. What can be reclaimed for the present, however, is the *performance* enacted by both bodies—the signifier of the actress's performance and the signified of those performances drawn from her subject's life—and the metanarrative that the dialectic between the past and the present creates to reinforce the connection between them.

The notion of the dialectical image helps account for the relationship of the represented past to the representing present and also mirrors reading and performance strategies that locate a similarly reciprocal relationship between author and subject. Carol Hanbery McKay, surveying the seven one-woman biographical performances that precede her piece in the 2003 collection *Voices Made Flesh*, identifies this relationship, noting that "although these historical figures presumably take center stage, they in fact compete with their authorial personae, who frequently turn them into reflections of themselves in order to expand their territory beyond traditional boundaries of gender and sexuality."[24] This is not an uncommon strategy: it populates many feminist readings of women's biographical narratives.[25] And it is not without merit, either; it further personalizes the political, creating a dialectical intertextuality between the work of the historical and the performing artist. Such a metadramatic effect, McKay argues, breaks down the discrete subject of biography, "rais[ing] for us the epistemological issues unleashed by postmodernism. Seeing the self as refracted and multiple is both freeing and disturbing," as it invokes "the interplay of 'multiple levels of performativity.'"[26] To a certain degree, such a strategy can disintegrate, testing the plausibility of historical reference on the one hand, and dispersing across the collaborative chain of theater artists on the other. To interpret a conventional biographical play as autobiography, the audience would have to take into account not only the life of the playwright (as this biography-as-autobiography strategy would suggest) but also the lives of the director, dramaturge, actress, and any number of others who contribute to the task of bringing the subject "back to life."

But when it succeeds—when the historical reference remains plausible and applicable across the collective of theater artists, this reading strategy illustrates precisely the idea of the recovered performance. Here,

the subjectivity of the biographical figure and the author alike is fragmented by the presence of other contributors to the dramatic process
such that any unified subjectivity refers instead to a community of collaborators—the particulars of any individual are erased by the commonalities of the whole group. Yet we can speak coherently about a community of collaborators, feminists who share specific political positionalities
in relation to themselves and society at large. So if we refigure this biography-as-autobiography strategy as one that reads like the kind of dramatized connection of inner and public lives that Rosenthal advocates,
then these biographies become as much about the communities that produce them as they are about the history they seek to recover. When cast in
this light, such a strategy can indeed become a significant way to gain an
understanding of these texts and their function for the contemporary
feminist stage.

Performing the Biographical Act

While a focus on the dialectical relationship between subject and performer opens up the notion of a more thoroughly dialectical image across
the performative transaction from playwright through performer to spectator, McKay also attends to the metadramatic valence of the one-woman
performances that she considers. But the postmodern emphasis on *meta*
implicates the generic constructions of biography, as well as drama; that
is, these plays call attention to the performance of the biographical act itself in order to revise it in favor of an epistemology that interrogates subject construction even as it constructs that subject. These generic concerns
are pervasive: in addition to the theoretical problems of staging history,
feminism has taken ideological issue with the form of the traditional male
biography. Feminist critics such as Anna T. Kuhn are quick to note that
"biography has traditionally been a male domain," and in their preface to
Women's Lives/Women's Times, Trev Lynn Broughton and Linda Anderson
note that the confluence of feminism and autobiography has resulted in
"the location and problematization of the 'subject,' an answer—or part of
one—to the claims of enlightenment epistemology."[27] This critique of
course extends to biography, for if traditional autobiography assumes a
discrete subject with a unified, apparently authoritative perspective on
the world, then those claims to singularity and authority are heightened
by the claims of biography, in which the biographical subject is repre-

sented in a supposedly objective fashion by a transparent narrator,[28] who erases his own presence in service of what Elizabeth Kamarck Minnich identifies as "a falsely abstracted nonrelational objectivity not only on the part of the author, but also for readers of the biography."[29] This subject formation, which imagines a great man doing undoubtedly great things in the public sphere, reinforces the Enlightenment epistemologies that privilege the relationship between man and the world around him as centered and authoritative, to the exclusion not only of women but of any disenfranchised voice not empowered by the hegemonic impulses of an invisible narrator.[30]

While the issues of perspective in traditional prose biography pose problems to the feminist critic, staging the biography creates even more pressing concerns. Despite the language surrounding the "biographical subject," it is clear that we are also in part talking about an *object* of biographical scrutiny—that we as audience members are often positioned as the subjects examining the object of our inquiry. Add to this condition the tendency of realist staging tactics to promote unidirectional viewing practices that indulge the male gaze, and our protofeminist biographical subject quickly becomes a spectacle—an object for the biographer's gaze. Epstein crystallizes this observation in his reading of Norman Mailer's *Marilyn,* arguing that in this exemplary case, we see the "biographical narrative as the scene of an abduction, a discursive practice through which the biographer can detain and defile his biographical subject."[31] And Epstein suggests that this scene of abduction is not necessarily limited to the male-author/female-subject relationship; instead he argues that the gap between self and other becomes what Mailer describes tellingly as a "wound." Invoking the Freudian associations of "wound" with penis envy and lack and using multiple definitions of the idea of abduction, Epstein generalizes Mailer's case to the entire course of traditional biography, which

> habitually reenacts the scene of an abduction because in order to discursively repair the biologically irreparable fracture (the alterity, the otherness, the discontinuity) between any two human individuals (reified generically as biographer and biographical subject), biography recesses the broken parts and causes the gaping of a wound. Moreover, as I have suggested, this wound is metaphorically associated with that which is repressed and excluded—women in a patriarchal culture, the racial subject in an imperialist economy, the underclass in a capitalist economy, gays and lesbians in a heterosexual

culture. Hence its desire to heal the break between self and other by generically arguing for a generic procedure that bonds biographer and biographical subject in a more or less "sympathetic relationship" . . . biography inadvertently demonstrated the hidden and not signified proposition.[32]

Epstein here not only suggests that this relationship is endemic to cultural others but suggests that biography generically reinforces this power gap in the very attempt to cross it.

In fact, several of the plays I will examine grapple with this paradox, choosing subjects who were notoriously objectified and spectacularized during their lifetimes, and abducted by power in various ways. The Restoration actress Nell Gwyn is just one example. In her case, as dramatized by April De Angelis's *Playhouse Creatures* (which I will explore more fully in chapter 5), the objectification that seems to have been a fact of life for Restoration actresses is set in direct contrast to the emergent professional status that actresses of this period were beginning to enjoy.[33] By using carefully juxtaposed plot points and metatheatrical performance, De Angelis highlights the degree to which the sexualization of the actresses's bodies may have actively inhibited their freedom as professional and sexual subjects. And yet De Angelis also asserts performance as the very basis for her characters' empowerment: the consummate professionalism of Mrs. Betterton (wife of famed Restoration actor Thomas Betterton), the comic skill of Nell Gwyn, and the intelligent performances (both onstage and in the salons) of Mrs. Marshall are held up as the source of the women's status as emergent professionals, and their growing influence in the company. That these very same performances led to their downfall at the hands of the men who sexualize them doesn't diminish the initial power of their performances, but it does underscore the abuse that women who seek to empower themselves (including these Restoration characters and the contemporary actresses who portray them) have been subject to for centuries. Feminist biography, then, seems to make this representational problem part of its polemic by using Brechtian strategies to problematize and call attention to the very practices that configure these women as objects in the first place, thereby (one hopes) subverting that same process in the present.

We therefore might find solace in the focus of these plays on creating community, and on the gendered sameness of subject, author, actress, and spectator, a series of relationships in which the gap that Epstein locates is not explicitly built into identity categories. Certainly the emphasis in these plays on a reclaimed *performance* over a reclaimed *identity* mitigates this effect to a certain degree, but such textual emphasis is not enough to counter such deeply ingrained viewing practices, which are themselves mimicked by the very practices of biographical research. Stacy Wolf notes in her biographical pursuit of Mary Martin, "My search for 'evidence,' then, became intimately linked with my desire—my desire for knowledge, answers, and proof, and my desire to see a lesbian presence in musicals and to see 'lesbian' on Martin's body, to hear it in her voice, to read it in her self-presentations."[34] Wolf casts her desire for her biographical subject in terms not too distant from those we hear in Epstein's reading of Mailer, but crucially, Wolf also frames that "desire in evidence" as a transgressively queer performance in and of itself. Like these plays, then, Wolf struggles with the tension between reclaiming a radical performance *through* radical performance, while simultaneously echoing the abduction of another woman's body that characterizes the most insidious of gendered and sexualized biographical relationships.

Thus we might object to the unified conception of the subject as an object of scrutiny, even as we find fault with the alleged objectivity with which the traditional biographer presents the subject. If these claims of objectivity assume a patriarchal authority in their implications of an absolute truth, feminist revisionists must respond in their biographies not only by revising the representations but also by revising the methodologies in such a way that their own "authority" is contextualized. As a result, feminist playwrights do not often simply "do" biography (even as Wolf refuses to simply "do" biographical scholarship). Instead, these plays work to fulfill the promise of Sharon O'Brien's recommendation that the biographer "dramatize the contingent nature of the biographical narrative."[35] They turn their critical eye to the historical gender performances being recovered, as well as an investigation of the process of that recovery, the performance of doing biography itself, and the paths by which we as postmodern readers and audience members have access to these historical acts. This scrutiny typically bears itself out in these plays in three ways: a presentation of the range of historical documents that serve to reconstruct the subject's performances, an examination of a biographer figure alongside the biographical subject herself, and an examination of the subject through writing and of writing as a means of representing a historical subjectivity.

The first strategy, the presentation of the documentation of history, implicitly reveals the constructed nature of the historical work being done in these plays. Texts that work this way typically do so by breaking into the representational action of the play by reading supposedly "objective" accounts of history that usually stand in stark contrast to the action we see onstage. Brechtian moves like this have a dual destabilizing effect. Fiona Templeton's *Delirium of Interpretations* serves as a relevant example. In her author's note, Templeton prescribes, "Only [Claudel] has an invented or subjective voice—the play is specifically about subjectivity, not biographical objectivity. Mostly the characters speak in voices borrowed from history. Since reality is multiple, some of these are contradictory in their apparent facts."[36] Instead of assigning any of the other characters a unified subjectivity, the playwright specifically has them speaking text from a wide range of historical sources, which she meticulously annotates in the margin. And while her notes indicate that this is a dramaturgical tool, it also provides some provocative staging possibilities; for the reader, at least, Templeton has "staged" the process of biography in every word that comes out of her characters' mouths. They are literally and overtly mouthpieces—Templeton makes every effort to lay bare her own process in order to represent what she calls "the very excess of subjectivities in all of their contradiction."[37] Such a staging tactic reveals the inherently unreliable nature of the historical documents by contrasting them ironically with the apparently reliable narrative the audience witnesses on the stage. But this tactic is not merely an attack on masculinist history, because in contrasting these two epistemologies of the life in question, the move also implicitly acknowledges the constructed nature of its own narrative. In doing so, these plays often avoid falling into the same traps of feigned objectivity for which they critique their sources.

In the case of Templeton's play, the body of the actress becomes a dialectical image that highlights the very process of biography, the "delirium of interpretations" that marked Claudel's life,[38] and, as the title of the play, marks the audience's experience of the play. Templeton claims here that only Claudel has what we might call a subjectivity, while the other characters are representatives of various self-proclaimed "objective" perspectives. The play reveals that in their conflicting nature—and in conflict with the only voice of subjectivity onstage (Claudel herself)—these supposedly objective sources are as subjective as the voice assumed by the biographical subject, if not more so. The difference here seems to lie in the body as a site for construction—the claims of these other voices are conflicting precisely because they do not have the bodied experience to support the claims. By representing the bodies that surround Claudel with a patchwork of various voices, the play points to the very project that these voices enact—the construction of the female body without the benefit of that body's experience to bolster those claims. Of course the irony here is that the actress who supplies the theatrical body relies on sources as much as do the "objective" and alienated voices. The Brechtian tactics that *Delirium of Interpretations* deploys work to reveal that the bodied performance of the actress is as much a construction as anything else. In this excess of subjectivities, supported by a host of historical sources and an imagined bodied subjectivity, Templeton reveals the degree to which her biographical subject is overdetermined. What we are left with returns us to the title of the piece, the contemporary term for the paranoia that marked Claudel's experience, but also the ecstatic experience of excess subjectivities, all bound up in the process of interpretation that the play invites its audience to enact. As a result, the audience is prompted to recognize that "we are all inscribed by prior, interdependent, and multiple evidence and interpretations of the world, and participate, creatively or not, in the constant formation of its present and future interpretation, including that of its past."[39]

While Templeton and others contextualize the textual sources of their own biographical work, still other plays examine their own methodologies by staging the biographers alongside the subjects they purport to examine. Whether casting these figures as witnesses, scribes, analysts, journalists, or scholars, many staged feminist biographies *perform* the process of biography even as they undertake that process. From the very first, this tactic destabilizes the notion of the unified subject, since subjectivity here is at least partially distributed across two figures: the biographer and biographical subject. This effect seems to have several effects. Among others, it offers a way "for the biographer to find ways of interrupting her own voice," as O'Brien exhorts.[40] Furthermore, the effect fragments the subject, ascribing the audience's knowledge of the biographical subject not only to her lived experience but also to the interpretative lens of the figure who chooses, for whatever reason, to put that life to paper. Lynn Kaufman's *Shooting Simone* portrays just this divide. The second act of that play narrates the experience of a young feminist TV journalist who interviews French feminist Simone de Beauvoir and ends up applying her observations of Simone's relationship with existentialist Jean-Paul Sartre to her own relationship with her cameraman.[41] The last image of Simone that the audience is presented with comes in the form of the younger couple's documentary, foregrounding the degree to which Simone's narrative is embedded in theirs. Moreover, if the abstracted objectivity of traditional biography implicates the audience in its obfuscating processes, then it seems that by subjectifying the biographer, plays like *Shooting Simone* equally reveal to the audience their own subjectivity and their own role in constructing the biography.

Furthermore, in revealing the constructed nature of these biographical portraits, these plays reveal the tenuous relationship between the representations being presented on the stage and the "truth" that they might otherwise seem to represent. While Templeton reveals the inherently contradictory nature of multiple biographies, Kaufman points out the same discrepancies embedded within representations by the subject herself. Indeed, while biographical inquiry reveals uncertanties in de Beauvoir's life as simple as her date of birth, Kaufman's portrayal of Simone links these incongruities to the slippery nature of subjectivity. Through these contradictions, Kaufman comes to her thesis about biography and "truth," as Simone states: "That's all we ever get to know, our version. . . .There are so many [truths] . . . [that if] you believe in a solitary truth, life is quite simple and quite dull."[42] This conception of a personal and subjective truth certainly speaks to a feminist sensibility of biography and illuminates the interpretive preference for autobiography. And yet the degree to which Kaufman's play relies on a correspondence between the known of de Beauvoir's life and the narrative of the play belies a sense of radical subjectivity in truth construction. "Our version" of the truth, then seems to call for an exploration of the past but also for understanding what constitutes one version against another. This notion highlights the degree to which historical precision for these plays does not appear to be a primary concern and in fact troubles some feminist constructions of the historical past through a reliance on the real, or a notion of objective truth. And yet it also reveals a concern for recognizing versions, the tension invoked by constructing a biographical narrative that itself identifies truth as less than objective.

Eliding Feminist Performances

The final tactic of many of these texts, besides recovery of feminist performances and a contextualization of the biographical act, is a performance of the processes of erasure that have made such recovery work necessary in the first place. At first glance, this may seem a curious and counterproductive endeavor for feminist biographies, to reproduce the processes by which their subjects are elided, but the presence of this element in many of these texts suggests that not only is this plot element not damaging to the entire recovery effort, it is essential to it. Joan Schenkar's *Signs of Life,* for example, makes explicit and frequent reference to Henry James's destruction of Alice's journals—but also to the subsequent role of Katherine Loring in their reconstruction. By representing the patriarchal elision of the historical subject (burning the journals) alongside the process of recovery, Schenkar seems to be justifying her own recovery work, and justifying the revisionist nature of that work by highlighting the tyranny with which the patriarchy asserts itself against female subjectivity. By giving body and voice to these historical figures, such discourse of elision and recovery serves to produce dialectical images that uncover the performances that feminist biographical plays are reclaiming even as they represent the historical process by which these women were hidden from history. Essentially, plays that use this tactic work to perform women's history by performing the elision of that history.

I recognize that there is a crucial difference between representing the silencing of these stories and actively participating in this silencing process. The matter of why the erasure of these stories must be enacted onstage in order to justify their writing recalls Griffin and Aston's claims in *Herstory:* first, that "women's theatre groups' work disappears as it appears . . . a perpetual silencing the result"; and second, that "Against this, the *Herstory* volumes [and, I would argue, feminist biographical drama] seek to work."[43] It seems that the work of recovering a tradition of transgressive performances is dependent on the very silencing processes against which such a project struggles. I do not wish to suggest that without the oppressive influence of masculinist discourse feminist theater could not exist. However, combating the silence is no longer just a political goal for the genre: it is its inspiration as well. That is, feminist theater has so invested itself in this archaeology of the past that the project has created its own aesthetic of polemic wrapped in history. The past that these plays unearth, then, must be one worth the dig. Therefore, in order to legitimate the very recovery work that they are doing, staged feminist biographies must represent the reasons why such recovery work is necessary. In doing so, these plays arm the audience members to whom they hope to pass on these models of feminist performance with a sense of the resistance they will face.

Conclusion

These dramatic depictions of feminist biographies reclaim and reimagine feminist performances while simultaneously scrutinizing the processes by which they do so. Moreover, the ways these plays deal with both the biographical subject and the biographer suggest that the "problems" of dramatizing biography often solve the issues that feminists have with this traditionally masculine form. There is something to be said about the function of history in legitimating and justifying the political work of feminist theater. If feminist polemic is a subject that is often met with shudders from the average newspaper theater critic, then history just as reliably evokes coos of respect and admiration. The example of the London reviews of De Angelis's *Playhouse Creatures* illustrates this very point. The fact that the play *doesn't* play like a polemic is its salvation: "The piece *could have* been a grim whine or a thinly disguised Open University programme" writes one reviewer. Instead, however, "it emerges as a funny and gutsy evocation of life on-stage and backstage in the attiring-room."[44] The evocation of life here, that whiff of historical legitimacy, apparently makes watching the play palatable. Nor is it simply that the historical politics aren't acknowledged: almost every review picks up on the feminist content as it relates to history. Another reviewer writes, "Women, De Angelis implies, irrevocably changed the English theatre but were victimized in the process."[45]

And yet the use of history to soften polemic runs the risk of confining that polemic solely to the past. While it is easy for reviewers to feel morally superior to our predecessors, few are willing to make the connection that these historical actresses (not coincidentally played by—gasp—actresses) offer to the present. Only one review of the play to date—written notably by a woman—extrapolates the political content of the play as relevant for the present. "In our time, actresses have acquired not just the properties of glamour but almost totemic quality," writes Carole Woddis. "But glamour is only the half of it; breaking free of the stereotype of 'sexual object' continues to haunt the profession now as then."[46] That so few informed audience members are able to identify the dialogue between past performances and present ones is unsettling. Certainly there is the question of readerships and the conventions of the theater review. But while these plays seem to solve the dilemma that both theater and feminism have with biography, there remains the question of how effective they are for feminists' primary political goals. If feminism is best received when cloaked in history, we must wonder whether all that we see onstage is the cloak itself.

This dilemma seems to be the sticking point for staged feminist biography. Confronted with the need to resurrect historical performances from the erasures of the past, challenged with the task of recovering them in a new, counterpatriarchal fashion, and then further charged with a mission of making political arguments both evident and palatable, playwrights working in this form seem doomed to come up short. And yet, as Woddis's insightful review of *Playhouse Creatures* demonstrates, failed outcomes are not inevitable. Even in the case of reviewers who merely recognize the oppressive tendencies of history, these images serve to shore up the rhetoric that the plays espouse, whether or not the reviewers are conscious of it. In doing so, they reinforce the dual appeal of history and biography for feminist playwrights—that history not only serves to frame feminist rhetoric but legitimates it by extending and verifying its narratives of oppression at the hand of authority. And if these plays can accomplish this in form, as well as content, then their tasks are even further buttressed.

As Tony Kushner writes in his manifesto on "difficult art," the most that these plays can do is to teach a stance to their audiences, to interrogate "by example, not by preachment."[47] These plays serve as performative examples by exploring and critiquing the past, and by looking at their own role in constructing the lives of the past. Instead of simply offering audiences great lives to admire, they offer them performances that have historically resisted restrictive gender norms and can be duplicated. Instead of offering an obscured process of unearthing lives, they offer audiences a critical approach to history that they can adopt beyond the space of the stage. And instead of offering a romanticized narrative that imagines women's history as an unfettered tradition, these plays reveal the very processes of elision that have sought to remove the records of such resistant performances from the records of human experience. So as feminist playwrights continue to shape this evolving form, their tactics do not merely reveal their own tenuous relationship with the history they seek to bring to light; they also illuminate what history can tell us about women's performances in the present.

CHAPTER 5 : A Life in the (Meta)Theater

WRITING/REHEARSING/
ACTING OUT

Inherent in a wide variety of feminist biography plays, as the previous chapter argues, is the notion that the act of biography is itself a performance—a performance that is scrutinized alongside the acts and performances of these plays' purported subjects. This phenomenon calls attention to, among other things, the degree to which women's lives in history are already deeply mediated and textualized, even prior to the mediation and textualization of playwriting. The idea of performing biography *as performance* already lends a certain element of metadramatic tension to feminist biography plays, which implicitly present their own representational practices in a critical fashion. This effect is even further magnified when the subjects of the plays are in fact writers or performers, subjects whose own lives within the public spheres of text and performance lend themselves neatly to a self-conscious examination of the representation of women's lives, and the imaginative constructions being fiercely negotiated by the subjects, their own audiences, their biographers, and ultimately the performers and audiences engaging them on the contemporary feminist stage. While these plays certainly engage in a kind of anxiety of production—an antitheatrical anxiety resident in their metatheatrical effects—their concerns are not *merely* about theatrical representation. Central to these metatheatrical experiments in staging women's lives is a doubled anxiety, one about the dangers and potentials in representing historical women onstage, but yet another about revealing that anxiety too vividly to an audience for which complex representations may seem to be politically counterproductive. At stake, then, are not only political stakes of representation in the material lives of the historical women these plays represent but also of the living actresses who reanimate them, and the contemporary audiences that participate in the ongoing circulation of written and performed life narratives.

If the metadramatic mode is a particularly fruitful, if fraught, one for feminist playwrights, then the simple choice of biographical subject can reveal a great deal about the rhetorical and political aims of the play. Of all the possible subjects for a staged feminist biography, for example, Charlotte Cushman might be the most overdetermined. An eighteenth-century actress known for her performance of breeches roles onstage and off; her appearance in a biography play *about* the performance of gender, as in Carolyn Gage's *Last Reading of Charlotte Cushman,* is clearly an apt pairing of subject and genre. The same must also be said about Pam Gems's *Marlene,* about early film star Marlene Dietrich, and *Playhouse Creatures,* April De Angelis's staging of the rise of Restoration actress and royal mistress Nell Gwyn. It is perhaps similarly little surprise that female playwrights should look to other writers for both subject matter and inspiration, as Polly Teale's *After Mrs. Rochester* (about the novelist Jean Rhys), Alma De Groen's *The Rivers of China* (about Katherine Mansfield), or the playfully titled *Do Something with Yourself! The Life of Charlotte Brontë* by Linda Manning all demonstrate. The list of such plays—representations of the lives of women who were in the business of constructing representations—goes on and on, and the playwrights who write them, like Maria Irene Fornes and Suzan-Lori Parks, have often been at the center of discussions of feminist drama in the last forty years. The concerns about self-representation, objectification, and metaphorical relevance that populate the whole corpus of feminist biography plays are particularly magnified in this subset of performance texts that seek to represent the lives of women whose own lives were bound up in textual production, either as subjects or producers of literary and theatrical works. It is no surprise, then, that in many of these plays, performances of writing and stage performances come under particular scrutiny as appropriate, radical, or deleterious modes of cultural representation for women's work and women's lives.

We might take as a brief example Liz Lochhead's *Blood and Ice,* about Mary Shelley and her creation of *Frankenstein,* a biography play that specifically and compellingly foregrounds the representation of subjectivity through the act of writing. The play, which Adrienne Scullion argues "is as much a memory play as it is a history play,"[1] uses the confluence of memory, history, and writing to create a space in which the experience and subjectivity of the author are posed as the defining parameters. That is, the play follows Mary Shelley *after* the death of her husband and through the process of writing her landmark novel and situates her not as a famous spouse but as a major artist on her own. By foregrounding the voice and experience of Mary Shelley, "in whose consciousness," Lochhead states, "my *entire* play takes place," Lochhead is able to place the context of Shelley's life—her famous mother, father, and husband, her husband's infamous reputation, and his early death—in conversation with her status as the author of *Frankenstein*.[2] The path of the protagonist, then, is not directed by her spouse, nor oriented toward achieving fame on completing a novel, but focused on writing as its own goal. "The dominant trope of *Blood and Ice*," writes Elaine Aston, "is Mary's quest for her own story, which is emblematic of the feminist quest to find the lost woman writer."[3] But while this dramaturgical tactic emphasizes the voice of Mary Shelley by calling attention to its famous and enduring manifestation in *Frankenstein*, the play also highlights the transgressive nature of that writing and underscores writing itself as transgressive. Scullion compares Shelley's writing to the "'transgressive' progeny of the novel," and the element of performance reinforces this, since it is Shelley's *act of writing*, itself a performance, that stands as the historically empowered moment.[4]

There is a great deal to glean from the conflation of women's writing with the transgression of gender norms, one that is reflected not only in the depiction of the historical subject but also in the work of the playwright whose own work is to write. Similar conclusions might be drawn from the persistence of plays about actresses, written as they are for actresses to perform. Lochhead and other playwrights who represent writing as a performance of subjectivity, or acting as a performance of visibility, highlight their own tradition as female authors and stage practitioners at the same time as they resurrect writers and stage practitioners as dialectical images for current feminists. Their plays work metadramatically to consider not only the lives of these historical figures but also the roles that writing and performance played in shaping these lives within the public sphere. Here I include plays like Lochhead's, about writers, more specifically metatheatrical plays about actresses and other practitioners, as well as plays like Hélène Cixous's *Portrait of Dora*, not because it resurrects a writer (Sigmund Freud hardly needs resurrecting) but because it considers the life of a specific woman as it is contained by a specifically male text. And while little work has been done to engage these texts as a specific subset of history plays or biography plays, the sheer number of them and the varieties of their engagements with representation itself tell us that the staged inquiry into the representational politics of women writing and performing at once reveals a common set of anxieties about representing women's lives, even as those plays occupy a variety of positions on how to address those anxieties.

While in Lochhead's play, writing and performance seem to operate as symbiotic systems for establishing a central character subjectivity, other examples of feminist biographical metadrama pose them as uncomfortably compatible or even directly competing representational systems. Many plays seem to be staging the relationships among lives, writing, and performance in a variety of ways, each locating different implications for performance and writing in the task of establishing women's voices in history.

Metadrama as Mode

To invoke metadrama as a mode for discussing these plays is to raise a loose set of critical approaches and traditions that have spread out unevenly and intermittently across the last fifty years to describe a phenomenon that is neither entirely formal nor entirely thematic in its iteration. From Lionel Abel's first breezy attempt at a systematic introduction of the term with 1963's *Metatheatre: A New View of Dramatic Form* to a few disparate contributions to the study throughout the 1970s and 1980s and finally to Martin Puchner's reintroduction of Abel's work with the reedited *Tragedy and Metatheatre* in 2003, studies of metatheatricality have only occasionally reached the depth, significance, and influence that metatheatricality itself, as a dramaturgical tactic, has consistently exercised over the same period.[5] Indeed, even the slipperiness of the terms *metadrama* and *metatheater* suggests a kind of imprecision in our usage. And yet this imprecision persists largely because the terms tend to refer to a broad range of effects—from the formal frame shifting of Pirandello to much simpler depictions of characters who happen to work in the theater—that exercise some notion of self-reflexivity about the entire universe of activities and concerns that are wrapped up in the enterprise of theatricalized representation, both onstage and off.

In recognizing this dispersion of such self-reflexive effects, I will generally use the notion of metadrama as a *writerly* concern, wherein acts of writing, performing, and spectating all fall under the lens of the playwright's purview, while *metatheater* describes an effect *in performance* in which the production and acting of the play give rise to a sort of audience consciousness that the content and form of the play reflect back on the real existence and consequences of writing, performing, and spectating in the audience's own world. We might imagine, of course, that one would give rise to the other, that the dramaturgical techniques employed by a playwright would precipitate specific theatrical moments that refer the audience back to theatrical representation, but we know that such chains of causation are neither inherent nor reliable.

When such links between metadramatic technique and metatheatrical effect do happen, however, we must consider in what way they occur. In *Drama, Metadrama, and Perception,* Richard Hornby identifies what he calls "the drama-culture complex," the cultural frames of reference that an audience uses to apprehend the metatheatrical effects of a given play, including the play at hand, as well as "other systems of literature, nonliterary performance, other art forms (both high and low), and culture generally." Only through this complex tissue of cultural and representational systems, he suggests, do serious plays engage real life.[6] Representational theater, then, achieves referentiality (if not efficacy) by referring more or less explicitly to itself as a representational and interpretive system rather than by referring mimetically to the real world beyond its borders. And, indeed, serious theater operates for Hornby not through its mimetic achievement but rather for its metadramatic engagement with this complex: "The hack play merely reinforces the drama-culture complex in effect at the time of its composition, while the serious play attempts to attack that system in some way."[7] In effect, by engaging (and *only* by engaging) the representational systems of drama and theater themselves, metatheatrical effects are able to critique the cultural systems in which they are bound.

If we take the momentary popularity of the metadramatic mode in feminist biography plays, we can begin to see how they employ this mechanism of engagement with the drama-culture complex to variously consider writing-as-an-act, biography-as-a-mode, and performance-as-a-condition for women who enter the public sphere. Of Hornby's varieties of the metadramatic, literary and real-life reference comprise a specific subset of tactics. Composed of parody, allusion, adaptation, and citation, such metadramatic moments are "signs of a healthy theatre" for Hornby, indicating a rich engagement in addressing and innovating theatrical tradition, as well as a "fair degree of literary and theatrical sophistication" on the part of the audience.[8] But more than just revealing a healthy and so-

phisticated theatrical communicative exchange, these tactics in feminist
biography plays represent a particularly complex case of metatheatrical
effect. Through both literary and real life reference, these plays present
lives as rooted in the real, but also as undoubtedly exhumed from the
pages of the literary. If, as the previous chapter argues, a common tactic of
these plays is to call attention to the performance of biography itself, we
can certainly see metadramatic operations already functioning in these
plays' engagement with and critique of the drama-culture complex
(which is itself bound up in what Judith Butler calls "matrices of power").
So we can see the critical stance of many biography plays through their
metadramatic tactics: by calling attention to the very processes of biography that they undertake, these plays implicitly reference the entire drama-
culture complex as it represents women's life narratives. Hornby (disin-
terested though he may be in feminist or indeed any political claims that
theater may make) might find in these plays not only "the signs of a
healthy theatre" but also, importantly, a serious engagement with not only
the real world beyond the stage but also the drama-culture complex that
mediates it. Reframed within the space of the theater, these women's already theatricalized lives, preserved in the already textualized modes of
biography (and its sources), refer persistently and critically to a drama-
culture complex that exists not only as a stage tradition but as the very cultural conditions under which women's lives are lived and viewed.

In revisiting the metatheatrical mode as not only a critical concern but
an epistemological one, Elinor Fuchs sheds further light on the appeal of
the metadramatic for feminist playwrights working in biography. While
Fuchs prefers the term *theatricalist* to refer to structurally metatheatrical
plays, her assertions about these plays apply broadly to less structurally
self-conscious plays within the body of feminist biographical metadrama.
For while she admits that "[t]raditionally, theatricalism has been the re-
doubt of metaphysics, ontology, and epistemology," increasingly "theatricalism offered many playwrights a dramaturgical model that welcomed
. . . scepticism into representations of the material world," representations
that had once been exclusively "the province of realism."[9] In these plays,
then, we find a mechanism for examining the specifically material effects—couched within the frame of the historical real—of the ontology
and epistemology of gender within the public sphere. Indeed, metatheatricality as a performative mode appears widely as a critical mode in
feminist theater, particularly in plays that invoke the materiality of gender within the representational field of literary representation. I have ar-

gued elsewhere, in fact, that the metatheatrical impulse of staged feminist parody has several effects that extend from the epistemological play of literary parody and adaptation to the social and political realities of gender performances.[10] There I have argued that not only do the metatheatrical impulses of such literary and theatrical reference offer up critiques of representations of women, vis-à-vis Linda Hutcheon's theory of parody, but they also teach a stance of parodic spectatorship that extends past the individual theatrical event into the politics of gender performance in other performances, in the theater and in the world.[11] Similarly, we might say that the metatheatrical effects that arise from these instances of feminist biographical metadrama teach a kind of spectatorial stance. That is, because they frequently invoke not only the *production* of representation but also the *reception* of representation, these plays ideally create effects that prompt an audience to consider the ways in which representations of women's lives are systemically bound up in political processes of power.

This means that the metadramatic impulse in these plays is rarely simply celebratory of public writing and performing as conveying women's lives. Indeed, as Fuchs suggests is frequently true of modern theatricalist plays, a deep antitheatricalism runs beneath. "The delight of the theatre and the mist of dream" she writes, "are ultimately, sometimes sorrowfully, left behind for a turn, or a return, to an ontological 'gold standard,' whether located on the plane of a Platonic ideal or the mundane real of lived life."[12] In these plays, the metadramatic skepticism of writing and performing may reject the theatricalized lives that these characters live, but just as frequently they suggest that for women such theatricalization, or at least textualization, is inescapable, for the specularized woman is always in some ways on display. In fact, when Fuchs identifies the antitheatrical bias of theatricalism as rooted as deeply as Plato's allegory of the cave, we might in fact also find echoes (shadows even) of the very case of gender production as a performative spectacle. That is, if the allegory of the cave enacts "an epistemology of ontological levels" that "expresses an ontological, moral and performative hierarchy,"[13] then the performative valences of gender itself are invoked as forcefully (if less explicitly) as the ontological valences of theatrical representation. So we can see as concomitant in these plays a critical exploration of both the conservative and subversive nature of a performative gender construct alongside the conservative and subversive nature of writing and performance as systems that purport to represent women's lives. So what Fuchs characterizes as an antitheatrical undercurrent in theatricalist plays might be understood in less evaluative terms as experimental, exploratory, and skeptical. The metatheatrical effects of these plays provide a mechanism through which to read critically (if not always overtly attack) writing, performing, and spectating as acts in the representational exchange, precisely while they read critically the performative codes of gender that are both oppressively and subversively deployed within these modes of representation.

Nor is the antitheatricalism (or perhaps more broadly, antirepresentationalism) of these plays as consistent, either in its form or in the final analysis, as Fuchs finds in her test cases. While it is impossible to find a particularly unified front in these plays and their competing, often contradictory portrayals of writing, performing, translating, and rehearsing as ways of representing women's lives, what we do find is that the triad of writer, actress, and spectator form what Ariel Watson has called "the anxious triangle."[14] In her exploration of metatheatrical forms, she notes that at the core of such forms is "the question of how power is distributed among the participants in the theatrical event itself."[15] She goes on to argue:

> The power of an individual in this triangle is always under threat from the other participants, always fending off encroachments, and the theatrical event can only be born out of this tension produced by this continual struggle, this perpetual sense that the project is on the brink of collapsing. In metatheatre we see a dramatization of this struggle, and of the trigonometric processes through which each creative element calculates its own strengths and weaknesses in relationship to those of its collaborator-antagonists.[16]

For Watson, what is at stake in the metatheatrical moment is control of the meaning-making processes of theater itself. But for staged feminist biography, the stakes of metatheatricality extend beyond the inwardly focused anxiety of stagecraft to the material political stakes of representing women's lives.

What Watson does acknowledge importantly in this passage, however, is the degree to which metatheatricality is bound up in the negotiation of power, a negotiation that continues and is amplified in the staging of women's lives: the power of the author and playwright to "possess" a woman within the text, the power of the actress to "act out" against traditional roles, and the power of the audience to objectify the performing body. Metadramatically, this negotiation happens within the boundaries of the text and the performance. In the case of Lochhead's *Blood and Ice,* for ex-

ample, written representation is a specifically female expression of subjectivity, while writing decidedly specularizes the subject of Freud's Dora
even as Cixous's *Portrait of Dora* finds her eluding writing by "acting out"
in the material world beyond Freud's analytical impulses. We find a similar
dissensus about acting as a profession operating in De Angelis's ambivalent
Playhouse Creatures and Fornes's more positive depiction in *The Summer in
Gossensass.* It is this decided disunity of opinion in these plays that suggests
that the metatheatrical mode in feminist biography plays is not a reliable
signal of a specific stance but rather a site for exploring the multiple, often
conflicting, vectors of representing women's lives on the stage.

Curiously, though, while these texts represent a kind of metatheatrical anxiety about their subjects' performances within the objectifying impulses of their own audiences, they seem eager to protect their audiences
from those anxieties. Typically, while many of these plays exercise a historical critique of the kinds of gaze that would wrest their subjects into
subjection, the historical metaphor of the dialectical image, while frequently made explicit for the actress, is rarely made so clear for the audience. That is, while we are encouraged frequently to make the connections between transgressive performances in the past as a precursor for
such performances in the present, these seem to be largely celebratory
metaphors, basking the audience in the warm glow of the possibilities of
gender. Rarely, however, are the anxieties expressed about historical spectatorship mapped so clearly onto contemporary audiences, and when
they are, they are met with a deeply conflicting reception, even among
those whose political stances might suggest sympathies with the critiques
espoused.[17] There appears, then, an oscillating set of anxieties, both in the
critique of the negative potentials of spectatorship and performance and
in the impulse to protect the audience from feeling too acutely the force of
that critique. This pairing points not only to the inwardly focused anxieties of metadrama but also an ourtwardly focused anxiety about material political efficacy, one that implicitly imagines that in order to achieve
rhetorical effectiveness, audiences must be assuaged and congratulated
for their own critical capacities, without being implicated as the possible
site of that critique.

While we ourselves might note these countervailing anxieties, they
suggest that these plays are not simply performing the kind of self-in-
volved representational examination often associated with a blank postmodern metafictional approach. Instead, their roots are in a perceived political real, one that implicates both representational systems and material

realities (the very nexus that written and performed lives negotiate). In what follows, I will examine three plays—Hélène Cixous's *Portrait of Dora*, April De Angelis's *Playhouse Creatures*, and Maria Irene Fornes's *The Summer in Gossensass*—that together suggest a phenomenon that we can trace across the entire cultural moment in which they appear. In this period—the last quarter of the twentieth century—while neither wholly preceding nor wholly following ideas appearing in feminist theory and criticism, the feminist stage served as a performance lab for testing the representational problems and potentials of a variety of approaches to understanding the textualized and constructed nature of women's lives, and in particular in the case of biography, of women's lives that are already deeply entrenched in the textual through a history of written representation. Each of these plays takes up lives of women that were textualized and theatricalized during their lifetimes, and using writing, performing, rehearsing, and translating as literal and metaphorical methods for representing women's lives, these plays stage anxious experiments in their own representational processes. At the same time, these plays also gesture outwardly to their audiences, offering them safe spaces for imagining gendered transgression while also seeking to persuade them to import those performances into the world beyond the stage.

Hélène Cixous's *Portrait of Dora:* The Subject Acts Out

While the most common appearance of the metadramatic mode in feminist biographical drama tends to feature performers and writers, the concern of the form with representing women's lives also calls us to look critically at women as the subject of writing, particularly writing that carries a specifically gendered valence. Certainly this is true for the life of Ida Bauer, the real-life subject of Sigmund Freud's *Dora: An Analysis of a Case of Hysteria,* whose life narrative first entered the public sphere as the psychoanalytic test case par excellence not only of female hysteria but also later as an exemplar of the ways in which Freudian psychoanalysis reaffirmed specific gender codes of women as submissive and dominated. Essentially a retelling of Freud's case study, Hélène Cixous's *Portrait of Dora* reframes the case history of "Dora," Freud's chosen pseudonym, within the site of the analysis itself. While Cixous's play is first and foremost an engagement of psychoanalysis as an exercise of the diagnostic gaze as a

particular tool for circumscribing women's lives, it also operates as a biography play, an intervention into the already textualized life of Ida
Bauer as mediated in Freud's case study of Dora. In liberating the life of
Ida Bauer from the "portrait of Dora," Cixous offers up performance as a
mode of transgressing and escaping the circumscribing impulses of both
psychoanalysis and its written artifacts.

Instead of presenting a coherent narrative that claims to know the
historical reality of Ida Bauer's case, Cixous resets the events of the life of
Dora and therefore a life narrative already bound up in a textual history.
Accordingly, then, avoiding the events of the life outside of Freud's portrait, Cixous situates Dora's case specifically within the conversation between analyst and analysand. These conversations are punctuated, illustrated, revised, and complicated by what goes on behind the dialogue:
images in various forms acting out what words can't express—memories,
fantasies, projected still images, scrim-shadowed tableaux, bodied performances. And framing these conversations and enactments is the disembodied Voice of the Play, whose third-party interjections question, reinter-
pret, and reexamine the events that the audience witnesses. The
phallocentric narrative of psychoanalysis that preorders and shapes lived
experience is displaced by what we apparently are to understand as the
raw material, the fragments of Dora's life as they are experienced, re-
counted, and interpreted by both the psychoanalyst and his patient. In
short, Cixous sets male biographical language against the performed bodied experience of women at the poles of a continuum of representation.

Much of the critical work on *Portrait of Dora* examines the play as a
feminist intervention with psychoanalysis, in both its Freudian and later
feminist incarnations. "'Cracking' the case, breaking the frame of the portrait," says critic Sharon Willis, "this spectacle of circulating voices and
images stages a particular theoretical encounter: that of feminism and
psychoanalysis."[18] Still others attend to the confluence of the play's inter-
ventionary subject (psychoanalysis) and its formal presentation (theater),
making analogies between Cixous's fragmentation of Freud's version of
Dora's case and her unstitching of traditional theater's linear narrative
and objectifying modes of viewing.

But there are both metadramatic tactics and metatheatrical effects at
work in this making of theatricalized portraiture; I therefore understand
the play as less about the epistemology of psychoanalysis than about biography as the template for that epistemology. For what is psychoanalysis if not life writing, the transcription of lived (and dreamed) experience

into narrative, subject to interpretation, shaping, fictionalizing? What we have, then, is a play as much about a male biographer struggling with the narrative demands of his determinedly female biographical subject as it is about an analyst and analysand puzzling over the pathology of the hysteric. We can then translate much of the criticism of the play's engagement with psychoanalysis into an engagement with the life writing that lies at the heart of Freudian analysis: the problem for Freud (as character and historical figure) inevitably shifts from a diagnosis of Dora's hysteria toward a narration of her hysteria as history. In fact, as Elin Diamond notes, "the 'presence' of historical figures [in *Portrait of Dora*] creates a sense of history as an assemblage of patriarchal narratives that are ripe for revision. If there is a referent in [this text] it is historical experience, never fully describable, but invoked as nodal points of memory and desire."[19]

Indeed, when viewed as historical *experience,* Cixous's play, like the others in this study, foregrounds not only the biographical subject but also the biographical act, examining not only Dora but also Freud—just one way in which the play splits its subject. In fact, Dora is not even as much a historical figure as is her narrator, for in a sense, she exists only in Freud's narrative. Freud elided the real-life figure of Ida Bauer as the biographical subject by his publication of the narrative in 1905, and as Ann Wilson notes, "Arguably then, the only traces of Ida Bauer . . . are evident in Freud's portrait of her in the case history. Dora is really Freud's Dora as Cixous' Dora is clearly a construct mediated not only by Cixous' textual practices but by Freud's."[20] So when Cixous chose the case as her own material, she had already chosen the biographical *act* as her object of scrutiny, more so than the biographical *subject,* the life having already entered into discourse through psychoanalysis-as-biography. In this sense, the recovery becomes secondary to the contextualization of the process of life writing. Dora and Freud, as the dialectic image of history, become discursive formations rather than real people. Again, Diamond notes of Dora, "neither her character nor any other is a unitary object under scrutiny, but rather a tangle of textual-cultural references, what [feminist director Simone] Benmussa calls 'texts from elsewhere.'"[21] This shift from unitary object to discursive field also signals a focal shift from the biographical subject to historical experience and the very subjective (and in Freud's case, patriarchal) practice of biography.

In fact, while we might read psychoanalytic biography as one of this play's concerns, Sharon Willis, among others, suggests that theater itself is equally crucial to this interrogation. She suggests that Cixous's main tactic in pressing on the assumptions of traditional theatrical viewing is to disrupt scenic coherence, the unifying, ordering impulse that theater (particularly mimetic theater) imposes on the messy business of life, in much the same way that Freudian analysis imposes a narrative order on lived experience. To achieve this, Willis argues, Cixous presents us with an array of images that can be interpreted in multiple ways: fantasy and memory, seen and unseen, unseen and heard, split apart and doubled.[22] In particular, Willis looks at the first scene of the play (as realized most famously in Simone Benmussa's 1976 production), wherein "the scene by the lake"—Mr. K.'s supposed seduction of Dora—is projected in film and still images as Dora relates the incident to Freud—here she both speaks to Freud as if relating the story ("I never loved Mr. K., I was never crazy about him") and as if experiencing it ("I'm not staying, I'm leaving with my father").[23] As the audience, we never know how to interpret this split image of the scene of analysis and the scene(s) of the crime. Is it Dora's memory of the real-life instance? Freud's fantasy? Or can we take her father at his word when he says, "She has probably imagined the whole scene."[24]

Destabilizing the referent of lived experience by making its interpretation ambiguous, Cixous undermines the authority of Freud's biography as a representation of objective truth and calls into question the very act of life writing itself. Willis asserts that at moments like this, the narrative coherence imposed by Freud in his case study is " 'pricked, pierced, stitched, unstitched. It's all women's work,' as Dora comments. . . . 'Women's work' here consists of fragmentation, juxtaposition, and interruption."[25] In an interpretive move that echoes the essentializing impulses of Cixous's own writing, Willis ties this strategy not only to the epistemology of "women's work" but also to hysteria. Male narrative, male viewing, and male authority are all frustrated by the embodied (and in Dora's case, pathologized) woman. In the specific context of biography, Diamond's characterization of the play's history as "nodal points of memory and desire" becomes all the more apt; Cixous's form revises the patriarchal epistemology of psychoanalysis, the masculinist impulses of biographical representation, *and* the objectifying gaze of the traditional theater.

Indeed, a good deal of critical work has already been done on the ways in which Cixous's narrative frustrates traditional viewing practices. Erella Brown traces this disruption to the fragmented narrative of the hysterical body, which facilitates a mise-en-scène that frustrates the objectifying gaze.[26] Other accounts, such as Mairead Hanrahan's, focus on the disruption of voice, both in the play and in the historical account of Dora, as central to the play's efforts to unseat the written authority of Freud's master text. A number of oppositions are set up in the criticism, then: experience and authority, fragmentation and coherence, visual objectification and vocal disruption, written circumscription and embodied transgression. Each of these, as Hanrahan suggests, underscores the fact that the "critical difference between Freud and Cixous concerns their willingness to accept that their account of Dora is precisely a *version,* one of a number of possible accounts."[27] By disrupting the coherence of Freud's text, Cixous calls into question the rhetorical authority that Freud's biography has over its subject. And *as biography,* these tactics contextualize the biographical subject (Dora) not as a fixed object of historical scrutiny but as a discursive formation, constructed through narrative and subject to interpretation. This notion of the biographical subject as discursive formation, a tangle of cultural references, is further foregrounded by the fact that the play, even more so than many other plays examined here, splits its focus between its two biographical subjects: Dora and Freud. Like many feminist biography plays that stage biography as a kind of performance in itself, *Portrait of Dora* contextualizes its status as a portrait, as biography, making both the life being written and the life writer its dual concern. As much as the Brechtian strategies of the play undermine the authority of Freud's narrative, they also redirect the viewer's gaze to the image of Freud himself, the transparent narrator whose interpretive authority over Dora's life goes unquestioned in his own narrative. Freud, like Dora, becomes both spectator and spectacle, subject who interprets and object of interpretation. Cixous subverts the conventional notion of Freud as site for male identification and Dora as object of the gaze; instead, both Dora and Freud are sites for identification and objectification, and in this way, the gaze is diffused and subverted.

Cixous's account differs from Freud's primarily in its formal elements, often through self-conscious theatricalization, which disrupts the authority of Freud's narrative control over the subject, if not his epistemological authority of diagnosis. Furthermore, the resistant performances imagined through Cixous's text are utilized not only as a way to interrogate the body of the subject itself (which here is split, fragmented, doubled) but to put into question the conventional modes of viewing that subject. These tactics have decidedly metatheatrical effects because they force audience members to not only view differently but to view self-consciously. Cixous's dream states and film sequences so thoroughly thwart transparent, passive viewing that an audience member can't help but to reflexively ask herself how best to watch such a production. The play is so overtly theatrical that, given Cixous's own emphasis on women's *writing* as a source of empowerment, one must wonder how theater functions within such a representational framework. How, we might ask, is this re-visioning of Dora's case, this re-presentation of her life, specifically suited to the theater instead of the written page?

Sharon Willis suggests that part of this question is answered in the term *acting out,* aligning the notions of rebellion and performance. To put it another way, performance becomes a way to resist masculinist writing and the subjection that it often entails, just as acting out is a way of resisting other kinds of masculinist authority. Therefore, Dora's acting out signifies metatheatrically, at the level of both the character who acts out against male authority and the playwright and performers who act out against the discursive authority of Sigmund Freud. This tendency of performance to provide for this kind of transgression has been well documented by feminist performance theorists. Peggy Phelan argues, for example, that performance exists only in the present and disappears as soon as it is enacted. In this way, it cannot be reproduced "or participate in the circulation of representation *of* representations: once it does so, it becomes something other than performance."[28] In reproduction, performance becomes coded, inscribed, part of the system of gender codes that Judith Butler argues are consistently reified, made compulsory through repetition and reproduction, and ultimately circulated within of the matrices of oppressive power. By resisting repetition, performance becomes an apt mode of expression for Dora's hysteric body, one that resists its "proper" reproductive function. Instead, as Phelan argues, "[W]ithout a copy, live performance plunges into visibility—in a maniacally charged present—and disappears into the realm of invisibility and the unconscious where it eludes regulation and control."[29] Dora's performance, then, in its sheer temporality, resists the ordering that Freud's narrativization seeks to impose on it. Instead, Dora here is performed by a live body, which, as Phelan suggests, "implicates the real," which disappears at the very moment of its presence. And "the after-effect of disappearance," Phelan argues, "is the experience of subjectivity itself."[30] We might speculate, then, that Cixous's play demands performance in order for the revision of Freud's biography of Dora specifically to resist the tendency of Freudian narrative to force lived experience into a phallocentric narrative, to continue to fight against the impulses of reproduction and to approximate the imagined experience of Dora's subjectivity as it disappears.

In short, because performance disappears in the moment of writing, *Portrait of Dora* must be performed and not taken simply a piece of writing. The play thematizes not the object—the piece of writing itself, the inscribed body of the biographical subject, which is subject to the control of power—but rather *experience,* the experience of the real and the experience of narrating the real. Cixous represents Dora's performance but also writes in her own position through the Voice of the Play, which, in establishing its own subjectivity through writing, distances itself from Dora; as Hanrahan notes, "The crucial difference between Dora and Cixous is that Dora does not write."[31] In this sense, Cixous's play stands not only as a biography but also (and perhaps more important) as a performance of biographical construction, as it presents Dora's resistant narrative and Freud's oppressive one. While the text is not explicitly metadramatic in presenting actual theatrical representation, it creates metatheatrical effects in two ways: first, by self-consciously disrupting and reconfiguring the theatricalized viewing practices by which we might ascertain the object of biography; and then by posing a kind of transgressive performance that resists and ultimately escapes writing, just as the character of Ida Bauer ultimately escapes her erstwhile biographer in the form of Sigmund Freud. It is the final moment of Cixous's play, in which acting out resists the circumscribing impulses of biographical writing, that we must acknowledge as significantly metatheatrical, for it poses performance as specifically powerful not only for representing women's lives but for living them as well.

April De Angelis's *Playhouse Creatures:* Women's Theater as History/Women's History as Theater

While Cixous chooses the everyday metatheatricality of acting out, we might find more overtly metadramatic impulses in those plays that position actresses as their biographical subjects, making explicit the interrogation of performance and a tradition for women in the theater. April De Angelis's *Playhouse Creatures* reconstructs the life of Nell Gwyn, one of the first famous Restoration actresses on the English stage—although she is perhaps more renowned as the favorite mistress of Charles II than as an onstage performer, where her skills were nonetheless noteworthy. De Angelis's play represents simultaneously a number of the rhetorical possibilities and the representational dangers of metadramatic narratives and metatheatrical performance effects, for inasmuch as her play holds up a number of specifically feminist concerns, and translates them quite directly to the contemporary stage, she does so in a way that is deeply suspicious of theatrical performance as vulnerable to the objectifying gaze, even as her play is extraordinarily guarded against her audience, in terms of her careful manipulation of the historical record, as well as her hesitance to implicate contemporary audiences in the critiques that she levels on historical spectatorship.

De Angelis's play exists in two published versions: the shorter 1994 version was first produced as a British touring production and focuses on Nell Gwyn and four other actresses in the King's Company circa 1670.[32] The play charts Nell's rise from serving strong drink in Covent Garden to her introduction to the stage and ultimately to the peak of her stardom and her decision to leave the stage to become the king's more permanent mistress.[33] The longer version, expanded for a 1997 production at the Old Vic in London and published in 1999, adds three characters: Elizabeth Barry, often cited as the greatest actress of her age; the playwright Thomas Otway; and the Earl of Rochester. While much of the play remains the same from edition to edition (notably most of their respective first acts), De Angelis's second version drastically alters the ending of the play, highlighting the rise of the ambitious Elizabeth Barry and reducing Nell to an apoplexied, desperate woman, thereby altering how the play ultimately imagines its historical subjects.

And "historical subjects" is very much the purview of this play, as it tries to negotiate the ambiguous situation of these actresses as both notoriously sexualized objects and emerging professionals.[34] To accomplish this De Angelis draws heavily on famous circumstances and incidents as touchstones for her play. Deborah C. Payne identifies a number of commonplace assumptions and extant tales of these women as they are traditionally cited when describing the oppression of the Restoration actress, and the vast majority of them appear in De Angelis's play: general conditions like the gender-based discrepancy in pay, the paltry number of parts available to women, the threat of firing as punishment for pregnancy, the dangerous lure of leaving the stage to become a mistress, and more specific instances such as Rebecca Marshall's run-in with thugs hired by Sir Hugh Middleton or a jilted Elizabeth Farley's destitute fate.[35] Other moments throughout the text reveal, at the very least, the playwright's familiarity with the history in question.

And yet to say that this is a work of history is also something of an overstatement.[36] Several characters, although they bear the names of real Restoration actresses and share a very few incidents from the real women's lives, seem to be substantively fictional characters constructed to advance a thesis about the state of the actresses in the seventeenth century. For example, Nell's first entrée onto the stage is presented in the play as a tribute to the character's wit and cunning—convincing Mrs. Betterton, wife of the actor-manager, that she was told that she was to have a line in the play in rehearsal, Nell makes her first appearance on the stage something of an accident from the standpoint of the company. Biographies of Gwyn paint a different picture, however, suggesting that she first met Thomas Killigrew, master of the King's Playhouse, because her sister was the mistress of Killigrew's son, and that she got her earliest roles because of her sexual relationship with Charles Hart, a leading actor.[37] So not only was her historical debut at least partially the result of sexual nepotism but the very company she debuted with is misrepresented in order to get all the necessary characters onto one stage.[38]

More important to the historicity of the play than the particular details of the lives of individual actresses, however, is the narrative employed to frame their lives and the conditions of their presence on the stage. Again I return to the previous chapter's consideration of Joan Schenkar's metaphor of historical facts as hinges in a larger narrative: although De Angelis quite liberally alters the surface details of her play, she grapples more substantively with the hinge facts, which not only reveal the compromised position of actresses in the Restoration but also underscore the degree to which this remains true in the present. In this case that narrative involves a split in the twin tropes of "actress as object" and "actress and professional." Payne argues:

> Modern criticism reproduces this split, construing the Restoration actress as either a reified object or an emergent professional. . . . Objectification and professionalization, far from opposing each other, can be seen as an effect of the late seventeenth century shift toward the primacy of the visual. And, like most cultural "logics," this one is also marked by contradiction. Thus while feminist critics are right to show how objectification undoubtedly diminishes actresses, they also fail to note how, in a public sphere with an increasingly pronounced sense of the visual, objectification simultaneously *amplified* actresses, situating them at the new nexus of power.[39]

Payne's argument poses a serious problem for the feminist playwright: in order to represent the Restoration actress' position at the "nexus of power," she must also represent objectification as a precondition of that power. This becomes a difficult task for De Angelis, one that is more successful in the earlier version of the play, in terms of both her representation of the Restoration and her presentation of Nell's stage as a cipher for twentieth-century feminist concerns. The 1994 edition of the play suggests, to a point, this paradox. Nell's first appearance on the stage is a result of her own cunning, but this first incident is by any professional measurements a disaster: she is struck dumb by stage fright, and after the rest of the actresses leave the stage, she can only think to dance. And yet Nell describes "in a special box, a man in glitter, cheering."[40] Nell's ability to please the king as a spectator is crucial to her success as an actress later on. In fact, the next time we see her "onstage," she is performing a comic breeches role, the kind of role historically said to be her specialty. Here we see that her objectification leads to her success, a success, it may be argued, that depends on her objectification, since, as Marjorie Garber, Kristina Straub, and others argue, the breeches role is a spectacle that sexualizes the actress in a number of complex ways.[41] Moreover, the play seems to consciously set up a link among poetry, consumption, and sexuality. At least three times throughout the play (between the two versions), we hear singsong rhymes that involve selling food by using double entendres. By linking the recitation of a poem with consumption, and then marking that consumption as sexual, De Angelis seems to be underscoring the decidedly object-oriented nature of the stage, and it is this very fact that facilitates Nell's rise to her position of empowerment at the king's side.

The 1999 edition (and, indeed, many moments in the earlier version), however, reinforces the divide that Payne critiques. The introduction of the plain Elizabeth Barry, who is historically cited as the most accomplished actress of the age, provides a dualizing counterpoint for the sexualized figure of Nell and, to a lesser extent, the characters of Mrs. Farley and Mrs. Marshall. In the cases of both Farley and Marshall, the play represents the sexualization and objectification of the actress as the key to their downfall, a case in which objectification distinctly undermines professionalization. Contrasted with this moralistic patterning of objectification resulting in ruin, Elizabeth Barry is represented as an ambitious, greedy woman who lets nothing stand in the way of her success on the stage. In polarizing her actresses this way, De Angelis seems to insist on the same false divide between objectification and professionalization. The sense that we get from Mrs. Barry, that she must suppress emotion "to make room for money and success," relies on the precise myth of professionalism that underpins Payne's argument: "Professionalization, by forcing the subject into the public realm to be judged according to external criteria, functions as another version of Cartesian dualism. Once again the actress is looked at, objectified; only this time she is framed against the perspectivist backdrop of taste."[42] So not only is Mrs. Barry not claiming sexual subjectivity, but she is not rectifying her status as object either.

It becomes fairly clear, then, that as a narrative of historical fact, De Angelis's text is a failure. But given her relative conversance with incidents that did documentably happen in the lives of these actresses, it appears fair to say that her bad history is not the result of ignorance or bad research. And while we might easily write off De Angelis's prerogative to take some fictional license with her characters, we must examine how and why she deploys history in the particular way that she does, especially given that she refers to her use of history in interviews, noting that while *Playhouse Creatures* isn't purely a reflection of contemporary theater, there are significant points of similarity and relevance between Restoration and contemporary actresses.[43] One might note that her flexible use of historical fact on the one hand works in service of feminist rhetoric, but we might also note that for audiences unfamiliar with the conditions of Restoration actresses, such poetic license with the historical material masquerades as fact. In doing so, De Angelis takes advantage of the audience's ignorance without self-reflexively casting doubt on their own complicity in perpetuating the same kinds of conditions she critiques. Certainly the notion of the dialectical image again becomes useful, since these images are quite literally "blasted out of history's continuum" as Diamond suggests, thus diminishing the historical divide between the audience and the world of the play.[44]

This effect is achieved in part by the metatheatrical passages within the play itself, moments that are at once contemporary and simultaneously doing some of the historicizing work of biography. Throughout the play, we see the actresses performing Restoration drama onstage. For the most part, however (with the exception of passages from Shakespeare's *Antony and Cleopatra* and *Macbeth*), the lines they speak are not those of seventeenth-century playwrights. They are De Angelis's approximations or reconstructions, and even in cases in which the play in question is extant (as is true of George Etherege's *The Man of Mode; or Sir Fopling Flut-*

ter), the playwright still replaces the text with her own. In these passages, De Angelis introduces into the metatheatrical performance the larger issues that she addresses in the play itself. The epilogue performed by Nell and Mrs. Marshall at the opening of Act II specifically demands shares in the company. The scene, supposedly from Etherege's play, addresses the issue of Mrs. Betterton's aging. Another scene involving Betterton comically represents the male fear of women's sexual appetites, which of course contrasts neatly with the sexual appetites of the male spectators with whom the actresses must contend during every performance. And finally, another scene that presents the actresses as an Amazon tribe very much mimics the kind of utopian community that De Angelis seems to be presenting in the tiring room. And so the Restoration stage, as staged in the audience's presence, is presented as an analogue of the lives of the first actresses who populated it.

But it is also an analogue of the lives of the actresses who populate today's stage. That is to say, while the play is not presenting a precise history, it does attempt to address many of the issues that confront contemporary actresses. Of Susan Bassnet-McGuire's seven requirements for a feminist play, De Angelis's play addresses no fewer than four of them: "equal pay," "equal job opportunities," "abortion on demand," and "freedom from sexual coercion."[45] By setting up this conduit by means of which the actresses bring their concerns to the stage, De Angelis recontextualizes these debates in the twentieth century: if the stage of seventeenth-century actresses reflected their lives, then it follows that in this play the stage of the actresses performing it similarly reflect concerns that extend off the stage. If we revisit the typical claim that feminist biographies are masked autobiographies—or perhaps more accurately, the overt application and manifestation of the dual nature of the dialectical image—we find its appropriate application here: because the biographical subjects are professionalized counterparts to the actresses who create them, their biographies span history to tell a story about contemporary lives. Here, then, the body of each actress onstage serves to diminish this historical divide: the problem of the objectified Restoration actress becomes the problem of the objectified modern actress. The issues of equal pay and sufficient roles for characters like Mrs. Marshall begin to reflect the legitimate labor concerns of actresses right now. As an image of the past, De Angelis's play may be imprecise in its details, but as a metatheatrical conceit it provides an image of the present, one that is reinforced by its grounding in the real.

And yet the issue raised by an exploration of this play is more complex than the commonplace that says the past is used to reflect the present. In a sense, the playwright is using the past here not only to reflect the present but to legitimate her task by both recovering the past's voices and replaying their erasure. The recovery work is quite evident: in her interview with Stephenson and Langridge, De Angelis notes that the play was "trying to say that there is a history there that is quite vital and it's a positive thing to know about."[46] And the relevance of that recovery is similarly evident, even if that relevance is dependent on the ideological mediation of the playwright. Specifically, *Playhouse Creatures'* actresses struggle with the problems of representations of women in the roles they perform but also the problems of representing those roles. Meanwhile, the contemporary actresses who play them enact those same struggles: actresses recovering a history of actresses seeking to establish a history. And by giving body and voice to these historical figures, such metatheatrical discourse serves to produce dialectical images that uncover the history that the plays are reclaiming even as they reproduce the historical process by means of which these women were "hidden from history." Essentially, this play works to perform a history of women's theater by performing the elision of that history. As I suggested in the previous chapter, in order to legitimate the very recovery work that it is doing, *Playhouse Creatures* must also represent the reasons why such recovery work is necessary.

The past that DeAngelis is unearthing, then, must be one worth the dig: hence the emphasis on contemporary feminist issues as plot motivators in the play. The prime movers of the plot include the push for shares in the company; Mrs. Farley's, Mrs. Marshall's, and Nell's individual interactions with various lovers; and the disastrous consequences of those interactions—unwanted pregnancy, accusations of witchcraft, life-threatening diseases, and the like. But underneath the issues of the company shares and jilted lovers is the notion of a community of female theater practitioners. At the center of this play is not the story of an actress's rise to fame, or a moral about the dangers of succumbing to sexual objectification, but rather a portrait of an almost utopian collective of women's voices that can accomplish virtually anything. The scenes between the middle of the first act and the beginning of the second play like comedy, with each dilemma being neatly remedied on the stage or in the tiring room: Mrs. Marshall's run-ins with Oxford are rectified by the homunculus she constructs backstage; Nell's inexperience and seemingly disastrous first stage entrance move from "shameful!" to "a reprieve!" in a

matter of less than fifty lines, and she is promptly taken under the tute-
lage of the expert Mrs. Betterton;[47] and a call for shares leads to an agreement that is ultimately cut short by disaster. By representing this community as politically informed and capable, De Angelis makes her
biographical subjects worth reviving at the same time as their stories reflect the work of the actresses reviving them.

Perhaps the best expression of interplay between recovery and elision
in De Angelis's play comes in the focus on the female voice. At one level,
Playhouse Creatures places voice in opposition to the objectified body. Witness Nell's first moments of instruction from Mrs. Betterton.

> *Doll and Mrs. Betterton go to the exit. Nell attempts her line as they are*
> *leaving. It stops Mrs. Betterton in her tracks.*
> Nell: . . . the live long day.
> Mrs. Betterton: Never underestimate the value of opening one's
> mouth while speaking. One may go a long way in the theatre
> with an open mouth.
> Doll: And not just in the theatre.
> *Nell opens her mouth but gestures wildly.*
> Nell: Watching my fellows fork the hay.
> Mrs. Betterton: A word. Stillness.
> Nell: Stillness?
> Mrs. Betterton: (*with stillness*) "Here I stroll the live long day
> watching my fellows fork the hay." See?
> Nell: Oh yeah.[48]

Mrs. Betterton introduces Nell to the profession with a lesson that, while
fairly simplistic, teaches her to emphasize her voice while minimizing the
role of her body as spectacle. By placing body in opposition to voice, De
Angelis equates objectification with silencing, a move that will become
important in representing the elision of the community she establishes
early on in the play.

But voice and performance, while powerful, also seem to be treated
with suspicion in this play. While the performance of the women onstage
represents their growing professionalism, intelligence, and means to
power (witness Mrs. Marshall and Nell's call for shares while taking on
breeches roles), it is also cast by de Angelis as inherently suspect. While
De Angelis cites voice as a key to women's empowerment, threats to that
empowerment inevitably lead to a destruction of the professional identity
of those who inhabit the stage. And in *Playhouse Creatures,* that threat
seems to be the sexual objectification that Doll Common's play-framing

monologues seem to best express. Her opening monologue recalls the Elizabethan days of bearbaiting and her sympathy for the bears that were treated with such cruelty. The metaphor (if it wasn't clear at the outset) is made explicit in the last scene: after telling another story about the bears, and the degree to which her father, the bear keeper, abused the bears to make them dance, she turns to Nell and says, "Playhouse creatures they called you like you was animals."[49] It is precisely the objectification that underscores women's professionalization on the Restoration stage that Payne identifies as central to the position of these actresses. But performance is not suspect in this play simply because it encourages objectification; performance is also cast as ultimately incapable of sustaining women's power precisely because of its ephemeral nature. We must recognize that every character that exists in De Angelis's utopian tiring room of Act I ends the play disempowered: deranged, destitute, or exiled. Mrs. Marshall's economic victory in achieving company shares for the actresses, like performance itself, disappears when she leaves the stage.

Interestingly, while public performance is implicated as a kind of subjection to the objectifying gaze, the audiences that take advantage of this specular vulnerability are never represented: that is, while we are presented with potentially powerful, often joyous moments of metatheatrical performances, that metatheatrical effect is never extended to the staging of audiences. We hear about the king admiring Nell from his box, and other gentlemen who eventually take advantage of the actresses' exposure, but we are rarely if ever shown clearly how contemporary spectatorship might *also* function dialectically with historical spectatorship. Instead, we are offered the safety of a critical distance: brought into the tiring room to hear about these terrible behaviors but never implicated in our own duplication of the mechanisms that make them possible. This casting of performance as transgressive but ultimately powerless, and potentially endangering, contrasts starkly with the disruptive potential that Cixous seems to assign "acting out" in *Portrait of Dora.* While Dora's performances are private transgressions, the public nature of the actresses' performances, the degree to which objectification became a precondition of their very professionalization, renders their resistance to oppression far more compromised.

Instead, while Cixous frames writing in her play as suspect and perhaps even integrally patriarchal, De Angelis seems to position it as a remedy for the inability of performance to signify women's empowerment in history. For De Angelis, this comes in the form of the playwright's hand, both in the seventeenth century and in the present. While the acted scenes throughout this play seem on the surface to come from plays extant in the Restoration—Mrs. Betterton reads a list of plays that includes Etherege's *Sir Fopling Flutter,* Vanbrugh's *The Provoked Wife,* and three plays by Shakespeare, in addition to the unattributed *Reluctant Shepherdess*—almost all of the passages acted onstage are rewritten by DeAngelis herself. So what we have here is a consolidation of female voice: contemporary actresses reciting lines written by a contemporary female playwright, lines that reflect the lives of the female characters whose voices this play is resurrecting. For example, an early stage appearance finds the actresses dressed as Amazons who proudly declaim:

> For Amazons we still remain
> And live without the rule of men.
> Fierce warriors both we be
> And will go down in history.[50]

It is hardly coincidental that at the introduction of this community of actresses, they are themselves acting the roles of a utopian homosocial community. Nor is it coincidental that Mrs. Marshall and Nell are in dressed in breeches and carrying swords (carpe phallus!) as they deliver the epilogue that makes their most outrageous demands.

> And while we're at it, playing for your pleasure
> We'll ask shares in your payments for good measure
> The price of our glorious forms you see
> Is shares in this very company.[51]

The 1999 version reinforces this emphasis on the connection of women's voices and words in a nod toward Aphra Behn. In a scene that represents the peak of her career, Nell offhandedly remarks that Behn (who herself does not appear in either version of the play) has specifically written a part for her (even though Gwyn never appeared in a play by Behn). In pairing her biographical subject with perhaps the most famous female playwright before the twentieth century, De Angelis places women's voices—both performed and written—front and center in her version of the Restoration stage. Professionalism and the business of women's theater, therefore, are doubly represented onstage and in history as a direct result of women's writing.

The Epistemology of Rehearsal: Maria Irene
Fornes's *The Summer in Gossensass*

Among her later plays, Maria Irene Fornes's *The Summer in Gossensass* is a
muted affair, one less deeply theatrical than some of her more charged
work, like *The Conduct of Life* or *Tango Palace*. First produced by the
Women's Project and Productions in 1998, Fornes's play depicts the efforts of two American actresses—Elizabeth Robins and Marion Lea—to
produce the first English-language performance of Ibsen's *Hedda Gabler*.
And yet, despite its reserved theatricality, it is both deeply metadramatic
and unexpectedly *meta*theatrical. While Cixous's and De Angelis's plays
pose writing and performance against one another, Fornes's play shifts
the perspective from this particular dyad to other interstitial moments in
theatrical exchange, considering most closely the ideas of reading, translating, and rehearsing as modes of engaging women's lives.

Set in 1891, *The Summer in Gossensass* covers the lead-up to Elizabeth
Robins and Marion Lea's production of *Hedda Gabler*, beginning with the
first word of the play's impending arrival in England. Marc Robinson
notes, "Hardly a profile of her appears without the familiar anecdote:
Maria Irene Fornes had not read a single play except *Hedda Gabler* before
she began writing in 1963."[52] Certainly, then, as a fond engagement with
Ibsen's play, Fornes's play appears as a love letter to reading itself, as the
characters replay a theme common in the contemporary playwright's
work: the squeezing of meaning—creatively, vitally—from a mere scrap
of writing.[53] Yet we might also find another sort of love letter in this play,
to Elizabeth Robins, as well as to *Hedda Gabler*. The action of the play, set
entirely in Elizabeth's drawing room, revolves around the frustrating
process of gaining access to the play and then access to the character who
would launch Elizabeth's career. The actresses are aided by Vernon
Robins (Elizabeth's brother), Lady Florence Bell, and a young theater en-
thusiast and collector, David. Together they obtain the script, first in its
original Norwegian, then in fragments pilfered from a competing production (said to feature Lillie Langtry, the historical mistress of the Prince
of Wales), and then in full translation. From there, we see Elizabeth and
her supporting cast excavate Hedda's character through careful close
reading and research on Ibsen and prepare to finally bring the controversial character to life in front of London's intellectual elite. While we never
see any of Elizabeth's performance of the role, the final image closes on an

older Elizabeth as she delivers a speech that recalls the heady days of Ibsen's first appearances on the English stage. It is an image that both acknowledges the import of both actresses (Robins and Lea) in bringing the landmark playwright to the English theatrical repertoire and implicitly, by depicting Robins as a notable public figure, establishes her significance in broader ways.

In Robins, the play's primary biographical subject, Fornes finds a woman who is at once an important suffrage feminist, a playwright, and an acclaimed actress. Having first earned fame for her portrayal of Hedda Gabler, Robins continued on to a successful onstage career, but she also worked as a playwright, novelist, and suffrage activist. In fact, her suffrage play *Votes for Women!* still commands scholarly attention as an important early feminist play. Fornes chooses to stage neither playwriting nor public performance as pathways into our experience of this woman's life, opting instead for less public moments that precede her entrance into the public eye. Yet Fornes seems far less interested in either the oppressive impulses of masculinist writing that we find in *Portrait of Dora* or the dangers of objectification found in the life of the actress—both potential subjects in a play that addresses the male text and female performer. Instead, she seems to locate the meaning making of a life through metaphors of life offstage but still decidedly connected to the performance. That is, only through reading, translating, and performing do we find Robins grappling with the identity and life of Hedda Gabler (and Ibsen's model for her, Emilie Bardach), while at the same time these processes offer audiences strategies for grappling with the life of Elizabeth Robins.

Because none of *The Summer in Gossensass* takes place on a stage, it *seems* to be less directly metatheatrical in effect than we might conclude it to be. On the one hand, it is a play about reading and bringing to production a landmark play in the history of modern Western theater. And in this way it is at least *subtly* metatheatrical in that its realist drawing room staging and generally muted theatricality together create a metatheatrical effect by pointing back at *Hedda Gabler's* similarly realist tactics. But Ibsen's play itself is hardly hypertheatrical, as realist drama in general tends to mute or even ignore entirely its own theatricality, so as a reference point *Hedda Gabler* offers little in high theatricality to *The Summer in Gossensass.* Yet while *Gossensass* remains a comparatively understated affair, the play is nonetheless insistently meta*dramatic*, particularly in its depiction of the communicative acts bound up in writing and reading. Marc Robinson's chapter is particularly persuasive on the centrality of this theme, noting not only that every character is depicted at some point with reading material but that several scenes depict characters reading single texts together, reading multiple texts on their own while together on stage, and analyzing and debating the importance of the many texts they have just read. Indeed, for Robinson, this is what the play is *about*.

> Fornes envisions a style of analysis, and hopes to cultivate it in her critic-readers. She even seems to agitate for such a style, while maintaining her customary tact: The play imagines a critic who will be as feverish as the reading characters in Fornes's other plays, yet as single-minded as Elizabeth Robins or Marion Lea—someone managing to combine the two temperaments so that the art under examination will regain its original force from the force of its reader's attention.[54]

The importance of reading, then, is well established—with characters as readers, Fornes as a reader, and Fornes's audiences as readers as well—and these reading figures become the site of inquiry on both why we read and how to read as well.

In seeking out Fornes's argument on the nature of reading, Robinson articulates an expressed ideal of both "feverish" passion and careful attention, but Fornes also stages commentary on what we might call the wrong ways of reading. Prominently, translation—particularly literal translation—comes under particular scrutiny as an insufficient, rote kind of reading. At the outset of the play, the actresses anticipate the arrival of Ibsen's text in its original Norwegian, a language neither of them knows. When the text finally arrives, we see Elizabeth struggling with simple word-for-word translation. After she vacillates on the possibilities of one simple passage, we see her as *"she takes the book in her hands and holds it against her chest"* and says, "I have the play. . . . It's in my hands. But I can't read it."[55] It's the only thing we see of Elizabeth's own translation efforts, but they reveal in the gesture that shifts from reading-with-dictionary to the pressing of the book against her chest a tension between reading as a rote, literal activity, and as a more affective process, one felt (almost literally, here) in the heart. Indeed, after we have learned of a competing production of the play, translated by Edmund Gosse and starring Lillie Langtry, we hear translation again articulated as a particularly sterile form of reading. Here Elizabeth's brother Vernon reads a printed review that declares that "Gosse's translation is the exercise of a fourth-form schoolboy. [The reviewer] speaks of Gosse's 'hopelessly wrong, awkward, silly, and misleading phrases'" and later asserts that "Gosse is a man of letters, but not a man of the theatre."[56]

Here being "of letters" is decidedly inferior to being "of the theatre," but Fornes further damns the competing production through the figure of Langtry, who "cannot do" sections of the play, further contributing to the butchering of its anticipated final form. Langtry is only mentioned a small handful of times in the play, but her characterization is specific, particularly in its deviation from the historical record. For, although Lillie Langtry began acting as early as 1882,[57] nearly a decade before the action of this play occurs, here she is characterized as having "taken up acting . . . to please the Prince of Wales."[58] This sort of acting-as-ambition (and by the sexual object of a spectating royal) is precisely the sort presented anxiously by De Angelis in *Playhouse Creatures;* conversely, in Robins and Lea, Fornes presents us with readers and actors who conform to a readerly ideal that is both professional and guided by affective instincts, rather than purely literal "schoolboy" processes or overtly sexualized ambitions.

We see this balancing of intense professional scrutiny and deeply affective sensitivity in the play's third and most overtly theatrical register: rehearsal. For soon after we see Elizabeth struggle with translation, Marion enters the scene, breathlessly having stolen some discarded pages of the competing script. We see Elizabeth and Marion encounter the roles of Hedda Tesman and Thea Elvsted, as they read through the scene three times, each time gaining more insight into the characters as they pause to speculate about who these women are and what their relationship must be. These scenes lie at the center of the play, for as Robinson asserts, "[I]t is in rehearsal—a synonym for reading together . . . —that Fornes finds her ideal for all forms of interpretation. Unsure of Ibsen's new play, yet determined to know it intimately, Elizabeth and Marion have the right combination of purpose and restraint—passionate tact—that Fornes deems essential to good criticism."[59] Given the importance of rehearsal as the play's central metaphor, it is perhaps felicitous, then, that Fornes's own rehearsal process for *The Summer in Gossensass* has itself been documented in Susan Letzler Cole's *Playwrights in Rehearsal: The Seduction of Company,* which devotes a chapter to the debut of the play, directed by Fornes herself.[60] As Cole describes it, Fornes's writing process for this play was much like the process of discovery that her characters undergo. As Fornes says to Cole, "In rehearsal, I hear it over and over, and make changes . . . it's like smoothing a wrinkle. The line didn't go with the sense and the rhythm."[61] Fornes's own emphasis on "sense" and "rhythm" coming into accord with "the line" seems to locate the same negotiation in rehearsal for both writer and reader, something operating on both the logical plane of language and the affective plane of sense. Rehearsal, for both writer and reader, becomes itself a sort of revision (as the multiple drafts of the script described by Cole and still extant in the Women's Project and Productions archives attest). On this point, Fornes has embedded into the play a clever little bit of direct commentary, when Elizabeth speaks of a playwright, a friend of a friend (who could not *possibly* be named Maria Irene Fornes) who talks about a play as a riddle, "And a riddle, of course, must have a question. The question is an important part of the riddle. . . . She says that by the time the author gets halfway through, she knows what the question is. Then, answering the question begins to shape the play. She says every answer creates another question. And each answer makes the play grow."[62]

Here we have, alongside the scenes of rehearsal, one of the play's most overtly metadramatic moments, and yet instead of throwing us more deeply into textuality, deeper into an engagement with a play set within and behind this play, Fornes's barely disguised commentary on discovering the riddle of the play pushes us out of the frame, back into the world in which Fornes is an author and in which we are audience members at the turn of the millennium, rather than the turn of the previous century. And it is on this point that my reading diverges from Robinson's. For, while he reads Fornes's play as positing rehearsal as a kind of reading, I argue the inverse: that reading is a sort of rehearsal, and one that throws us back, somehow, into life. For while Fornes-reading-Ibsen may rest at the center of this play, that play is framed by real life and real lives, not only by the real lives of Elizabeth Robins and Marion Lea but also, spectrally, by Emilie Bardach, the failed seductress on whom Ibsen is purported to have modeled Hedda herself. That is, we might initially see this play as a highly intertextual interaction between Fornes's play and Ibsen's, where *Hedda Gabler* gives rise to *The Summer in Gossensass*. But I would argue that the textualization of lives completely frames this interaction, such that a diagram of the frames of the play might look like this: Emilie Bardach → *Hedda Gabler* → Robins → *The Summer in Gossensass* → audience. As much, then, as I am interested in this play's critical response to Ibsen, I am perhaps more interested in what the play says about the real lives that exist both centrally and spectrally on the stage, and how these lives transform through textual mediation. For while the dialectic between reading and rehearsing certainly suggests *The Summer in Gossen-*

sass's deep interest in the dynamics of reading deeply and thoughtfully, it also models for us the relationship between a life spent reading and the life being read. In doing so, Fornes suggests that for both her characters and for her own audiences, reading other lives becomes a kind of rehearsal for living life beyond our contact with the page or the stage.

In many ways, of course, this play seems to be missing some of the more common features of the feminist biography play. It spends virtually no time ruminating on how Robins's and Lea's lives in the theater have been preserved for us, in part because Lea and Robins appear at first to be merely ciphers for readers of Ibsen. But if we shift our critical lens from reading texts to reading lives in texts, we might still see the echoes of critical reflection on the translation of lives into text, and the reading of past lives as a rehearsal for present ones. One way that this comes out is through the emergence of Emilie Bardach from the most obscure shadows of Ibsen's play. In scene 5, we meet David, a man "whose interest in the theatre has caused him to collect documents and memorabilia of theater artists of whom he has special admiration. He has papers on Ibsen and papers from Ibsen's hand." David, a lover of theater first, and a collector and archivist second, offers up the letter that first mentions Bardach, "A very interesting Viennese girl I met in Gossensass. . . . A demonic little wrecker.—Like a bird of prey."[63] Here David immediately works information from this reference into the collective sense of who Hedda is, playing out how one might feel to be with a woman like this: "You die and then you are reborn. How often does someone have the opportunity to experience being possessed by someone else? Owned by someone else! Be it a demon or not. An angel or beast. Owned by a demon, or an angel, or a beast. Be owned. Be possessed."[64] David's rapturous language of possession is troubling to some degree, certainly because of the way it imagines Bardach in such stereotypical forms—woman as simultaneously angel, demon, and beast. But more troubling are the lines from Ibsen's letter about Bardach: "She wanted to possess me. But instead, I possessed her. For! My! Play!"[65]

That Emilie Bardach herself disappears behind Ibsen's texts is itself disconcerting, while Fornes's choice to continue to frame her as a possessing demon possessed by Ibsen seems to precisely articulate the dangers of writing women's lives. But just before the actresses finally receive their own English version of Ibsen's play, we briefly hear Bardach's voice, as Marion reads one of her letters: "'He is a volcano! So terribly beautiful.— Passion comes to me when it cannot lead to anything.' She wrote this.

'Eternal obstacles. This! And only this! Is true love! But oh, how sad I feel . . . for he fears his love for me.'"[66] In this way, we get a sense that Bardach herself is translated from the writer of this letter into the "little Viennese wrecker," whom Ibsen met on his summer stay in the Tyrolean town of Gossensass, and again to the destructive protagonist of Ibsen's play, another "wrecker" who has just returned to Norway from a Tyrolean honeymoon. Just as Elizabeth struggles to overcome a simple transliteration of the play, she also struggles to avoid simple transliteration of Bardach onto the role she is given. For Fornes, then, translation becomes one metaphor for writing a woman's life to the stage: an act that avoids the simple transliteration of facts and instead finds in the rehearsal of language the affective dimension of performing a feminist biography, squeezed from the foreign text rather than copied dutifully in schoolboy's hand.

Translated again in Gosse's "schoolboy" edition, Emilie Bardach appears to Robins only as a ghost, but she becomes the ghost on whom Robins later built her career, for, as Penny Farfan reminds us, "Robins, who lived to the age of ninety, identified her performance of the title role in the English-language premiere of *Hedda Gabler* in London in 1891 as the defining moment of her long and varied career as an actress, writer, and suffragist."[67] Yet Farfan is too well aware that Hedda is hardly an ideal feminist figure; she notes that "in willfully producing and performing such a provocative piece of drama, the actresses had . . . gone as far beyond the pale of accepted standards of femininity as Ibsen's title character herself."[68] Indeed, Farfan argues that "Robins's theatre career . . . became noteworthy with *Hedda Gabler* and ended with *Votes for Women*" and that her "feminist critique of Ibsen . . . developed over the course of her career and resulted in an unresolved tension not unlike that inherent in the figure of Hedda Gabler as suffragist icon."[69] It is in this way that I argue that Robins is not only translating Bardach but is also, through Hedda, rehearsing herself. Indeed, in the program note to the 1998 performance, entitled "The Coming Woman," literary manager of the Women's Project and Productions, Lisa McNulty, notes that "Robins eventually turned from acting to writing, and wrote several plays, novels, feminist essays and *The Coming Woman*, an unfinished novella based loosely on her own life, before her death in 1952."[70] The note goes on to quote Robins herself, who relates an anecdote that ends with the line "Hedda is all of us."[71]

On the one hand, such framing mechanisms in the program insinuate what Farfan has more explicitly articulated: that reading, rehearsing, and performing Hedda as a character was a starting point for Robins's own extraordinary, and less ambivalently feminist, life. That is, her life's work exceeded the feminist potential of the "unresolved tension . . . inherent in the figure of Hedda Gabler as suffragist icon." The reading of Hedda is only a rehearsal, and never the life itself. We see this embedded in the play in two ways. First is the way that Fornes's script inverts the destructive choice central to Ibsen's: Hedda's defining act (aside from her suicide) is the burning of Eilert Løvborg's manuscript, an action often read as emblematic of Hedda's destructive femininity—impeding the birth of the scholar's text is concomitant with her own sterility (or at least the insinuation of her unhappiness with the possibility of her pregnancy). But here we see our actresses struggling hard to rescue a manuscript, as Marion saves pages discarded by the competing performance and together they bring the text to life in performance. Hedda's textual abortion, then, is a rehearsal for Marion and Elizabeth's textual re-production. And as if such a re-production, a rehearsed translation, were not enough, we get a more direct discussion of the value of the unsavory character for the actress. As David and Vernon discuss the difficulty for the actor of "finding the character in oneself . . . even if you're playing a horrible person," their discussion suggests the importance of reading character critically, of negotiating character and self.

> VERNON: Yes. Elizabeth says yes. When she's rehearsing,
> sometimes she behaves strangely—she says it can be troubling.
> But then, it's not. She says in performance it's not painful.
> Except sometimes.
> DAVID: Yes. I can see how finding the character within oneself
> could inspire a performance of greater magnitude. However,
> there are things that are not part of our existence, but are
> outside of ourselves, like imitation, which could also be of
> great value to creation.
> VERNON: How would you play a horrible person?
> DAVID: Well I would say you have to study the character of a
> horrible person. I have files on a number of them.[72]

Here we see Vernon and David hashing out the problems of engaging a life, and the process of reading and performing Hedda (and reading and performing Emilie Bardach behind her) is one that involves finding the character inside oneself, rehearsing, behaving strangely, imitating, imagining, and studying.

It would be foolish to suggest that, like the other two plays examined in this chapter, *The Summer in Gossensass* is primarily *about* writing and performing as modes for representing women's lives. But by using lives that historically played out on the stage through writing and performing, the frame for the intertextual mediation between *Hedda Gabler* and *Gossensass* weaves the metadramatics of staged feminist biography into that central engagement. For these lives are always textual, already spectacle, and the care with which we approach them must be both deeply analytical and intensely affective. Our engagements with such figures must always be approached with the care and awareness of them as translations of life, as imitations of difficult characters, but they are always rehearsals for how lives can be lived. And if we take the complex of engagements that Robins makes with Hedda and Emilie Bardach as exemplary, we as audience members might also find a model for the complex of engagements that Fornes has, and that we might make with the figure of Elizabeth Robins, one that first holds up the compelling, complex character but returns the responsibility of reading, studying, analyzing, and translating that life back into our hands.

Conclusion: Translating Lives in the (Meta)Theater

As a set of anxious considerations of the representational consequences of writing and performing women's lives, the plays discussed here reframe what Ariel Watson casts as jostling for power instead as a distribution of responsibility. De Angelis gives Nell Gwyn responsibility for emphasizing voice over body; Cixous gives Dora the responsibility to escape the scene of diagnosis and the writing into submission that Freud represents; and Fornes endows her audiences with a responsibility to read her characters both critically and passionately, empathetically and analytically. Circulated among the participants of this anxious triangle are the stories of women's lives as subjects, artists, and speakers whose prerogative to speak out and act out stakes a claim for a female subjectivity whose place in history and on today's stages is still not sufficiently established.

Yet even as these lives are written for and performed on the stage, the metaphor of translation arises as a leitmotif across all three: lives are translated into texts, which are translated into performances; narratives are translated across languages; and performances are translated across often wide historical gaps. Translation theory is quick to identify a distinction between literal word-for-word translation and free translation, and many who study translation are quite adamant that translation itself is an art rather than a science. Working with the often competing goals of transparency, effectiveness, and efficiency, while always cautious about the ways in which translation itself mediates meaning, translation becomes an apt metaphor for understanding lives written for the stage. Certainly, in the case of Cixous, we see these concerns arising at multiple levels. At the first level, we find Cixous reading a translated Freud, and I am reading a translated Cixous. Only the most rudimentary knowledge of poststructuralist theory will tell us that each translation magnifies the slippage between sign and signified, one already inherent in any language.

This very effect, of *différance* amplified in the layered translation of texts, is similarly inherent in the language of staged lives. De Angelis, for example, is often sacrificing literal history for a free translation of Gwyn's life, one drawn along lines of narrative structure and rhetorical effectiveness. While we might debate the value of her liberal choices to translate history, one that values narrative transparency over fidelity to the historical record, we might note that the invisibility of that translation of history also facilitates De Angelis's own mediation of that historical record. It is in the very idea of free translation, then, that we find historical lives translated into late-twentieth-century performances of lives. And in Fornes's play, we find the very idea of translation self-consciously considered as a metaphor: translation—both linguistic and narrative—facilitates reading, which facilitates rehearsal, which facilitates performance. This metatheatrical process might well be used to describe the logic of the operations of each of these plays, which themselves translate historical lives to the contemporary stage, that their audiences might read them as rehearsals for performances off- and beyond the stage. While these operations are always fraught with slippage, with ideological mediation, and accordingly with anxiety, many playwrights also seem acutely aware of the specific material consequences that their metadramatic engagements with history might contain. And so we find them cautiously engaging an anxiety turned inward toward performance but only rarely turned outward toward the audiences whose lives they hope to affect.

CHAPTER 6 : Performing Race and the Object of Biography

The corpus of staged feminist autobiography and biography admittedly has been, like the body of feminist drama in general over the last decades of the twentieth century, a largely white affair. Typically, the texts and performances that comprise this corpus, like many of the plays examined in the previous two chapters, have consistently taken a protective, nonconfrontational approach to its audiences, often formulated in the name of fostering a supportive community of women who can, in solidarity, confront and critique the circumscribing discourses of gender that are often written onto male characters, many of whom are themselves only ever imagined offstage. For white performers and playwrights, however, the active critique and reframing of gender constructions often elide the equally important work of critiquing and reframing racialized constructions, particularly when race and gender interact discursively to generate mutually supporting lines of subjugation. For performers of color, autobiographical performance has yielded a small but significant number of staged interrogations of the performativity of both gender and race; individual performance artists like Robbie McCauley, Carmelita Tropicana, and Laurie Carlos have compellingly introduced race into the discourse of feminist lives, while playwrights such as Adrienne Kennedy have brought autobiographical material that directly engages discourses of race to scripted drama. These texts and performances frequently turn out to be challenging theatrical events and just as often create an almost Artaudian sense of discomfort in engaging their audiences. Yet biography plays have proven far less popular, and perhaps less fruitful, for interrogating race and ethnicity as historical constructions. Even when they are staged, they can come off either as dangerously naive to the operations of racial discourse or as so deeply suspicious of their own working mechanisms that their rhetorical success is always in question.

While the notion of the performative nature of gender, primarily as articulated by Judith Butler, has gained enough traction that it has been usefully applied to other nodes of identity construction, discourses of race have not seen those concepts imported so easily. Certainly we can imagine ways in which cultural performances of race could be considered a stylization of the body, although the compulsory nature of the repeated and repeatable codes of race is more complexly arranged, if for no other reason than the variety of racial categories historically deployed to make meaning of biological and genetic distinctions. Given the often arbitrary ways in which racial distinctions have been drawn, the many vectors along which racial hierarchies are deployed between cultures and groups, and the inconsistencies between various exercises of racinated power, it becomes clear that racial performativity can only be conceived under very specific historical and cultural contexts, without which the codes of a performance of race dissipate into meaninglessness. Accordingly, while racial logic (especially in imperialist contexts) deploys a kind of binary logic not unlike the binary logic of sex, racial binaries themselves are articulated on both biological and cultural lines that do not succumb quite so easily to simple charges of essentialist stereotyping, making specific stylized acts simultaneously reifications of and challenges to the logic of racialized power.

So while we might say that racial identities can be imagined as performative, the mechanisms and theories used to unpack gender, sex, and sexuality cannot be used in precisely the same way in exploring power dynamics exercised across racial categories. Instead, I turn briefly to Saidiya V. Hartman, whose theorization of the performative of African American identity offers one template for imagining the constitutive nature of the stylized body through cultural articulation. For Hartman, performing blackness, particularly in the antebellum period, "is defined here in terms of a social relationality rather than identity; thus blackness incorporates subjects normatively defined as black, the relations among blacks, whites, and others, and the practices that produce racial differences."[1] That is, instead of coming to rest specifically on the definition of an individual body through specific performances that stylize that individual body, "blackness" for Hartman is produced spectacularly through social relations that specify and orient difference along specific lines of power, and in normative terms, implicate the black body as abjected and the white body as dominant. This dominance is typically rendered invisible by what Charles W. Mills has called "The Racial Contract," noting that "in a racially structured polity, the only people who can find it psychologically possible to deny the centrality of race are those who are racially privileged, for whom race is invisible precisely because the world is structured around them, whiteness as the ground against which the figures of other races—those who, unlike us, are raced—appear."[2] It is through acting on this invisible privilege, then, that white bodies perform race and through the exercise of this privilege over black bodies that white bodies perform the social relationality of blackness through performances of domination, social privilege, and an apparent naturalization of white agency.

Hartman's notion of performative blackness arises specifically in the context of antebellum America. But using the notion that *racial* categories are performed primarily through social relationality, while a Butlerian approach to *gendered* categories coheres as identity, we can see the ways in which performances seeking to address both gender and race in performance are likely to meet a particularly tangled web. Nor is it simply a matter of multiplying the social concerns under examination; such concerns multiply exponentially, as the comparative "anatomo-politics" (to use Hartman's term) of sex and race may appear to operate through similarly performative mechanisms but ultimately diverge in the sites of instantiation—individual identity and social relationality. For white playwrights, then, the appearance of the possibility of performing race—that race might be taken off or put on like the costumes of gender—becomes a particular kind of trap, for in seeking to unmake racial codes, or to reveal them as arbitrary, such performances underscore precisely the white privilege that such playwrights and performers rely on to enact such performances. For playwrights seeking redress from within racial categories, then, the issue of performing identity must become secondary, as the very possibility of identity is called into question through the processes of performing otherness (blackness included) that always imagine the racinated body as subject to power and an object under power's particular force.

Writing particularly about African American performance from 1850 to 1910, Daphne A. Brooks deploys a concept that can nonetheless be said to apply to many contemporary black playwrights as well. The phenomenon that she calls "Afro-alienation" brings together the Brechtian alienation effect and the condition of raced alterity, in which we can "consider these historical figures as critically defamiliarizing their own bodies by way of performance in order to yield alternative racial and gender epistemologies."[3] Brooks cites Elin Diamond's Brechtian-feminist approach to contemporary feminist performance, in which "the female performer . . . connotes not 'to-be-looked-at-ness'—the perfect fetish—but rather 'look-ing-at-being-looked-at-ness' or even just 'looking-ness.'[4] For contemporary black feminist playwrights, then, this tactic of "calling attention to the hypervisibility and cultural constructions of blackness" is not historically limited to the period of Brooks's analysis but can be seen running across the corpus of black women's drama, from the realist concerns of Lorraine Hansbery through the dramatic experiments of Adrienne Kennedy up to the work of (as we shall see) Suzan-Lori Parks.

Of course, race is present in every play (though often in the form of an imagined-invisible whiteness), and so all playwrights are inherently writing about race; our awareness of that fact typically depends on the degree to which the playwright and performance make race a visible axis of interrogation, or alternatively assume it as an invisible given. I want to examine two case studies of plays that seek to make race visible, although they do so from different cultural vantage points, and with varying success. Taken individually, they help us tease out two particular binds (themselves suggesting a false binary) of the deceptive performativity of race for white women and the doubled otherness of performing both black and woman as a black woman. I will look to Timberlake Wertenbaker's *New Anatomies,* which on the one hand is an excellent example of an early use of feminist biography to explore the performative possibilities of gender through the life of Isabelle Eberhardt, but which on the other hand overplays its hand by insinuating that the same subversive potential is available in racialized crossings, despite the fact that its availability to Wertenbaker and Eberhardt depend on the whiteness of both. By comparison, I will look at Suzan-Lori Parks's *Venus,* about the Venus Hottentott, based loosely on the life of Saartjie Baartman, the nineteenth-century African woman whose appearance on the freak show circuit in England eventually evolved into the trope of the black Venus as exoticized, naturalized, and sexualized other. In Parks's play, which itself has been the subject of considerable debate, we can see a notion of performing blackness playing out as spectacle both in the world of the play as subjection and metatheatrically as a scene of redress, suggesting, as Hartman puts it, "the entanglements of dominant and subordinate enunciations of blackness."[5] Taken together these plays underscore what *Venus* takes as its central subject: that even under the critical lens of feminist inquiry, race is produced through spectacle; and that the spectacular consciousness that theater engenders means that the production of racial categories is always in place, even if it is not always in play as an object of scrutiny.

Timberlake Wertenbaker's *New Anatomies:*
Performative Gender and the Orient Performed

New Anatomies depicts the life of Isabelle Eberhardt, a Russian Jew who, while dressed as a Muslim man, integrated herself into Sufi culture in turn of the century Algeria. Eberhardt's life is intriguing and important on a number of fronts: her cross-gendered performance, her complex relationship to imperialism in northern Africa, and her position as a woman in Islamic culture. She infiltrated the highly gendered culture of Islamic Sufism by dressing as an Arabic man to become the first known woman to take part in the rituals of the Qadria, a mystical sect of Sufism. In doing so, she flouted the strictures placed on both women and colonialized Arabs by French rule, traveling freely in Algeria and intermingling with the subaltern culture. Wertenbaker recounts Eberhardt's life relatively closely, but while she alters only minor details, she also omits potentially major ones.[6] Constructed chronologically, but framed by the events surrounding Eberhardt's death, Wertenbaker's play follows Eberhardt from childhood to early contacts with Islamic culture to her infiltration and participation in the Qadria and finally to her death in 1904 at age twenty-seven. In creating this portrait, Wertenbaker suggests a particularly radical scope for the possibilities of performance for subverting identity categories, bringing race, culture, and religion into a discussion of the performance of gender, with the insinuation that such performances can be enacted in similar ways, across similarly constituted fields of power.

Of the feminist biography plays that emerged in large numbers from the late 1970s onward, *New Anatomies* is an exemplar of the critical concerns and dramaturgical trends sketched out in chapter 4. Wertenbaker's purpose here seems to be a project of reclaiming Eberhardt as a protofeminist hero, highlighting her gender and cultural crossings as an analogue to the performative identities that were coming under scrutiny in Wertenbaker's own cultural moment (the play was first performed in 1981 and published in 1984). And Wertenbaker's script encourages productions to recognize this analogy, pausing on moments in which Isabelle changes clothing from European woman to Arabic man. If the project of reclaiming a feminist history is crucial to this mode of feminist theater, then Eber-

hardt is certainly a model of a woman "put away" by history for her social and political transgressions. The process of reclaiming Eberhardt simply for the sake of her traditional historical value seems less than relevant—while the French government did apparently commission her to do
a bit of spying on a rival sect of the Qadria, she seems to have had little
impact on the course of human events as we currently understand them.
Her relevance to contemporary feminism as a dialectical image is much
more apparent—Eberhardt can be rearticulated in 1981 as a second-wave
wrench in the patriarchal machine. For example, Marjorie Garber writes,
"Cross-dressing for Isabelle Eberhardt thus became both a way of *obeying*
the paternal and patriarchal law ([her father] permitted her to go into
Geneva only if she dressed as a boy) and a way of *subverting* it."[7] In not
presenting her audience with the figure of Isabelle's father, Wertenbaker
chooses to emphasize the latter of these functions.

Throughout the play, what Elaine Aston has called "the gestus of the
cross-dressed body" does the work of presenting Isabelle as a dialectical
image for the audience.[8] While Eberhardt herself may not be particularly
useful by traditional biographical standards, her transgressions were certainly useful for the political agenda of 1980s feminism, and to some degree they remain so today. And those transgressions are numerous: her
cross-gendered performances in both European and African settings challenge traditional gender categories, and her sexual habits while cross-
dressing avoid easy classification. When approached by a potential female lover, Isabelle asserts, "I am not a woman. I'm Si Mahmoud. I like
men. They like me. As a boy, I mean. And I have a firm rule: No Euro-
peans up my arse."[9] Meanwhile, her cultural crossings—not only assimi-
lating into an Islamic sect but doing so as a woman—appear at first glance
to resist cultural stereotypes of orientalism even as they violate the patriarchal customs of Islam, a point that becomes increasingly complicated as
the history of Western relations with Islam grows increasingly complex,
as we get further and further from the first productions of Wertenbaker's
play.[10] Nonetheless, the body of the actress must do double duty: serving
in a sense as a biographer herself by performing the life of Eberhardt; and
also serving as the recovered object, since it is her use of costume and presentation of the body that embodies the historical transgression of her biographical subject.

Wertenbaker extends this image outward from the lead actress to the
supporting cast as well. While Isabelle is the only *character* to enact these
various transgressions, Wertenbaker calls for every character onstage to

be played by a woman, making the theme of gender crossings even more explicit. Five actors play seventeen parts, eight of which are male. The actress playing Isabelle is the only person who doesn't double, and, by extension, the only person who never plays a man or an Arab, although she moves fluidly between genders and ethnicities. The four other actresses mirror this gender crossing by playing both male and female characters, often making costume changes right onstage, a choice suggested by the script. This foregrounding of costume as a tactic of gender performance by the other actresses mediates the actions of Isabelle and makes them accessible to what presumably would have been a primarily white and female audience. In the real world, in which transvestitism provokes anxiety, Eberhardt is troubling; in a dramatized world where such gender passages are expressed in the familiar language of costume, her identity is made more palatable—her radical gender performativity is mediated for the audience by the fact that her crossings (and, by extension, those of the actress who portrays her) are normalized by the costuming of the other actors in the production. By enacting Eberhardt's transgression in the safe space of the stage, the rest of the cast demonstrates the power of gender performance but also defuses its most dangerous appearances as aberration. These Brechtian strategies for presenting the performativity of identity create what Susan Carlson calls "combustible dialectical energies . . . [that] urge audiences and readers to accept the philosophical challenge of experimenting with new selves."[11]

This recovery work is undertaken with remarkable ideological force throughout the play, and the Brechtian approach that foregrounds it makes that ideology visible. Wertenbaker uses dramatic possibility to move beyond conventional biography in her handling of the subject position in the narrative. Instead of presenting a single, unified perspective that encourages the audience to uncritically identify with Eberhardt, the playwright instead offers a fluctuating subjectivity with the point of identification moving between both Eberhardt and the character of Severine— a fin de siècle French journalist as notorious for her radical politics as she was for her lesbianism. Severine here is positioned as Isabelle's "scribe," an extreme exaggeration of their real-life relationship, which actually consisted of one disastrous meeting. The play is framed by the events surrounding Isabelle's death: in the first scene, she is incomprehensible and presumably insane, and in the final scene she is dead. In both scenes, Severine is the audience's means of contextualizing Eberhardt; we look at her through Severine's gaze. While the narrative that exists between these moments does conform more or less to a traditional positioning of the heroine as subject (Severine is not present for the early life, nor for any of Isabelle's travels across the desert), this narrative is bracketed by the frame structure, and so our entrance into and departure from Isabelle's life is mediated by Severine's perspective—one that is itself fictionalized in its access to offering a representation of Eberhardt. Severine is therefore quite literally a constructed perspective of radical politics through which our present audience can filter the subject.

This divided focus parallels Sue-Ellen Case's notion of the fractured subject.[12] While Case imagines this position as representative of women's displaced subjectivity, reflecting the woman as both subject and object (which is represented in *New Anatomies* by the protagonist's two identities, the European Isabelle and the Arabic Si Mahmoud), this split subjectivity serves a function for biography as well. Sharon O'Brien's vision of a feminist antibiography includes "taking into account that the female may occupy many 'subject positions'" in order to "challenge the focus of the unified self without discarding a focus on gender."[13] As much as Eberhardt is the biographical subject, she is also the object of historical scrutiny, both for the audience and for the characters around her. Not only does the audience see her through their own eyes but they see her through Severine's as well. Severine's position of subjectivity in the frame structure makes her an intermediary for the historical image of Eberhardt. She, like Isabelle, is both subject and object of the audience's gaze, but she also objectifies Isabelle. Severine, radical both for her politics and for her sexuality, desires Isabelle but can have her only by writing her. As her scribe, Severine is also her biographer. While in real life, biographers use Isabelle's own writings as a primary source, Wertenbaker imagines this intermediary figure—one who presents an interesting problem. For while Severine's gaze is not male, it is partially objectifying and desiring. The final scene in the play includes a conversation among Severine, a nameless judge, and Colonel Lyautey, the colonial functionary who facilitated Eberhardt's journeys in the last years of her life:

> JUDGE: Close the file. This person must be officially forgotten.
> LYAUTEY: We found some journals. Would you like to see them, Severine?
> SEVERINE: With pleasure.[14]

It is crucial to notice that Severine's answer here is not merely affirmative but an expression of pleasure. This pleasure, while not sexual, suggests the pleasure of biography, that by writing the subject, one possesses the subject, which suggests some of its danger to feminist scholars who note the way that the biographer/subject relationship mimics the relationship on which the desiring male gaze is predicated. The degree to which this notion echoes William H. Epstein's biographical abduction may be in doubt, but it certainly exemplifies Stacy Wolf's notion of "desire in evidence" in reading and rewriting the subject.

Therefore, if Severine is the biographer in the play, she must certainly be a metaphor for the biographer outside of the play as well, one who, like Wolf, writes against the eliding effects of history on women's subjectivities. And it is this last scene that thematizes this role: while the judge declares that Isabelle must be officially forgotten, her journals and her scribe ensure that she will be remembered and—in a performance such as the very one the audience is watching—revived in the live, albeit mediated, three-dimensional image they see. In the bracketing structure of the play's frame, Severine is simultaneously the historical object watched by the audience; the subject gazing, like the audience, on Isabelle's image, already acknowledged as significant; and, like Wertenbaker herself, the biographer serving as an intermediary between the object in the past and the audience in the present. This alternating subjectivity not only reclaims Eberhardt from the depths of official forgetfulness but it also subtly thematizes the mediated image that such a reclamation necessarily provides against the erasures of history. Yet because the "biographer" here is also marginalized, also female, not unlike Wertenbaker herself, this mediation is posited as the best possible type.

The conversation between past and present prompted by the dialectical image of the actor's body and the presentation of the biographer figure resists the closure that traditional, male-driven biography encourages. Instead, a feminist biography such as Wertenbaker's foregrounds an open passage between the text and the audience and subverts the classic teleological narrative associated with biography. Although the framing device might suggest that the entire narrative is leading toward Eberhardt's death—her last days, the mental incomprehensibility, the fact that her death is announced in the last scene—her death is, crucially, *not* the last action in the play. If this is a play about writing lives, the most important action takes place in the last three lines, quoted earlier, when Colonel Lyautey hands the journals to Severine and they walk off arm in arm. Had the play ended on the Judge's line, "This person must be officially forgotten," closure would have occurred seamlessly. But the moment in which the colonel announces the existence of the journals to Severine pries open the narrative, suggesting both that the content of the narrative continues and, more significantly for biography, that the *construction* of the narrative continues as well. The disruption of closure that this final moment enacts not only opens up Eberhardt's life but hands it to the biographer, and by extension to the audience in the form of this very play. By opening the narrative up like this, the analogy that Eberhardt provides for contemporary audiences is permitted to pass freely. While Eberhardt herself cannot exactly be reclaimed, Wertenbaker seems to suggests that her transgression can.

So from a white feminist perspective, one that only takes race into account insofar as it supports the white feminist project visible on the 1980s British stage, *New Anatomies* espouses the idea of gendered performativity as a fluid boundary that can be crossed with a gesture as easy as a costume change. This is certainly a simplistic view of the notion of performative gender, and while in some ways it expresses a utopian impulse to imagine a world in which such crossings happen so easily, even on only gendered terms, the suggestion of the mere possibility of radical performativity may be overstated, for as Moya Lloyd critically asks, "In what senses are drag and gender parody ipso facto transgressive activities?"[15] Lloyd here is responding to a fallacy, persistent in queer and feminist criticism, that imagines that subverting racial performativity is as simple a matter as performing gender parodically. This facile impulse understands the performativity of gender as belonging specifically to the individual volitional subject, which from the standpoint of Butler's theories of gender can never precede the performance of gender themselves. That is, for Butler and Lloyd, the acting subject *is produced by* performances of gender, not the other way around. To imagine otherwise, Lloyd argues, is to indulge in a misreading that indicates an *authorial* understanding of performativity that locates transgression in the intent of the person performing, which in the case of *New Anatomies* might be too easily ascribed to either the historical Eberhardt or the actor who plays her. So while Wertenbaker's play might be imagined as successfully doing biography even as it subtly interrogates biography, the gendered performances that it seeks to offer up as a model may themselves be naive.

Yet if the notion of a fluid gender performativity offered up by this play is simply naive, the notion of a fluid racialized identity is dangerously so. Verna Foster takes up this issue, arguing on the one hand that "The Brechtian-Churchillian dramaturgy of *New Anatomies* . . . performs

Wertenbaker's exploration of gender," yet on the other hand that her casting and costuming choices "can too easily deny autonomy to the Arab characters (four men and a silent woman) by folding the performance of national identity into the performance of gender identity."[16] Foster goes on to quite exhaustively list the ways in which Wertenbaker's play, viewed from a post-9/11 perspective, one more deeply attuned to the cultural complexities of Western and Arabic encounters, "illuminates the difficulties of negotiating historical changes in the circumstances of reception," particularly in "the play's problematic and only partial accommodation of the renewed interest in East-West relations."[17] Specifically, Foster notes the way that lack of historical evidence already serves to elide the Arab characters in the play, which is itself compounded by Eberhardt's own lack of detail about her Arabic friends in her own journals. Furthermore, Wertenbaker herself excises Eberhardt's Arab husband, Slimène, a figure whose less desirable patriarchal presence may nonetheless have offset the comparative absence of autonomous Arab characters in the play.

This phenomenon, at least from this vantage point thirty years on, seems not only to be an omission but also a reification of the orientalist position that the play itself may, on the surface, want to dispel. Certainly, Isabelle's integration into Sufi culture is expressed as a dissatisfaction with and implicit critique of European culture. There, Wertenbaker suggests, the strictures on performing femininity were stultifying to Isabelle, who found a measure of personal freedom in the desert cultures of Morocco. Foster lists multiple sources that offer up postcolonial critiques of Eberhardt herself as a Western woman exploiting the colonial encounter for personal gain; I would take the critique a step further and suggest that in conflating the performance of gender and the performance of ethnicity, Wertenbaker inadvertently replays the colonial encounter in much the same way that we might imagine Eberhardt having done, depending specifically on her whiteness as a kind of empowered privilege to enable both gendered and racial crossings. That is, while we might find the play's somewhat simplistic casting of cross-dressing as an effective transgression of gender roles, Wertenbaker's version of gender performance still only comes off as potentially less effective offstage than it would be onstage. But to fold Arab identity into the male identity that Isabelle assumes is to elide the social relationality that Saidiya Hartman locates at the center of the performance of race. That is, while Wertenbaker offers up a fluid performance of identity, that performance depends on the colonial power already in place to guarantee Isabelle's protection, an effect under-scored by the inclusion of a colonial court scene trying Isabelle's at-tempted murderer. So in attempting to "put on" the identity of an Arab man, what Isabelle explicitly performs is orientalism. She performatively invokes her own privilege as a white agent in colonial Africa and depends on imperialist domination to guarantee (and, historically, to fund) her own pursuit of freedom. What Wertenbaker seems to pose, then, as a transgressive performance of race ultimately turns out to be its opposite, a radical gender performance that depends explicitly on the normative performativity of oriental racism and subjection.

If there is any way to suggest the play's apparent intention to ethi-cally perform race, it might come in the attempt to make visible the spec-tacle of race, performed as it is by Eberhardt, and potentially by the ac-tresses performing the roles that surround her. If, as Foster points out, even initial reviews of the play commented on its less than deft handling of the other, then at least we can say that the presence of race as a con-struction has been, to some degree, exposed by the play. And, if anything, what it exposes in this post-9/11 moment is the degree to which white-ness itself is a spectacle—of power, privilege, and the performative pre-rogative. As much as we might critique Wertenbaker, and even Eberhardt before her, for posing whiteness as a given, a blank onto which marked racial performances might be written, we must also note that the play does more than many other plays examined in this section by bringing the vector of race into the discussion of gender, acknowledging, albeit imper-fectly, the common reliance on spectacle and theatricality in the produc-tion of gendered and raced identities. The degree to which this is fairly unique in feminist biography plays, particularly by white playwrights in the 1980s, is as telling about the perhaps limited focus of a feminist poli-tics, especially during the second wave, but also more generally about the degree to which whiteness is still imagined *by white people* as invisible, as the given norm onto which other identities might be sampled like so many costumes.

Suzan-Lori Parks's *Venus*: Implicating the Present by Interrogating the Past

While we might seek to recuperate the Isabelle Eberhardt of *New Anatomies* as heroically transgressive, we can see the ways in which the folding of gender performances into racialized ones can easily elide violent histories of oppression, even as they seek to open up others. Perhaps, then, it is inherent in the celebratory mode of white feminist history making, and in the quintessentially second-wave feminist project of recovering women's lives, that the complexities of power are simplified so that (usually white) audiences can rally around a specific image, embodied by the actress who performs the historical life. Plays that offer more ambivalent, less celebratory images, then, are at once more likely to make audiences uncomfortable and, by extension, to generate a varied, potentially controversial reception. Specifically, because race and gender are constructed along different vectors of discourse, performances of those processes must necessarily be more complex, more fraught, and likely less palatable, particularly when they turn their critical gaze back on the audience itself. Here metatheatricality is inwardly focused not only on the dynamics of performance itself but on spectatorship as complicit with, if not even largely responsible for, the circumscribing constructions that inhere on the raced and gendered body.

This seems to be precisely the case in Suzan-Lori Parks's *Venus*, in which the audience is persistently made aware of its own complicity in the operations of raced and sexed constructions of the black woman's body as freakishly hypersexual. In the first scene of the play, we learn that not only is the eponymous character dead but "exposure iz wut killed her." Over the course of the play the Venus Hottentott (the stage name of the historical Saartjie Baartman, a South African woman exhibited in British freak shows for her allegedly enormous buttocks and genitals) is exposed to a host of discursive regimes—individual desire, the freak show stage, the courts, the anatomy lab, and even the present day stage—all of which relentlessly cast the character in the object position. *Venus* is best described by one of the play's own characters, the Negro Resurrectionist.[18]

> "Early in the 19th Century a poor wretched woman was exhibited in England under the Appellation of *The Hottentot Venus*. With an intensely ugly figure, distorted beyond all European notions of beauty, she was said to possess precisely the kind of shape which is most admired among her countrymen, the Hottentots."
>
> The year was 1810, three years after the Bill for the Abolition of the Slave-Trade had been passed in Parliament, and among protests and denials, horror and fascination her show went on. She died in Paris 5 years later: A plaster cast of her body was once displayed, along with her skeleton, in the *Musee de l'Homme*.[19]

Parks does not name her biographical subject as such. That is, the name Saartjie Baartman, or Sarah Baartman as it was anglicized, never appears in Parks's script; she is only ever "Venus" or "The Girl" in the script. In her critical reading of Parks's play, Jean Young provides a more detailed biographical picture.

> By the early nineteenth century the conquest of the peoples known as the Khoikhoi, Hottentot, and Bushmen was nearly complete. The few remaining survivors of this slaughter were dispersed throughout the colony, totally subjugated and forced to work as servants for the Dutch. Saartjie Baartman was one of the survivors in service of a South African Dutch settler, Peter Cezar; and Hendrik Cezar, thought to be Peter's brother, brought her to London.[20]

By focusing on the historical record, Young paints a picture of a young woman who was perhaps never free to exercise agency over her removal to England, her display in Piccadilly Circus, or her presence in the anatomical theaters of Georges Cuvier, the doctor on whom Parks bases the character of the Baron Docteur.

Parks's play, unlike Wertenbaker's, is not nearly so sympathetic to its biographical subject or its audience, ruthlessly objectifying Venus, implying her complicity in those processes, and forcing the audience into complicity with this objectifying process. Parks makes the objectifying processes of history evident, even unavoidable, for her audience through staging historical text, creating analogues for her audience in moments of what Brooks calls "Afro-alienation," and representing the body of Venus as a site of convergence for any number of "traumas of self-fragmentation resulting from centuries of captivity and subjugation."[21] In doing so, Parks presents to her audience not only the uncomfortable matrices of power operating throughout history but, more appropriately, how these operations still work in the very theaters in which her play is presented.

That Parks's play is about history is without question. Parks's entire oeuvre is to a great extent an interrogation of history and the way the present constructs the past, and *Venus* is no exception. The degree to which the play seeks to write history for the sake of *good* history, however, is negligible, particularly since Parks has been questioned on her revisionist stances. For example Young critiques the playwright by arguing that:

> Baartman was a victim, not an accomplice, not a mutual participant in this demeaning objectification, and Parks's stage representation of

her complicity diminishes the tragedy of her life as a nineteenth-century Black woman stripped of her humanity at the hands of a hostile, racist society that held her and those like her in contempt."[22]

And Parks does indeed suggest complicity: we hear Venus say very little in the play: her voice is often circumscribed by those who seek to make meaning of her body. But often when the character does speak, it is to assent to the silver-tongued coercions of those who would gain from her body: The Man who brings her to London, the Mother Showman who runs the freak show in which Venus is staged, The Court that seeks to prove its beneficence, and the Baron Docteur who would seek to make her both his lover and his specimen.

And while *Venus* does reobjectify and recommodify its subject, such a reading also misses the point of Parks's historical meditation. That is, by following this claim with a detailed historical refutation of the points in which Venus's (the character's) complicity runs up against Baartman's (the historical figure's) victimhood, such a reading understands the play only as historiography, rather than as *about* history—as mimetic, rather than metatheatrical. It misapprehends the play's historicism as "what really happened" rather than how the audience experiences history, lives it, and duplicates it in the present. In an interview published in the play's program, the playwright asserts that "the butt is the past, the posterior, posterity."[23] Anne Davis Basting's review of the play echoes this, musing that "the past is quite literally, Venus's and our own collective behinds—carried with us as we step into a future more aware of the deadly effects of colonialism, gazing, and racially and sexually marked standards of beauty."[24] The emphasis here on "us" and our relationship with history seems to more accurately grapple with Parks's thesis: that our relationship with our constructed past is perhaps more important to our present conditions than the accuracy of that construction. And yet this quote also suggests the appeal of history for feminism—when Basting notes the degree to which history is "carried with us" she also recognizes the unshakability of the past as real. To extend Parks's metaphor: while the details surrounding Saartjie Baartman's posterior may vary, what remains true is the kernel of Baartman's celebrity—that she was commodified and objectified, ruthlessly, and that if this play in some way duplicates that phenomenon, even with an audience supposed to know better, it at least proves the degree to which this past, this posterior, is still connected to us. Moreover, the size of the butt—the enormity of the problem, its longevity—only suggests that the problem deserves address.

This framing of the past is in keeping with our notion of the dialectical image, in which the body of the biographical subject is just as important for its bearing on the present as it is for its historical significance. And in the case of Venus, that body is loaded with meaning, for as Tony Kushner notes, "Here is a moment of incredibly *dense* history. All sorts of things convene at this moment, across and through the body of this woman."[25] Earlier he observes, "*Venus* also treads the fault lines of several American cultural sensitivities, moving racial clichés and stereotypes out of the unlit mutterers' corners and back to center stage, where the sight of them makes us wince."[26] Once again, the emphasis is placed on the "us," the audience of this play. For while the dialectical image of Isabelle Eberhardt represents gendered transgression to be celebrated in the present, the image of Venus represents a gross objectification that must be condemned in the present. But as Harry Elam and Alice Raymer argue:

> It is easy to condemn the past abuses of spectatorship. That is what is obvious about the play. But the obviousness conceals the fact that even in a re-production we, the contemporary audience members, are still viewing the Hottentot Venus with an assumption of superiority over those earlier spectators, thus ignoring our own complicity in the sight.[27]

On this last count, that the audience is left unaware of its own complicity in the objectification, there is reason to pause at frequent reports of audience discomfort, rather than self-satisfaction. That is why Kushner says "wince" and Robert Brustein's review of the play notes that much of the audience "decamped before the final curtain."[28] If the audience members were only left feeling smug in their own superiority, the artifacts that we do have of audience response would not likely register such emotional discomfort, yet reviews and accounts of the Richard Foreman production of *Venus* at the Joseph Papp Theater in New York all indicate precisely this discomfort.

Of course, a great deal of criticism has appeared since this first controversy over the reception of the play, and while much of it engages Young's initial excoriation of the performance, the critical consensus seems to be that Parks is circulating ideas of embodiment, history, race, and theatricality to ends that challenge racial hegemonies rather than upholding them. Several critics, taken together, help us interrogate the role of the historical body in performance, particularly as that body relates to notions of presence and spectatorial desire. Sanya Osha, for example, argues that Baartman's ontological status, perched precariously between human and animal, was historically decreed by white desire, a phenomenon savvily exposed and critiqued by Parks's play.[29] Greg Miller extends the analysis by connecting the theatricalized audiences onstage with those offstage, "showing how . . . those of us in the audiences slavishly pursue the fetishized objects of desire."[30] Miller astutely points out, however, that the fetishized object in this play comes in the form of Venus's bottom, typically staged (following Richard Foreman's premier production) as an exaggerated prosthetic, a visibly grotesque amplification of the corporeal bottom of both the historical Baartman and the actress who plays her. Johanna Frank examines this process of objectification in the play as a kind of dismemberment, arguing that "The Girl" who eventually becomes The Venus Hottentott becomes "a site of embodied absence, whose presence emerges in the performance of stories of corporeality *rather* than by corporeality itself."[31] What this trio of critics suggest to us is the degree to which the ontological status of Saartjie Baartman's body is completely overdetermined, a sign that bears so much discursive weight as to thoroughly erase the means by which subjectivity might come to connect to corporeality. Indeed, this play might be said to be about the *stripping* of subjectivity, one by which a potentially complicit subject is dis(re)membered, objectified, fetishized, and dehumanized.[32] The notion of embodied absence that Frank raises points us to the prosthetic prop as emblematic of Venus, the body without selfhood.

Moreover, we might note the degree to which Venus's body, and Parks's metaphor, might be seen as trafficking in the discursive territory of the *exceptional* body, one transformed into symbolic signifier rather than material signified, an idea that disability theory has recently called into question. Writing about Joan Schenkar's *Signs of Life* (discussed briefly in chapter 4), Carrie Sandahl notes that "*Signs of Life* reveals how gendered and sexed identities result from a process of systematic bodily discipline that in everyday life goes unmarked. Schenkar uses the metaphor of freakishness to show how feminine behavior is constructed as freakish."[33] She goes on to argue that "By focusing on how femaleness is performed, Schenkar's play calls less attention to the fact that disability is also performed, thus inadvertently reinforcing the negative association of disabled bodies as freakish."[34] While we have seen the folding of race and gender into a single set of performative acts in *New Anatomies*, we might be alert to the ways in which *Venus,* in already negotiating the different performative components of both race and gender, might casually "fold in" exceptional bodiedness as, if not a merely additional notion of othering, then at least as a metaphorical elision of the materiality of the body in question. Indeed, the insistent use of the "posterior as past" metaphor might suggest precisely this effect.

The question goes to the very heart of what we mean by the term *biography play.* For on the one hand, the notion of biography always insinuates a prior historical real, a materiality referenced explicitly *as reality* by the genre of the play. Certainly, following Hayden White, we can see that reality referenced in linguistic terms in two ways: as metonymy or metaphor. As White notes, "If we stress the similarities among elements [in this case, past and present] we are working in the mode of metaphor. If we stress the differences among them, we are working in the mode of metonymy."[35] That is, as metonymy, historical representations refer back to the totality of past events in an arbitrary but symbolic relationship, whereas we might see the metaphorical figuration of past events as posing an identifiable and ascertainable relationship to the present. If, as White suggests, a historical characterization "must utilize *both* metaphor and metonymy in order to 'fix' it as something about which we can meaningfully discourse," then no biography play can ever, by definition, escape the metaphoricization of the historical body, a fact that the notion of the actress as dialectical image of that body will almost necessarily underscore.[36]

In the case of *Venus,* however, the manipulation of history is so apparent, and history so deeply denaturalized, that we cannot focus on the play as primarily referencing a historical real, but rather as referencing the spectacle of history itself. Reading the play's own historical context against the transnational process of the reinterment of Baartman's remains, Sara L. Warner transforms the notion of dismemberment into a drama of disinterment, one that problematizes, among other things, "the assumption that the restoration of dignity is the goal of the recovery process."[37] In fact the play so deeply presents the staged body as metaphor—both of dismemberment and of disinterment—that its metonymic relationship to the past body of Saartjie Baartman is rendered untenable. Indeed, my student Sarah Einstein has argued this explicitly, noting that "we should not read the character Venus (or even the character The Girl) as representative of Baartman, but as representative of the social *construct* of the Venus Hottentot, and that instead of being a biography of Saartjie Baartman, this play is a history of the construction of The

Venus Hottentot."[38] Einstein follows Greg Miller in identifying Parks's re-fusal to name Baartman throughout the play and how this refusal turns the play away from a recoverable subjectivity for Baartman to an exami-nation of the historicized spectacle of the black female body as always al-ready metaphor, one that must be "recommodified" in order to achieve an efficacious critique of contemporary spectatorship.[39] Einstein continues by arguing that "it is exactly in that tension between efficacious and mimetic representations of bodily alterity that we find the difficulty in staging biographical, rather than autobiographical, life stories of those whose identity is shaped by experiences of physical alterity."[40] Arguing essentially that a biographical reading of the play is a failed reading, one that seeks out the historical body as staged metonymy, rather than as per-sistent metaphor for the spectacularization of the black female body itself, Einstein's argument pushes us toward imagining this play as *both* a recommodification of the exceptional body and a critical engagement of that very process by which the body is transformed into spectacle by ma-terializing the discourses of sex, race, and exceptionality.

Here we see clear connections with both Hartman's and Brooks's ar-guments about performances of blackness, which depend precisely on spectacle to establish their discursive meaning, as well as to potentially unpack those meanings. Hartman writes, "The emphasis on the joining of race, subjection, and spectacle is intended to denaturalize race and un-derline its givenness—that is, the strategies through which it is made to appear as if it has always existed, thereby denying the coerced and culti-vated production of race."[41] In similar language, Brooks argues, "By using performance tactics to signify on the social, cultural and ideological ma-chinery that circumscribes African Americans, they intervene in the spec-tacular and systemic representational abjection of black peoples."[42] It is not surprising, then, that Parks's play about a raced body in the nine-teenth century employs dissonant representational tactics congruent with both nineteenth-century *and* postmodern modes of resistant performance. Specifically, *Venus* emphasizes not only the persistent presentation of Venus's historical body as spectacle but also underlines those discourses that present the body's materiality as a given: the freak show, the court-room, the dissecting theater, the bedroom, even history itself. As a play about blackness, and about exceptionality, *Venus* points us early and often to those processes. As a play about gender, though, *Venus* pays less atten-tion beyond the linkage to the materiality of sex itself. Remembering that Hartman argues that the performativity of race depends on social relationality rather than identity, we come to understand that race, gender, and embodiedness are all performed on intersecting but divergent vectors of identity, materiality, and social relationality, all of which are materialized through spectacle, an understanding on which *New Anatomies* capitalizes invisibly but never acknowledges. Yet in the case of *Venus,* we also see that the persistent performance of race, and racinated freakishness, undermines the very possibility of gender as an identity category: that Venus's insistent materiality is *only* ever sexed—that is, produced as an effect of material sexed embodiment. In the meantime (with the exception of the first scene, when she is The Girl), socially produced gendered performances of identity remain as inaccessible within the trope of the Venus Hottentott as Saartjie Baartman's name.

The applicability of both Einstein's argument and a theory of performative blackness depends on the ability of a performance to make sufficiently visible the metatheatrical effects by which spectacles of the exceptional, raced, female body historically produced meaning, and were transformed into spectacular tropes, written onto the body of the woman once known as Saartjie Baartman (and, historically, the many other women who performed the role of the Venus Hottentot after Baartman's death). Here historical performance happens in much the same way that April De Angelis fears it did for Nell Gwynn, but for Baartman, the objectification of the female body is further circumscribed by the performative dimensions of blackness. Inasmuch as race is produced by spectacles of the "social relationship of dominance and abjection," *Venus* can be seen as precisely the unveiling of the "givenness" of race as produced through social spectacle, spectacle produced as much by stylizations of the black body by the acts of white characters as by those of Venus herself, even within the framework of complicity.

Obvious examples abound. The Mother Showman's first presentation is perhaps the most visibly spectacular, as when she introduces Venus by declaring, "She bottoms out the bottom of the [evolutionary] ladder / yr not a man—until you've hadder."[43] But other, less obvious constructing mechanisms are equally revealed as spectacular: The Chorus of The Court, for example, issues a writ of habeus corpus for Venus, which is quickly contextualized when Venus herself defines *habeus corpus* as "You should have the body," a moment that underscores the degree to which her body is already captive to English law, which will later on prove to only be using her body as a spectacle of its own specious judgment: "In closing, whatever happens to her / we should note that / it is very much to the credit of our great country that even a female Hottentot can find a court to review her status."[44] This series of scenes underscores the fact that while Venus's own embodied performance is quite a small component of the proceedings, the court's elaborate spectacle of deliberation and justice stylizes that body as subject to white dominance and at the same time (as it sniffs at her indecency) reifies the abjection of that body. Finally, the Baron Docteur's long intermission monologue, titled "*Several Years from now: In the Anatomical Theatre of Tübingen: The Dis(-re-)member-ment of the Venus Hottentot, Part I,*"[45] meticulously recites the results of his careful dissection and measurement of Venus's body, which both dismembers and dis*r*emembers her, both acts that further write racialized, sexed, nonnormate meaning onto her abjected body from the privileged position of the white male medical gaze. Indeed, it is the layering of these discourses and the insistent repetitions of their conclusions across the course of the play that refer us back to Hartman's discussion of the performativity of blackness as both the scene of subjection and the potential scene of "redress and emancipation."[46] Hartman writes, "The unremitting and interminable process of revision, reelaboration, mimicry, and repetition prevents efforts to locate an originary or definitive point on the chain of associations that would fix the identity of a particular act or enable us to sift through authentic and derivative performances."[47] That Saartjie Baartman's identity disappears in Parks's play can be attributed to all of these constructions, layered one on another: of *freakish, black, woman,* all markers with their own sets of cultural meaning, all overlapping and co-constructing and yet each operating on different vectors of materiality, identity, and sociality.

Reading the play closely, then, we find two particular ways in which *Venus* as a playscript makes history making and its objectifying impulses clear and stageable, and they work both to interrogate the machinations of the past and to implicate the audience as complicit with those workings. The first is the play's insistence on highlighting the role of spectatorship in constructing Venus as a sex object and extends that role specifically to the audience in the theater. Metatheatrical effects, far more than just Parks's own metadramatic tactics, are essential to the effectiveness of the play as political theater. Parks sets up the historical objectification of the aberrant body in a number of ways throughout the play through the constant display of Venus's body: as a "freak," a courtroom spectacle, the subject of a play, a medical specimen, and the Baron Docteur's lover.[48] Here the character is displayed, ogled, and anatomized in front of the audience, and in these scenes Young and Elam and Rayner locate Parks's reproduction of the very objectification that she seems to critique. Were these moments to be the entire narrative, the audience's "assumption of superiority" that Elam and Rayner claim would be unquestionable. Indeed, Parks seems almost deliberate (if not actually heavy-handed) in her replaying of the scenes of objectification and othering that mark Venus's narrative. As Roger Bechtel argues, "While the Negro Resurrectionist may turn away [at the final image of Venus] we, of course, don't—spectators to the very last. But at the same time, *Venus* has made us acutely aware of our spectatorship, and if the temptation to *watch* seems to overwhelming, we have also learned, in the course of the play, its great cost."[49]

Several moments in the text make all too explicit the connection between the past's spectatorship and the present's. For as Bechtel notes, "*Venus* has allowed us the rare opportunity to see ourselves seeing, to watch ourselves watching a history that shockingly, watches us back."[50] Bechtel reads closely each of these moments, just a few of which I will highlight here. The first is the interspersion of scenes from "For the Love of Venus," Parks's reconstruction of a contemporary comedy in which the Baron Docteur's wife's story seems to be playing out. In these moments, the audience watches the Baron Docteur impassively view this narrative. According to the stage directions, he "is the only person in the audience. Perhaps he sits in the chair. It's almost as if he's watching TV. The Venus stands off to the side. She watched the Baron Docteur."[51] These stage directions create an explicit diagram of objectification and implication. First, the audience is given one primary analogue for theatrical spectatorship in these scenes: the Baron Docteur—the most notorious of the nineteenth-century characters on whom we might locate our "assumption of superiority." By setting the Baron Docteur up as our most obvious site for identification, and positioning him just as we are positioned, as audience members watching the play, the play makes it difficult to imagine that a savvy theatergoer would miss the connection. And to foreground the implication of spectatorship in the process of objectification, Venus stands off to one side, looking at the Baron Docteur in order to draw our attention to the theatrical spectatorship itself, as opposed to the metatheatrical spectacle onstage. Following Venus's gaze, we are compelled to look critically not just at the historical objectifications of the Baron Docteur but also at those in which we continue to participate, at the very activity in which we are engaged. The metatheatrical conceit that runs through the play makes the dialectical image of the Baron Docteur as significant an image of spectatorship as Venus is an image of the objectified body.

Parks builds in other formal mechanisms for staging objectification as well. As Jennifer Johung notes in her essay on the curious phenomenon of Parks's "spells"—notations where characters' names are repeated on the page without dialogue following—these moments in the playwright's dramaturgy allow for a great deal of theatrical flexibility. But they also seem to be designed stage moments that draw the audience's *visual* attention, without the additional register of language. Johung notes one scene in which Venus is on display for the Chorus of Spectators, the spell that highlights Venus "pre-empting the look of the spectators, [as she] poses and looks at herself . . . further indexed by the looks of the spectators."[52] Here, the spell first finds Venus looking at herself, as the Spectators chant "Lookie-Lookie-Lookie-Lookie / Hubba-Hubba-Hubba-Hubba," all while the audience itself looks on, a layering of spectatorship that we cannot help but notice. But more than just indexing objectification and racist visual pleasure, these moments also call attention—in both text and performance—to the body of the actress in question, and the absence of the historical subject in question. "As such," Johung writes, "the spells initiate a constant negotiation back and forth—a flickering between the absent subjectivity of the historical figure and the present subjectivity of the figure in Parks's play, and between the absent subjectivity inherent in figurative presence and the material presence of the body of the performer."[53]

The play's implication of the present audience in replaying the spectatorial objectification of the past is also made explicit in its treatment of historical documentation. Like Fiona Templeton's *Delirium of Interpretations*, Parks's text demands that we stage the history that underpins the biography taking place onstage. We initially need look no further than the fact that the historical information is provided to us by the Negro Resurrectionist, a character who, as a gravedigger (a trope in Parks's plays), is already laden with metaphorical associations with grave robbing, body snatching, raiding the past, and exhuming the dead. If we imagine the introduction of the characters at the outset of the play as itself a kind of disinterment from the past, the play's critical approach to historical representation becomes clearer. Take, for example, the scene entitled "Footnote #7" in which the Negro Resurrectionist reads "A DETAILED PHYSICAL DESCRIPTION OF THE SO-CALLED VENUS HOTTENTOT," the entire text of which is listed in quotation marks.[54] Of course, a reader is left to wonder how one might stage a footnote, and whether the quotation marks around the text are relevant. And yet if we look at the excerpt quoted earlier to summarize the play's subject matter, we will notice that the first paragraph is set in these quotation marks, while the second is not. There seems to be some effort on Parks's part to demarcate her text from the texts of history (and a production of this play might devise ways to stage these punctuation marks—not unlike what I have suggested is possible in Templeton's play—so as to make Parks's own process of historical construction evident). More important, though, the quotation marks set the discourse of history apart from the discourse of the play itself, asking the audience to critically examine not just contemporary accounts of Venus but also by extension our own accounts, and the degree to which they, too, duplicate the sorts of racism, sexism, and othering that we might be tempted to displace completely on the past.

Taken together, the focus on spectatorship and on history itself would seem to press the critique insistently outward to encompass the very audience watching. In doing so, Parks makes the audience complicit not only in witnessing the spectacle of race but also in producing it. Indeed, under the conjecture of Parks's play, we can even say that the insistent metaspectacularization of the exceptional black female body forces the audience into their own performance of blackness. The play highlights the degree to which the audience's own dominance as paying spectators mimics the objectification and commodification of the trope of the Venus Hottentot, and perhaps even of the nearly invisible identity of Saartjie Baartman, who first lived in that embodied trope. The insistence on denaturalizing the materiality of race, and on unveiling the givenness of that materiality by emphasizing spectacle, discourse, and spectatorship, creates a scenario in which audiences perform blackness as a kind of domination and at the same time witness blackness performed as critique and redress. The confluence of these notions—the absent historical subject, the present performer (who herself is looking), the objectifying spectators (onstage and off), the black body subject to power—tells us a great deal about the difficulties of staging black women's lives, in which subjection and subjectivity seem to be in a constant struggle, and in which the objectifying impulses of biographical inquiry seem admissible only if tempered by both an explicit acknowledgment of the tropes of racial representation and a persistent critical focus that turns the critique back onto the audience.

Ultimately, whether Parks's audience is given enough cues to do the sort of self-critique that I am suggesting or instead is left with a feeling of smug superiority over the errors of the past is a matter of individual productions and individual audiences; a poor production of the play and an audience untrained in the dramatic cues that Parks relies on will not produce the Brechtian effects that engender critical self-reflection. Certainly the exaggerated fat suit worn by Adina Porter in the premier production of the play is one tactic that highlights these effects; the cables that bisected Foreman's stage to form "sight lines" in the mise-en-scène are another.[55] Einstein, in her analysis of the play, suggests that, in the style of other Parks plays, particularly *The America Play*, all actors be cast as African American to underscore the exceptionality of Venus's body distinct from all black bodies.[56] Yet even in the text itself, Parks leads her audience to think critically about the past, a task that the plays examined in this text seem to have in common. And as Kushner points out, "Difficult Art [especially the example of *Venus*] seeks to teach a posture to its audience, a stance. And I deliberately write that the art, rather than the artist seeks to teach, for this is instruction by example, not by preachment."[57] *Venus* interrogates history and its own role in re-presenting that history, and it asks its audience to do the same, to acknowledge that "Vision," as Roger Bechtel argues, "sees through historical eyes."[58] In doing so, *Venus* calls attention to a long history of representational injustices and oppression of women based on the object status of the female body, and thus hopes to help end the very objectification that it portrays, one implicated both in the past and in the present as they mutually construct one another.

And yet, the persistence of the play's reobjectification and recommodification of the historical body has implications not just for how we read this play but also for any feminist biography play. In chapter 4, I argue that one persistent danger of the biography play is that its focus on recovering the biographical subject elides the sense that we are watching an object of biographical scrutiny. Certainly, we have seen the ways in which *Venus* makes this representational problem part of its polemic, by using metatheatrical strategies to problematize and call attention to the very practices that cast Venus as a material discursive object in the first place, the sort of Afro-alienation that potentially subverts that same process in the present. Yet the critical ambivalence points to a lingering critical issue inherent in staging the historical black woman's body. Specifically, the historical and contemporary pathways to imagining those bodies as objects are so insidious and so deeply entrenched that it is virtually impossible to create an unambivalently subjective theatrical representation of the objectified black woman, even when that representation relentlessly and forcefully calls attention to and critiques those very pathways. So while I have argued that Parks confronts her audience with both the spectacle of power operating throughout history and the replaying of those spectacular operations in the theater in which her play is being presented, we must still ask whether *confronting* her audience is enough. For despite the admirable motives that might be found in depicting a biographical subject as a speaking subject, there remains a difficulty in reconciling the speaking subject of feminist biography with the sexualized object that appears in more traditional historical accounts of women. The resulting political gymnastics, then, often have no choice but to suggest the subject's complicity—even if it is only partial—in her own objectification. Some critics, like Christopher Innes, suggest that this is precisely the mechanism necessary to accomplish Parks's stated task of removing African American representations from the realm of the typical, legible, safe victim narrative.[59]

I want to close my consideration of *Venus* not with a nod to its now extensive professional production history but with an example of my own classroom experience with the play, one that highlights the representational dangers not only for the image of a historical Saartjie Baartman but also for the actress who steps into the costume of Venus's body. In my introductory classes on dramatic literature, I offer students a performance option, in which they choose a scene, perform it, and lead a discussion on their performance choices as interpretations of the play. In three different cases students have chosen a scene from *Venus,* and in all three cases an African American woman was part of the group, and yet never did one of those women play Venus; in two of those cases, a white man did. This phenomenon is instructive. I would argue that part of the rationale for these casting choices is that the scene of objectification is too uncomfortable when the students know the young woman whose body might come under scrutiny, when their classmate is already a speaking subject to them. Whether these performance groups could articulate this discomfort with such objectification when they cast their scenes I cannot say (although they always had logical explanations for the interpretive potential that their nontraditional casting choices possessed); nonetheless, I would argue that these students were able to intuit the uncomfortable fault lines they trod in their performances.

This phenomenon must give pause to any student of feminist biographical drama: how do the othering processes already inherent in both biography and staging women's bodies—particularly exceptional bodies, and raced bodies, with their intersecting performatives of sociality and materiality—construct not just the biographical figure but also the actress? Do the elisions of identity inherent in portraying the exceptional, raced, sexed body of the Venus Hottentot come to bear on the identity of the actress who plays her? How do we value the fact that not only might Baartman be recommodified and reobjectified but that the actress who plays her is commodified and objectified as well? Certainly she is made an object, of her own complicity, and certainly she is a commodity, though perhaps to her own profit. These questions remain unanswerable, to a large degree, although they unsettle what I have argued throughout has been a vibrant field of feminist drama from virtually its first appearances on political stages in the United Kingdom and United States. These are the questions that remain for discussion perhaps of all feminist performance, of autobiographical performance art, biography plays, and indeed any body art that risks objectifying the artist as a precondition for critiquing that objectification.

Conclusion: Raced and Gendered Spectacles and the Spectacular Space of the Theater

We could, certainly, look to the earliest forms of Western theater and find the roots of the present dilemma embedded even there. The *theatron* of ancient Greek theater has always been a watching space to produce spectacles that affirm gendered and national and racial identities. When the citizens gathered for the City Dionysia, they were affirming both gendered and racial distinctions between those other than themselves, and they did so to assert the commonality of the values that undergirded their very presence. This observation has been part of the discourse of feminist theater criticism ever since its first flourishing, with the publication of Sue-Ellen Case's "Classic Drag," and the inherent gaze of the *theatron* has been present in those discussions ever since.[60] But to contend that the Greek theater was as much about racial distinction as it was about gendered ones only requires us to recall that the very first history play was Aeschylus's *The Persians,* a play whose rhetoric of racial superiority of the Greeks over their invading foes spectacularizes the other as deviant as insistently as did the British freak shows that featured the Venus Hottentot as their main attraction.

My point here is that the theater, ancient or contemporary, has always been a site where gender and race are constructed as cultural spectacles, and that white feminist theater (biographical or otherwise), even inasmuch as it makes visible the discursive construction of gender, just as often makes invisible the production of race, no matter how insistently it may still be present. The two examples discussed here, despite their representational dilemmas, nonetheless make gender and race both visible as cultural productions, ones that have historically been utilized to turn othered bodies into subjugated objects. Wertenbaker's play works ambivalently, making visible gender as a transformable construction while inadvertently reifying white constructions of power to enact racialized performances that the play mistakenly poses as radical. *Venus* is not ambivalent, but it is deeply critical, forced to (re)produce the spectacular processes of objectification that the play scrutinizes. We must wonder, then, about the ambivalences built into all theater that seeks to undo the cultural constructions of otherness, constructions built in the *theatron* and other spectacular spaces. Perhaps, then, we must think about other forms, other spaces. Whatever way feminist performers and playwrights may seek to transform theater, as feminist theater moves forward into the next decades of the twenty-first century, we must ask how the performance of lives can continue to make visible the production of gender while acknowledging the place of gender within the tangled web of racial, cultural, and transnational identities with which gender interacts, and do so complexly while seeking to avoid the persistent objectifying processes that make such a theater so important.

CONCLUSION : Performing Global Lives

In November 2009, a working group convened at the annual conference of the American Society for Theatre Research (ASTR) on the subject of contemporary women playwrights. Tasked with advocating for the work of contemporary female playwrights of the previous twenty years, participants brought together a rich assemblage of playwrights, from established stars like Sarah Ruhl to less well known writers like Nigerian playwright and working group participant Julianna Okoh. Autobiographical texts, biography plays, and a more broadly construed set of history plays were unsurprisingly well represented. I presented an early version of this book's argument about Sarah Kane, while other texts, like De Angelis's *Playhouse Creatures* and Polly Teale's *After Mrs. Rochester*, a fantastical memory play about novelist Jean Rhys, were submitted for discussion. And while few of the dozen other texts are conventional biography or autobiography plays, several take up the concern of the historical female body: Rebecca Lenkiewicz's *Her Naked Skin* places a fictional love story within the documented historical context of suffrage activism, Wendy Wasserstein's *An American Daughter* is loosely based on the Zoë Baird "nannygate" case of the 1990s, Heather Raffo's *9 Parts of Desire* is a composite of Iranian women she met and interviewed, and Judith Thompson's *Palace of the End* stages monologues based closely on the lives of three real figures connected to Western intervention in Iraq.

Among other things, the prominence of life narratives and the historical real (overlapping, but not precisely congruent) is a testament to the fact that auto/biographical narratives in contemporary feminist performance practices have comprised a surprisingly large part of the already large and vibrant corpus of feminist performance texts that emerged from the United Kingdom and United States beginning in the 1970s. Encompassing texts from the most radical performance art to the most structurally conventional of history plays, the texts that make up this study focus on such core feminist lines of inquiry as identity, body, voice, community, history, and narrative. At the center of this study, we find a handful of key questions. How is the performing body linked to the historical body, and what role does narrative play in that link? How essential to the performing body is the historical identity that it claims? What use might the slippage between body and identity serve to those artists who intend to unmake the gender codes that govern women's bodies? And how might the artistic medium of theater be put to use doing so? Yet while these concerns appear across texts in remarkably consistent and often self-conscious fashion, the *ways* in which these questions are answered are stunningly diverse. A simple comparison of two of the texts studied here reveals the variety of approaches that an individual artist might take toward these issues.

An exemplar of autobiographical performance, Holly Hughes's *Preaching to the Perverted* relies on an essential correlation among the body of experience, the authorial voice, and the performing self. The embodied experience that she narrates explicitly involves a sexed and sexualized female body, and the degree to which that body was made into a public spectacle. Because the narrative relies on the speaking "I," the autodiegetic turn of her performance is crucial in supplying subjectivity as a response to the objectification, the feeling of being watched and judged, that the NEA Four controversy generated. Ultimately, by performing her own narrative, by verifying her experience through the presence of the same sexed and sexualized body that had been held up for vilification, Hughes's performance sought to reclaim her body and her experience from the discourse that would marginalize it. The performance could not have been effective had someone else performed it, in part because the narrating "I" relied on an audience expectation of truth that ultimately offered Hughes the political power to speak. In this case, subject, author, and performer are collapsed, because the truth value of the narrative depends on the truth value of the narrative voice as its verifying lynchpin. The rhetorical effect of *Preaching to the Perverted,* then, to further queer and feminist ends, depends on a congruence among historical body, narrating voice, and performing body. It is a kind of essentialism of experiencing body and narrativized identity that we can see operating to a greater or lesser degree in the work of Carolee Schneeman; in the queer, feminist, disability performance of Terry Galloway; or even, in equivocal ways, in the final devastating work of Sarah Kane, where the absence of the experiencing body signifies for the narrativized self.

In contrast, April De Angelis's *Playhouse Creatures* does not—and indeed cannot—require a similar congruence, since the subject of the bio-graphical inquiry, Nell Gwyn, is long since irretrievable. Her historical body is literally dead, her authorial voice silenced, her performing body a footnote in history. And yet De Angelis's narrative carries a political weight that is comparable to Hughes's performance, since even as *Play-house Creatures* describes the working conditions of the first professional actresses on the English stage, De Angelis implicates the working condi-tions of the present-day actresses who perform the play. In this case, the image of Nell Gwyn is radically dialectical, evoking at once Gwyn's ex-perience, De Angelis's voice, and the contemporary, living actress's body. This is drama's narrative third person, a representation of an other through the lens of performance. As such, the expectations of historical value are diminished, and what De Angelis's voice reclaims is less the specific experiences of Nell Gwyn than the radical nature of the perfor-mances with which Gwyn stylized her own body in history. Instead, a contemporary actress can stylize her own body through the image of Gwyn, thus interrogating both history and the present through the very conflicts that such a dialectical image onstage presents. While the play cannot literally reclaim the historically significant body of Nell Gwyn, the groundbreaking performances she enacted can be disembodied, taken off and put on by actresses and ultimately perhaps audience members; such a third-person performance as staged feminist biography enacts makes this process obvious. Indeed, the third-person nature of this performance, which tends to cut across a range of biography plays, also seems to be op-erating in many of the most performative of autobiographical perfor-mances, where Bobby Baker's or Carmelita Tropicana's denaturalizing performances self-consciously distance the body's discursive identity in a sexist culture from a discrete notion of selfhood, one that several of these performers implicitly seem to deny exists.

These examples tell us much about the breadth of theoretical config-uration that the field of staged feminist life writing can represent. To-gether, they represent several challenges to notions that apply not only to feminist performances but also to much larger concepts of authorship and political presence. I have suggested that the relationship between the real self and the performative self of autobiographical performance implicates notions of authorship in ways for which existing theories don't fully ac-count. Certainly a simplistic understanding of authorship is undermined by a reliance on the physical presentness of the author's body (as opposed to another speaker's) in autobiographical performance; anyone other than Holly Hughes performing *Preaching to the Perverted* would fall flat, even Karen Finley, who like Hughes was part of the same Supreme Court case. And even more complex notions of authorship have difficulty accounting for the imbricated nature of these multiple conflated identities, since poststructuralist accounts that unsettle the status of the author also unsettle the status of intent, always troubling within rhetorically and politically charged texts and performances. Certainly none of these examples suggests a return to a pre-new-critical one-to-one-to-one understanding of the relationship of the body that experiences, the body that writes, and the body that performs. Yet at the same time, theories that deny the importance of the identities of the body of experience and the writing body are confounded by these genres. As Dee Heddon puts it, "[T]hough many performances employ 'destabilizing' strategies, they also nevertheless continue to have, or make, political appeal, walking a fine line between reifying 'real' experience and erasing it."[1] This is the push and pull of the field, seeking variously to exploit a playfully deconstructive approach to gender and at the same time establish the speaking, performing woman whose presence as such carries political and cultural authority. And these have been the terms of discursive experimentation for many of the texts in this field, yielding as rhetorical results as diverse as the theatrical and narrative tactics they deploy.

Just as autobiographical performance often reaffirms the real of authorial experience, and therefore the link between experiencing body and performing body, biographical drama ultimately posits that transgressive performances (often transgressive performances of writing itself) can and must be recovered *without* the historical body that first performed them. In this light, we can hardly harbor the old humanist notion that the author and the performing voice are precisely the same. Surely the differences between Isabelle Eberhardt, Timberlake Wertenbaker, and the contemporary actress in Wertenbaker's *New Anatomies* help us tease out these identities, just as Carmelita Tropicana's "autobiographical-style" multiple identities reveal a layering of constructed selves. We must, then, account for authorship in a way that does not completely discount the life experiences of the historical bodies represented in *New Anatomies* or of the playwright as they come to bear on performances of the actresses who play Eberhardt as the biographical subject or Severine as a biographer figure. Yet neither can such a theory work too hard to conflate the biography of Eberhardt or Severine with the literary or dramatic performances with which we might otherwise associate them.

Ultimately, then, the dialectic created by staged feminist life writing serves as a means of asserting the relevance of the material historical body to the body of the performer. We must acknowledge the relationship of the historical woman's body to the image we see onstage, thereby reasserting her place in history and revalidating her experience, which less careful deconstructive approaches might invalidate as merely so much textuality. In the case of Holly Hughes's *Preaching to the Perverted*, acknowledging such a dialectic permits us to understand Hughes's narrative through the authority of her experience. This understanding encourages the audience to join Hughes in her critique of the Supreme Court and its institutionalized white male anxiety, and to understand the urgency of this critique by acknowledging its grounding in the real, a grounding that the elision of the author does not permit. It is Hughes's performing body—the same body that was made into spectacle by the NEA Four controversy—that verifies the experience of her performed narrative, and therefore underwrites the authority of her life performance. This effect similarly allows us to read and witness Sarah Kane's *4.48 Psychosis* as both autobiographical and not-autobiographical, understanding the collage of identities housed in the fragments of first-person performance as being both an expression of Kane's life narrative and an artistic construction.

In the case of biography plays, such a congruent connection among the historical subject, playwright, and performer is not necessary to establish the political connection, say, between the Restoration actresses of *Playhouse Creatures* and the contemporary actresses who play them, although to understand what is being reclaimed in this play, we must first understand how those disparate bodies function dialectically across history. And in plays like Wertenbaker's *New Anatomies*, we must also be able to read the authorial process of doing biography onto the biographer figure if we are to imagine audiences understanding the contextualization of biography as a potentially objectifying act. To read the objectifying gaze of Wertenbaker as biographer/playwright through the body of the desiring character of Severine forces us to understand precisely how the dialectic exceeds simply a pairing of historical body and performing body and includes the author's desiring body in its representational function.

In seeking to put forward the feminist theatrical practice of playing at lives through auto/biographical plays and performances, I am also advancing a few more mundane methodological assertions: that narrative study, despite the disciplinary turf battles that it inevitably invokes, can be usefully applied alongside performance theory in illuminating theatrical, literary, and real-life performances of gender; that life writing and life performances can be read and viewed through lenses that consider both their fictional aspects and the truth value they assert; and that the dialectic among the historical body, authorial body, and performing body must be scrupulously interrogated as a means of understanding how authorship functions, how women construct and assert their identities and political power, how transgressive performances can be reclaimed and disseminated, and how community can be propagated through single or multiple performing bodies.

While I stand by all of these assertions, we must also remember that the performing body is itself a historical body, and accordingly, we must remember that these texts, individually and as a collective phenomenon, are products of a specific historical moment. At the outset of this book, I listed a remarkable proliferation of feminist life-writing texts produced in a single regional theater community in 1998. That year, in their introduction to *O Solo Homo,* an anthology of queer performance texts, Holly Hughes and David Román contended with the idea that "queer performance is booming," an assertion that was borne out in my own experience as a theatergoer and practitioner.[2] And yet, writing a mere eight years later, Heddon notes about autobiographical performance that "one cannot help but think that what was initially intended as a radical, challenging and varied practice, in terms of content, form and purpose, has been appropriated and adapted for a different context, with very different aims and outcomes."[3] While Heddon suggests that a complete emptying out of political meaning from autobiographical performance is largely overstated, the shift from Hughes and Román's "boom" to Heddon's sense of appropriation is nonetheless striking. What happened in those eight years to shift the weight away from the apparent political vitality of these forms for feminist artists (and queer artists and other artists engaged in cultural politics)?

We can, of course, cite a whole host of historical events that contributed to a change in the political and cultural landscape on which these performances are built, and they begin in the very summer in which I observed the local effects of the life-writing boom in feminist performance: in 1998, *Time* magazine put the actress Calista Flockhart, star of the Fox television show *Ally McBeal,* on its June 25 cover with pictures of three prominent historical feminists and the headline, "Is Feminism Dead?"; the image sparked scores of serious conversations about the possible onset of a postfeminist moment. That issue of *Time* was on newsstands when, on June 27, the Supreme Court announced its *National Endowment for the Arts v. Finley* decision in favor of the NEA. That summer also gave us hour after endless hour of media coverage of Bill Clinton, Monica Lewinski, a stained dress, and "presidential kneepads." The Culture Wars were shifting decidedly rightward, and identity politics was being cast suspiciously as "gonadal politics" by Ralph Nader, who in two years would muster just enough progressive fervor to tip the national presidential election (dubiously) toward a Republican win. On September 11, 2001, al-Qaeda flew hijacked aircraft into the World Trade Center and the Pentagon, and by March 2003, U.S. forces had invaded Iraq. While none of those events was in and of itself a specific marker of an end to the Culture Wars and identity politics, together they form a chain of both causal and correlative events that suggest, if not the end of, then at least a pause in, the highest point of cultural contention over the politics of identity.

In its place? Certainly another potent, angry set of voices is arising from political theater artists. Feminist playwright par excellence Caryl Churchill's *Far Away* is a meditation on the absurdity of war, while her *Drunk Enough to Say I Love You* is a thinly veiled allegory for American and British international politics. Building on the success of documentary theater in the previous decade (forged on the identity-politics stages of Anna Deavere Smith, Eve Ensler, and Moises Kaufman), many erstwhile feminist playwrights and theater artists looked to documentary performance and verbatim theater to further establish the stakes of the real onstage. Vera Brittain and Gillian Slovo's *Guantánamo: 'Honor Bound to Defend Freedom'* stages few women in its critique of the "War on Terror," but its political framework bears certain hallmarks of the feminist documentary theater practitioners that preceded it. On the continent, Dutch playwright Adelheid Roosen's *The Veiled Monologues* and *Is.man* have brought feminist inquiries to bear on the global culture clash between Euro-American culture and various iterations of fundamentalist Islam. To suggest that feminist drama and performance have disappeared, then, is to miss their transformation.

This precise issue was raised in the "Contemporary Women Playwrights" working group at ASTR 2009. Confronted with debbie tucker green's *Stoning Mary*, Quiara Alegria Hudes's *Elliot: A Soldier's Fugue*, Heather Raffo's *9 Parts of Desire*, and Judith Thompson's *Palace of the End*, participants were asked to consider the persistence of plays by women that take global antiviolence stances more prominently than they do feminist stances. My answer, then, as it is here, was that as feminist playwrights had established themselves in the 1980s and 1990s as important voices, and as the terms of national and international discussion had shifted, the feminist epistemologies that governed more recognizably feminist drama and performance in earlier decades were still quite in operation in more recent plays that critique a range of political practices and stances on the global stage.

I take as evidence of this continuity Judith Thompson's *Palace of the End*, submitted for our consideration by Sharon Friedman. Winner of the 2008 Susan Smith Blackburn Prize, *Palace of the End* is itself something of a biography play. A triptych of monologues based closely on the events and circumstances of three real figures, the play brings a decidedly feminist sensibility to a number of issues surrounding the U.S. and British intervention in Iraq, while at the same time minimizing the overtly gendered politics it deploys. The first monologue, "My Pyramids," stages a soldier based closely on the experiences of Lynndie England, the U.S. soldier pictured in photos taken at Abu Ghraib; the second, "Harrowdown Hill," imagines the final suicidal moments of Dr. David Kelly, a whistle-blower on British intelligence efforts to trump up claims of Iraqi weapons of mass destruction; and the third, "Instruments of Yearning," presents us with Nehrjas Al Saffarh, a prominent member of the communist party in Iraq who had been tortured, along with her children, in one of Saddam Hussein's secret prisons, not unlike the Abu Ghraib we confront in the first monologue.

None of the monologues is overtly concerned with how gender is constructed or how patriarchal power comes to bear specifically on women, although, as I will show, both themes run through the play. Thompson's most obvious subject is the war itself, or as Robert's Crew's *Toronto Star* review articulates it, "She is firmly against the 'weapons of mass destruction' propaganda that was used to justify the intervention, firmly against the abuse and torture of soldiers and civilians, firmly against the inhumanity of war itself."[4] And yet her approach to this subject is decidedly recognizable within many of the very terms that this study has analyzed. Specifically, I want to return to a tension raised by disability scholar Susan Stocker, who considers the critical potential of a notion of Butlerian performativity against the potential of mutuality made possible and visible by a more essentialist, humanist notion of identity. I would argue that Thompson deploys both standpoints to decidedly feminist ends in her critique of Western intervention in Iraq, arguing along the way that women can be both conscripted into the service of that inhumane intervention and their identities as women used against them in inhumane scenarios. Ultimately, Thompson poses a kind of cross-culture mutuality, embodied in the figure of the mother, as the way forward.

In fact, it is the image of the expectant mother that we see when we first meet The Soldier in the first monologue. Lynndie England, on whom The Soldier is based, was the U.S. Army reservist who was captured in photographs depicting the torture and prisoner abuse of several Iraqi detainees in Abu Ghraib prison. The monologue shows us a very pregnant Soldier reflecting on her actions, her notoriety, and her future. While on the one hand, The Soldier is depicted as generally unrepentant for her role in Abu Ghraib, Thompson also lucidly imagines the world that would give rise to the attitudes that she espouses, and in this way, the character is as significant for being a woman as for being a soldier. That is, through the key details we learn about The Soldier before her time at Abu Ghraib there emerges a portrait of a poor young woman growing up in an economically depressed region (England's hometown in Fort Ashby, West Virginia, is only eighty-five miles from where I teach at West Virginia University), where the role models with which she is presented include fellow West Virginian Jessica Lynch, whose 2004 rescue from Iraqi forces elevated her to hero status. The Soldier is a woman deemed unattractive by conventional standards, although she proudly claims that she was "voted a six and a half outta ten at my school," who has so thoroughly internalized a regime of female beauty that she declares, "I *hate* ugly women."[5] She describes an unrealistic devotion to "Charley" (based on Charles Graner, England's real life lover and superior officer, largely purported to be the local ringleader of the Abu Ghraib prisoner abuse) and a willingness to repeat the actions that she did to curry favor with him and the other male soldiers.

Feminism for The Soldier is a dirty word: "I am definitely *not* nor have I *ever* been a feminist. I hate feminists man, now *feminists* are UGLY. Thas [*sic*] why they don't like men, they can't get theyselves a man. Is that why you think I'm a feminist because I am a soldier? I am a soldier because I love my country."[6] In these lines we see a complex representation of a particular failure of recent feminism to reach a whole group of American women—in this case, poor white women. The worst stereotypical images of feminists prevail for this character, who returns to patriarchal notions of heterosexual coupling and national fervor over an alternative framework that might privilege humane compassion over interpersonal and international domination. And we see the impossibility of that compassion when The Soldier describes the feeling she got when she held an Iraqi prisoner on a leash, a moment that triggers a memory (presumably fictional) in which she and her childhood friends invited a disabled classmate over for a party, only to torture her, sexually abuse her, burn her clothing, destroy her prosthetic leg, and send her crawling home. Here Thompson makes explicit the connection between the persistently demeaning and limiting discursive constructions of womanhood and the inhumane actions undertaken by an individual historical woman who found herself trying to live untenably within those constructions. For The Soldier, feminism is akin to communism (visible in the "I am not nor have I ever been" formulation of her particular distaste for feminists) and therefore anathema to the masculinist dogma of nation.

The performativity of gender becomes a site of critique, as the compulsory codes of femininity victimize the conventionally unattractive woman in poverty, who in turn victimizes the prisoners of Abu Ghraib, all in the name of country. Untenable as either a sexualized commodity or an active consumer, Lynndie England signifies for Thompson the almost inevitable result of a patriarchal culture that makes moral monsters out of its own unwanted children and then devours them for responding along precisely the same masculinist, jingoistic lines that it demanded of them. If there is any hope expressed, it is that The Soldier will escape into Quebec with her young child, to disappear and live the quiet domestic life of her fantasy. While Canadian exile is hardly an ideal (or likely) scenario, we hear in her fantasy The Soldier prioritizing maternity over nation—nurturing over fighting—and in that moment we glimpse a shred of hope, at the same time as we see its futility.

The Soldier's Iraqi counterpart in the play, Nehrjas Al Saffarh, died in 1991, the victim of a U.S. missile in the first Gulf War. Speaking the third monologue, "Instruments of Yearning," from beyond the grave, Nehrjas has already been a mother, as well as a prominent communist; Thompson leads us to believe that she may have been something of a feminist as well. On Broadway, Nehrjas was played by Heather Raffo, the playwright and performer of 9 Parts of Desire, and so we can see in the performance an intertextual care for the stories of Iraqi women coming to Western stages. Nehrjas's story, for example, begins with a nod to the constitutive gendered power of names. Her name, Nehrjas, means "daffodil." She continues:

Another thing I have observed is that a woman is never
called after a tree. Only a flower. Because the purpose of
the flower is to attract a bee.
And a tree,
The tree stands alone.
Blissfully—alone.
The tree provides air.
And shelter.
And food.
So I think, all mothers should be given a second name after
a tree.[7]

Nehrjas's monologue immediately stands in contrast to The Soldier's, for instead of detailing what she is willing to repeat to gain the favor of "a bee," she instead speaks of gaining a new name that stands for strength, independence, and protection. Simply, Nehrjas's impulse to protect is the opposite of The Soldier's impulse to abuse.

Her story is a harrowing one, for after she talks about trees, she tells us that she has committed the worst of sins, which we learn later is having allowed her sons to be tortured before her eyes, the younger one to his death at age eight. As the spouse of the leader of the communist party in Iraq on the day of a Baathist coup, Nehrjas and her family were obvious targets, and she tells us that hiding her husband's whereabouts will protect more people than simply her family: "If we give in," she tells us, "we are giving not only our lives but the lives of millions. It would be like giving up Nelson Mandela, you understand? It would be like saying yes; you can go and murder these million children. To save ourselves."[8] So instead, as she details, she was raped in front of both boys, her elder son's nose was battered in with a hammer, and her younger son was suspended upside down from a spinning ceiling fan until he lost consciousness and then left on the roof to die. As audience members, we are not only confronted with the horror of the moment but we are asked to feel empathy for a woman who could not protect her children, and who *would* not do so to protect what she believed might be the welfare of millions of others.

And Nehrjas's monologue is as politically complex for Western audiences as it is morally complex, for while the previous monologues are critical of recent Western involvement in Iraq (as is Nehrjas), her primary antagonist is Saddam Hussein, whom she unambivalently calls Satan. Here Thompson seems to undermine her own antiwar argument by villainizing the supposed target of the 2003 invasion. But ultimately Thompson

212 : LIVES IN PLAY

seems less interested in using her characters to make arguments about specific policies than in asking her audience to engage affectively with them. Indeed, Nehrjas's final image comes after her own death, one of flying around Baghdad with her younger son, who tells her:

> "Mummy, you must go back to Baghdad—and watch over our people with all the other ghosts. Me, I am a child, so I can go to paradise now. But you, you must watch, because the worst, Mummy, the worst is yet to come. . . . You must watch until there is finally peace. But I will wait for you." And so I am here, watching. With the thousands of other ghosts 'who are watching with me. There are more every day.[9]

The use of the historical figure of Nehrjas Al Saffarh is not likely to resonate deeply for most Western audiences, except perhaps in the fact that she was a real person, and in our failure to protect this real person, or her real son, we as audience members are perhaps more culpable. Because in the emphasis on protection, we hear echoes of Susan Stocker's claim that the possibilities afforded by mutuality, the common desire to protect and care for one another, outweigh the value of critique. For Thompson, moving from one soldier's life story to one victim's, we see both operations happening in the same play.

Importantly, between these two women's monologues is that of Dr. David Kelly, whose monologue is a testament to the impossible moral quandary of having to manufacture a case for invading Iraq and then deciding to uncover the deception. Of the three, his is the least obviously wrapped up in a politics that implicates gender roles, just the politics that typically passes between men. His story, though, centers on personal responsibility and the only ethical choice he feels he can make (although that choice leads him to suicide). Crucially, as he speaks his final words to the audience, he thanks them: "Thank you for witnessing."[10] By clearly identifying the audience's role as witnesses, he implicates their responsibility along with his own. Couched between the critique of ethical failure embodied in the figure of The Soldier and the maternal call to empathy, mutuality, and care embodied by Nehrjas Al Saffarh, David Kelly's monologue pushes the audience toward their own responsibilities: to witness, feel deeply, and watch over others.

We may notice, then, that while Thompson's play might be construed as a feminist biography play, it is not primarily concerned with equal pay or access to child care or even the representations of the women staged here. Instead, we find an epistemology of global politics through a decidedly feminist lens, one attuned to the damage done by masculinist, nationalist codes, enforced through sexual and physical violence, and enacted with disregard to the care and protection that feminist theorists like Susan Stocker, and Maxine Sheets-Johnstone before her, argue are unique to our very humanity. Indeed, it is this stance toward protecting the other that links feminism for Thompson to a global humanism. The Soldier, in telling us of the pangs of guilt she felt about having tortured the disabled girl in her hometown, quickly distinguishes her from the prisoners she abused in Abu Ghraib, for at least she was an American. Nehrjas's monologue, on the other hand, demands that we make no such distinctions. A feminist epistemology of otherness requires that we engage a common humanity. In constructing such an argument, Thompson also implicitly acknowledges the ontological push and pull of staging real lives, situating one as a site for discursive, even deconstructive critique in the figure of the female soldier, while invoking an age-old essentialism in the protective body of the mother who mourns her dead child and the dying children of her nation. In this way, we might say that *Palace of the End* is typical of staged feminist life writing, for in tying together the historical female body and performing female body through the rhetorically charged narratives of real life, this play expresses a specifically feminist view as politically charged as the performance art of Carolee Schneeman or Bobby Baker or the dramatic work of Timberlake Wertenbaker, Maria Irene Fornes. or Suzan-Lori Parks.

The United States is pulling out of Iraq as I write this, and small signs suggest that we might in fact find ourselves returning to the cultural concerns of previous decades: the 2010 retrospective of the work of Marina Abramovich, "The Artist is Present," at New York's Museum of Modern Art has returned performance-based feminist art making at least to the spotlight of white Western culture, while scholarly venues like ASTR and *Theatre Journal*'s March 2011 special issue are returning to contemporary women playwrights as sources of important critical and political work. Whether we will see the narratives of real lives working at the center of such a return remains to be seen, but if we do, we can expect them to continue to walk these fault lines between performed selves and real lives, between history and liveness, between cultural critique and an empathetic mutuality.

NOTES

INTRODUCTION

1. Deirdre Heddon, *Autobiography and Performance: Performing Selves* (London: Palgrave Macmillan, 2008), 160.

2. Feminist theater rose to prominence in English-language theater in particular with the careers of Pam Gems and Caryl Churchill in the United Kingdom, spawning a host of young, avowedly feminist playwrights in the late 1970s through the last years of the twentieth century. In the United States, the success of Marsha Norman and Wendy Wasserstein on Broadway mirrored the more radical feminist and lesbian work in small performance spaces around New York by Split Britches, Holly Hughes, Karen Finley, and many others. These rich years in feminist and lesbian theater and performance were mirrored by early and influential studies in feminism and theater that began in earnest in the late 1970s with Janet Brown's *Feminist Drama: Definition and Critical Analysis* (Metuchen, N.J.: Scarecrow Press, 1979) and reached prominence with the 1984 founding of the journal *Women and Performance* and the publication of Helene Keyssar's *Feminist Theatre* (London: Macmillan, 1984), Sue-Ellen Case's *Feminism and Theatre* (New York: Routledge, 1988), and Jill Dolan's *The Feminist Spectator as Critic* (Ann Arbor: University of Michigan Press, 1991). Throughout the 1980s, feminist performance praxis and scholarship both insistently worked at questions of women's identities in performance, from active advocacy for specific women's rights to explorations and explosions of traditional gender roles. Elaine Aston, writing about American scholarship while inaugurating a transatlantic scholarship of feminist theater in *An Introduction to Feminism and Theatre* (New York: Routledge, 1995), writes that "the work of American feminist theatre scholars has, therefore, raised the profile of feminist practitioners working in a variety of performance contexts, and has, for example, given attention to American lesbian performers, female performance artists, the theatre created by women of colour, etc." (7–8).

At the same time, feminist autobiographies and feminist theories of autobiography saw a similar growth as second-wave feminism crested. Beginning with Adrienne Rich's confessional poetry in the late 1960s and 1970s and continuing through feminist autobiographies such as Audre Lourde's *Zami: A New Spelling of My Name* (Watertown, Mass.: Persephone Press, 1982), Gloria Anzaldua's *Borderlands/La Frontera: The New Mestiza* (San Francisco: Aunt Lute Books, 1990), and bell hooks's *Bone Black: Memories of Girlhood* (New York: Henry Holt, 1997), women's autobiographies troubled the waters of autobiographical form while establishing the imperative to write women's lives. Building from the notion that "the personal is political," such work represented an overtly politicized notion of telling life stories that at once laid bare the local details of women's experiences and gestured outward to the broader fabric of women's lives and the material and discursive conditions that circumscribed them. In an early gesture in the study of women's biography, Estelle C. Jelinek, in "Introduction: Women's Autobiography and the Male Tradition," in *Women's Autobiography: Essays in Criticism*, edited by Estelle Jelinek (Bloomington: Indiana University Press, 1980), stakes out the distinctive character of women's autobiography in such terms: "The emphasis by women on the personal, especially on other people, rather than their work life, their professional success, or their connectedness to current political or intellectual history clearly contradicts the established criterion about the content of autobiography" (10). In response to such an approach, work by Leigh Gilmore, Carolyn Heilbrun, and Sidonie Smith has laid out a more complex basis for a feminist criticism of life writing, which, as Smith writes, "must grapple with the formal constrictions and rhetorical presentations, the historical context, and psychosexual labyrinth, the subversions and the capitulations of woman's self-writing in a patriarchal culture that 'fictionalizes' her" (*Poetics of Women's Autobiography* [Bloomington: Indiana University Press, 1987], 18). See Leigh Gilmore, *Autobiographics: A Feminist Theory of Women's Self-Representation* (Ithaca, N.Y.: Cornell University Press, 1994); and Carolyn G. Heilbrun, *Writing a Woman's Life* (New York: W. W. Norton, 1988).

3. Such a critique begins with the epistemological underpinnings of a canon of life writing that is populated almost entirely by male writers, whose lives are presented (by themselves or others) as coherent, unified narratives of a concrete, discrete self. Commenting on the classical tradition of autobiography that begins with Saint Augustine's *Confessions* and extends through Benjamin Franklin's autobiography and the bevy of biographies of great men that currently line bookstore shelves, feminist critics identify first, as does Jelinek, the dearth of women's voices. Of course, much has changed since the boom in memoir publication over the last two decades, a boom that has fostered a great deal of women's autobiographical writing. Even so, the distinction between women's personal memoirs and men's public autobiographies seems to remain entrenched in this discourse, one that Gilmore, among others, problematizes.

4. Gilmore, *Autobiographics*, xiii. Gilmore is careful here to note that even much early feminist criticism of autobiography "reproduces the . . . ideological tenets of individualism: men are autonomous individuals with inflexible ego boundaries who write autobiographies that turn on moments of conflict and place the self at the center of the drama."

5. Of course there are counterexamples from the canons of postmodernism and male writing (Roland Barthes, Vladimir Nabokov, Eugène Ionesco) that do not present this post-Enlightenment construction of the subject. Yet these remain outliers to the dominant tradition of autobiographical writing.

6. Martine Watson Brownley and Allison B. Kimmich, *Women and Autobiography* (Wilmington, Del.: Scholarly Resources, 1999), 1.

7. Brownley and Kimmich suggest, for example, that "the male autobiographer, whose narrative may suggest that he alone deserves recognition for his accomplishments," will ignore the fact that his "life is a part of a larger social fabric" (ibid., 1). This notion of the self as autonomous is particularly problematic for an ideological stance that privileges community among women (even though, as Gilmore points out, we must take great care not to essentialize women's self-representation just as traditional criticism of life writing has done with men's lives. [*Autobiographics*, xiii]). Nonetheless, performances of life writing (particularly biography plays) that position the exemplary woman in much the same way as the exemplary man risk alienating the "average woman" whom these plays often hope to persuade into action at the same time as they minimize the importance of community and collectivity in establishing women's empowerment.

8. Sidonie Smith, *Poetics*, 5. Smith here is following a line that prevails in contemporary theories of autobiography. Paul John Eakin famously argues in *Fictions in Autobiography: Studies in the Art of Self-Invention* (Princeton, N.J.: Princeton University Press, 1985) that "the self that is the center of all autobiographical narrative is necessarily a fictive structure" (3). Similarly, Timothy Dow Adams, in *Telling Lies in Modern American Autobiography* (Chapel Hill: University of North Carolina Press, 1990), asserts that "autobiography is synonymous with *lying* for many readers" (4, emphasis mine). These assertions, though counterintuitive to life writing's general truth claims, have become so much part of a poststructuralist sense of the genre that few critics working in the field today would dispute them. Certainly, teapot tempests surrounding the fictional liberties taken in memoirs by Rigoberta Menchu or James Frey seem vehement enough in the larger popular readership that Eakin and Adams might well have not made such pronouncements at all, yet on an ontological level, such criticism unsettles even popular expectations of referentiality in life-writing forms.

9. Gilmore, *Autobiographics*, 126.

10. Plato's *Republic* famously initiates the critique of representation; Aristotle's earliest definitions of theatrical mimesis posit the necessity of the suspension of disbelief; and the antitheatrical tradition in Europe was nursed along by Tertullian's claims in *de Spectaculis* that "The Author of truth hates all the false; he regards as adultery all that is unreal. Condemning, therefore, as He does hypocrisy in every form, He will never approve any putting on of voice, or sex, or age." Tertullian, "On the Spectacles," in *Dramatic Theory and Criticism: Greeks to Grotowski*, ed. Bernard F. Dukore (New York: Holt, Rinehart and Winston, 1974), 92.

11. Keir Elam, *The Semiotics of Theatre and Drama* (London: Routledge, 1980), 61, emphasis original. There is, or course a long tradition of earlier texts, from medieval plays such as Henry Medwall's *Fulgens and Lucrece* onward to Luigi Pirandello's *Six Characters in Search of an Author* and Peter Handke's *Offending the Audience*, that trouble this very separation of real and dramatic worlds. Such texts frequently use metatheatrical tactics to break down fourth-wall conventions, working against the idea of theatricality as decidedly false. I explore this idea more fully in Ryan Claycomb, "Curtain Up?: Disrupted, Disguised, and Delayed Beginnings in Theatre and Drama," in

Narrative Beginnings, ed. Brian Richardson (Lincoln: University of Nebraska Press, 2008), 166–78.

12. Tracy C. Davis and Thomas Postlewait, introduction to *Theatricality,* in *Theatricality,* ed. Tracy C. Davis and Thomas Postlewait (Cambridge: Cambridge University Press, 2004), 5.

13. While traditional theater makes no such claims to efficacy, much avant-garde political theater since the 1960s has aspired to precisely that end. In *The Politics of Performance: Radical Theatre as Cultural Intervention,* performance artist and theorist Baz Kershaw suggests that, while elusive, a sense of political efficacy underpins the assumptions of any overtly political performance, in "the potential that theatre may have to make the immediate effects of performance influence, however minutely, the general historical evolution of wider political and social realities." Baz Kershaw, *The Politics of Performance: Radical Theatre as Cultural Intervention* (London: Routledge, 1992), 1.

14. Jeanie Forte, "Women's Performance Art: Feminism and Postmodernism," in *Performing Feminisms: Feminist Critical Theory and Theatre,* ed. Sue-Ellen Case (Baltimore: Johns Hopkins University Press, 1990), 254.

15. Marvin Carlson, "Performing the Self," *Modern Drama* 39, no. 4 (winter 1996): 604.

16. Ibid., 602.

17. Jill Dolan, *Geographies of Learning* (Middletown, Conn.: Wesleyan University Press, 2001), 431.

18. Sherrill Grace, "Theatre and the Autobiographical Pact: An Introduction," in *Theatre and AutoBiography: Writing and Performing Lives in Theory and Practice,* ed. Sherrill Grace and Jerry Wasserman (Vancouver: Talonbooks, 2006), 15.

19. Judith Butler, "Performative Acts and Gender Constitution: An Essay in Phenomenology and Feminist Theory," in *Performing Feminisms: Feminist Critical Theory and Theatre,* ed. Sue-Ellen Case (Baltimore: Johns Hopkins University Press 1990), 270; Judith Butler, *Bodies That Matter: On the Discursive Limits of "Sex"* (New York: Routledge, 1993), 9.

20. J. L. Austin, *How to Do Things with Words* (Cambridge, Mass.: Harvard University Press, 1962), 14.

21. Ibid., 22.

22. Butler, "Performative," 278.

23. Ibid.

24. Andrew Parker and Eve Kosofsky Sedgwick, introduction to *Performativity and Performance,* ed. Andrew Parker and Eve Kosofsky Sedgwick (New York: Routledge, 1995), 5.

25. David Savran, *A Queer Sort of Materialism: Recontextualizing American Theatre* (Ann Arbor: University of Michigan Press, 2003), 260.

26. Judith Butler, "Imitation and Gender Insubordination," in *Inside/Out: Lesbian Theories, Gay Theories,* ed. Diana Fuss (New York: Routledge, 1991), 318.

27. Estelle Jelinek, preface to *Women's Autobiography: Essays on Criticism,* ed. Estelle Jelinek (Bloomington: Indiana University Press, 1980), ix.

28. Sherrill Grace, "Performing the Auto/Biographical Pact: Towards a Theory of Identity in Performance," in *Tracing the Autobiographical,* ed. Mar-

lene Kadar et al. (Waterloo, Ont.: Wilfrid Laurier University Press, 2005), 70; Grace, "Theatre," 29. In laying out these ideas, Grace cites Elin Diamond, *Performance and Cultural Politics* (New York: Routledge, 1996), 5; and Dolan, *Geographies*, 431.

29. Grace, "Performing," 70.

30. Susan Bennett, "3-D A/B," in *Theatre and AutoBiography: Writing and Performing Lives in Theory and Practice*, ed. Sherrill Grace and Jerry Wasserman (Vancouver: Talonbooks, 2006), 34–35.

31. Heddon, *Autobiography*, 9.

32. Ibid., 13.

33. Timothy Gould, "The Unhappy Performative," in *Performativity and Performance*, ed. Andrew Parker and Eve Kosofsky Sedgwick (New York: Routledge, 1995), 29–31.

34. Elaine Scarry, *The Body in Pain: The Making and Unmaking of the World* (Oxford: Oxford University Press, 1987).

35. Judith Butler, "Burning Acts: Injurious Speech," in *Performativity and Performance*, ed. Andrew Parker and Eve Kosofsky Sedgwick (New York: Routledge, 1995), 203.

36. Ibid., 205, emphasis original.

37. Marvin Carlson, *Performance: A Critical Introduction* (London: Routledge, 1996), 6.

38. Ibid.

39. I acknowledge that there is drama that is antinarrative in form, such as the later work of Samuel Beckett, just as there is dramatic narrative that is not designed for performance, such as Shelley's *Prometheus Unbound* or the Circe chapter of James Joyce's *Ulysses*. These boundaries of dramatic representation, however, are not ones tested by the works considered in this study.

40. Della Pollock, "Introduction: Remembering," in *Remembering: Oral History Performance*, ed. Della Pollock (New York: Palgrave Macmillan, 2005).

41. Susan E. Bassnet-McGuire, "Towards a Theory of Women's Theatre," in *Semiotics of Drama and Theatre*, ed. Herta Schmid and Aloysius Van Kesteren, Linguistic and Literary Studies in Eastern Europe, no. 10 (Amsterdam: John Benjamins, 1984), 447.

42. Janet Brown, "Feminist Theory and Contemporary Drama," in *The Cambridge Companion to American Women Playwrights*, ed. Brenda Murphy (Cambridge: Cambridge University Press, 1999), 155.

43. Elaine Aston, *Feminist Views on the English Stage: Women Playwrights, 1990–2000* (Cambridge: Cambridge University Press, 2003), 9–10.

44. Tim Miller and David Román, "Preaching to the Converted," *Theatre Journal* 47.2 (May 1995): 169–88.

45. Susan Sniader Lanser, *Fictions of Authority: Women Writers and Narrative Voice* (Ithaca, N.Y.: Cornell University Press, 1992), 3.

46. Ibid., 6.

47. Elin Diamond, *Unmaking Mimesis: Essays on Feminism and Theatre* (New York: Routledge, 1997), 146.

48. Bennett, "3-D A/B," 35.

49. Charlotte Canning, "Contiguous Autobiography: Feminist Performance in the 1970s," *Theatre Annual: A Journal of Performance Studies* 49 (1996): 74.

50. Bennett, 3-D A/B," 35.

51. Paul Taylor, review of *Playhouse Creatures*, by April De Angelis. *The Independent* (London), September 7, 1997, Features, 20.

CHAPTER 1

1. RoseLee Goldberg, *Performance Art: From Futurism to the Present*, Rev. ed. (New York: Harry N. Abrams, 1988), 174.

2. Heddon, *Autobiography*, 21.

3. Heddon is careful to note a shift in early-twenty-first-century auto-biographical performance, however, noting that "it is perhaps understandable why critics consider solo autobiographical performance to be little more than a vehicle for the aspiring actor who perceives it as an easy way to 'put on a show.' The solo work, demanding a versatile performance, is considered the ideal window through which to showcase that versatility (particularly when the auto/biography represents multiple voices). The hope is that the piece will be picked up and transferred to Broadway, or, at the very least, lead to the performer being cast in another production" (ibid.,159–60).

4. Goldberg, *Performance Art*, 196. The narrative element of these performances brings many of these pieces into the discussion of the more or less conventional plays that appear elsewhere in this study. While the divide between "drama" (the traditional text that describes a semiotic elsewhere and else*when* in a convention that suggests a live performance) and "theater" (the performed realization and interpretation of that drama) is fairly clear, the line where either of those categories end and performance art begins is less clear. While performance art certainly encompasses a broader range of practices, we can say that it overlaps with drama specifically when it makes use of a narrative text that is performed in a time and space inhabited by an audience. Of course, some of artists whom I discuss here do not precisely perform narrative drama. For example, Orlan's carefully conceived plastic surgeries, while they do involve the self (revealing a resemblance to autobiography), do not purport to narrate the self in the same way that Bobby Baker does in *Kitchen Show*. Nonetheless, Orlan's experiments with her own body reveal much about the rhetorical potential of the self in performance, an element that lies at the center of the narratives studied here. Accordingly, we must imagine the entire spectrum of performances that offer up a representation of selfhood, even if these representations are not precisely narrative, precisely because they illuminate more traditionally narrative performances that we can more clearly call autobiographical drama.

5. Carlson, "Performing," 599.

6. John Brockway Schmor, "Confessional Performance: Postmodern Culture in Recent American Theatre," *Journal of Dramatic Theory and Criticism* 9, no. 1 (fall 1994): 159.

7. In part because performance art is situated at the theoretical frontiers of theater, and therefore represents a scholarly hotbed of inquiry, an extraordinarily large body of work has already been produced on autobiographical performance, even specifically feminist autobiographical performance. Given

that the most exciting theatrical advances during most of the 1970s and 1980s came in the field of performance art, that much of that performance art was confessional or autobiographical, and that a significant number of the performers creating these pieces were self-identified feminists, it is no surprise that much of the most engaging feminist theatrical criticism of the last twenty years has examined precisely this phenomenon. Nonetheless, this chapter is intended to lay out the grounds on which the larger mode of inquiry (the function of narrated lives in feminist performance) can take place.

8. Heddon, *Autobiography*, 21.

9. Forte, "Women's," 254, emphasis mine.

10. Ibid.

11. Quoted in ibid., 257.

12. Brownley and Kimmich, *Women*, xi.

13. See, for example, Eakin, *Fictions;* and Adams, *Telling*.

14. Sidonie Smith, "Construing Truth in Lying Mouths: Truthtelling in Women's Autobiography," in *Women and Autobiography*, ed. Martine Watson Brownley and Allison B. Kimmich (Wilmington, Del.: Scholarly Resources, 1999), 37.

15. Ibid., 39.

16. Quoted in Tanya Augburg, "Orlan's Performative Transformations of Subjectivity," in *The Ends of Performance,* ed. Peggy Phelan and Jill Lane (New York: New York University Press, 1998), 288.

17. Butler, "Performative Acts."

18. Valie Export, "Persona, Proto-performance, Politics: A Preface," *Discourse* 14, no. 2 (spring 1992): 33.

19. Eelka Lampe, "Rachel Rosenthal Creating Her Selves," *TDR: The Drama Review* 32, no. 1 (spring 1988): 181.

20. Rebecca Schneider, *The Explicit Body in Performance* (New York: Routledge, 1997), 55.

21. Augsburg, "Orlan's," 303.

22. Ibid., 290.

23. Kate Bornstein, "Kate Bornstein," in *Out of Character: Rants, Raves, and Monologues from Today's Top Performance Artists,* ed. Mark Russell (New York: Bantam, 1997), 50–51.

24. Augsburg "Orlan's Performative Transformations," 292.

25. Linda S. Kauffman, "Cut-Ups in Beauty School—and Postscripts, January 2000 and December 2001," in *Interfaces: Women/Autobiography/Image/Performance,* ed. Sidonie Smith and Julia Watson (Ann Arbor: University of Michigan Press, 2002), 104.

26. Amelia Jones, *Body Art: Performing the Subject* (Minneapolis: University of Minnesota Press, 1998), 51.

27. Carlson, "Performing," 603.

28. Carmelita Tropicana, *Milk of Amnesia—Leche de Amnesia,* in *O Solo Homo: The New Queer Performance,* ed. Holly Hughes and David Román (New York: Grove, 1998), 19.

29. Alina Troyano, *I, Carmelita Tropicana: Performing between Cultures* (Boston: Beacon Press, 2000), 47.

30. Ibid., 24.

31. Ibid., 47.

32. Chon Noriega, introduction to *I, Carmelita Tropicana: Performing between Cultures,* by Alina Troyano (Boston: Beacon Press, 2000), ix–x.

33. Ibid., ix.

34. Sidonie Smith, "Performativity, Autobiographical Practice, Resistance," in *Women, Autobiography, Theory,* ed. Sidonie Smith and Julia Watson (Madison: University of Wisconsin Press, 1998), 109.

35. Kate Bornstein, *Virtually Yours,* in *O Solo Homo: The New Queer Performance,* ed. Holly Hughes and David Román (New York: Grove, 1998), 234.

36. Ibid., 234–35.

37. Ibid., 278.

38. Claire MacDonald, "Assumed Identities: Feminism, Autobiography, and Performance Art," in *The Uses of Autobiography,* ed. Julia Swindells (London: Taylor and Francis, 1995), 190.

39. Heddon, *Autobiography,* 43–44.

40. Smith, "Performativity," 109.

41. Tropicana, *Milk,* 19.

42. Bobby Baker, *Daily Life Series 1: Kitchen Show.* Written and performed by Bobby Baker. Filmed by Carole Lamond (London: Daily Life Ltd., 1991), VHS.

43. Indeed, *throwing* is actually a gerund and therefore a noun. But it is a noun formation that itself has a verb as its root: even its linguistic status is composed of an act.

44. Heddon, *Autobiography,* 119.

45. Lesley Ferris, "Cooking Up the Self: Bobby Baker and Blondell Cummings 'Do' the Kitchen," in *Interfaces: Women/Autobiography/Image/Performance,* ed. Sidonie Smith and Julia Watson (Ann Arbor: University of Michigan Press, 2002), 196.

46. Butler, "Performative," 270, emphasis mine.

47. Butler, "Imitation," 20.

48. Ferris, "Cooking,"193, emphasis mine.

49. Ibid.

50. Augsburg, "Orlan's," 308.

51. While semioticians note that theater is remarkable for its density, even excess of signification, Judith Butler notes in "Imitation and Gender Insubordination" that "psychic excess," the repeated and persistent play of compulsory gender codes creates ruptures in the efficacy of those codes. When brought together in performances like Baker's, the density of theatrical signification helps to produce the very psychic excess that Butler identifies as crucial to gender transgression. See Ryan Claycomb, "Staging Psychic Excess: Parodic Narrative and Transgressive Performance," *Journal of Narrative Theory* 38, no. 1 (winter 2007): 104–27.

52. Peggy Phelan, *Unmarked: The Politics of Performance* (New York: Routledge, 1993), 149.

53. Canning, "Contiguous," 74.

54. Holly Hughes, *Clit Notes: A Sapphic Sampler* (New York: Grove, 1996), 22.

55. Bornstein, *Virtually Yours,* 242.

56. Miller and Román, "Preaching," 176.

57. Jill Dolan, "Performance, Utopia, and the 'Utopian Performative,'" *Theatre Journal* 53.3 (October 2001): 455.

58. Ibid., 475.

59. Ibid., 471–72.

60. Ibid., 471.

61. Miller and Román, "Preaching," 176.

CHAPTER 2

1. Diana Fuss, *Essentially Speaking: Feminism, Nature, and Difference* (New York: Routledge, 1989), xi.

2. Bella Brodzki, and Celeste Schenck., *Life/Lines: Theorizing Women's Autobiography* (Ithaca, N.Y.: Cornell University Press, 1988), 1.

3. Hélène Cixous, "The Laugh of the Medusa," in *Literary Criticism and Theory*, ed. Robert Con Davis and Laurie Finke (New York: Longman, 1989), 733.

4. Ibid.

5. Lanser, *Fictions*, 19.

6. Carolyn G. Heilbrun, "Women's Autobiographical Writings: New Forms," in *Women and Autobiography*, ed. Martine Watson Brownley and Allison B. Kimmich (Wilmington, Del.: Scholarly Resources, 1999), 23.

7. Hughes and Román, *O Solo*, 2.

8. Carlson, "Performing," 600.

9. Heilbrun, *Writing*, 12–13.

10. Forte, "Women's," 254.

11. Cixous, "Laugh," 741.

12. Forte, "Women's," 254.

13. Quoted in ibid., 255–56.

14. Cixous, "Laugh," 736–37.

15. Kauffman, "Cut-Ups," 104–5.

16. Fuss, *Essentially Speaking*, xi.

17. Schneider, *Explicit Body*, 3.

18. James M. Harding, *Cutting Performances: Collage Events, Feminist Artists, and the American Avant-Garde* (Ann Arbor: University of Michigan Press, 2010), 27.

19. Ibid., emphasis original.

20. Schneider, *Explicit Body*, 21.

21. Ibid., 21–22.

22. Fuss, *Essentially Speaking*, 4.

23. Ibid., 6.

24. Ibid., 104.

25. Hughes and Román, *O Solo*, 4.

26. See a fuller discussion of this notion in chapter 4 on feminist biographical drama.

27. Schneider, *Explicit Body*, 65.

28. Smith, "Performativity," 109.

29. Smith, "Construing Truth."

30. Paul de Man, "Autobiography as De-Facement," *MLN* 94, no. 5 (December 1979): 919–30.

31. Bennett, "3-D A/B," 35.

32. Fuss, *Essentially Speaking,* 4.

33. Karen Finley, *A Different Kind of Intimacy* (New York: Thunder's Mouth Press, 2000), 254.

34. Ibid., 258.

35. Finley's choice to publish much of this in a written memoir as opposed to performed autobiography speaks to a certain degree of the psychic danger of such public performance. It is clear from the memoir and work that followed that the ordeal took a very personal toll on Finley. The degree to which her art was subversive is highlighted by the public brutality brought against her and the other performers as a way of maintaining the status quo.

36. Finley, *A Different Kind,* 255.

37. Ibid., 261.

38. Patrick Pacheco, "The Karen Finley Act Reacts," *Los Angeles Times,* June 27, 1998, F1.

39. Richard Meyer, "'Have You Heard the One about the Lesbian Who Goes to the Supreme Court?': Holly Hughes and the Case against Censorship," *Theatre Journal* 52, no. 4 (2000): 546.

40. Holly Hughes, *Preaching to the Perverted,* unpublished manuscript, 2003, 15.

41. Ibid., 6.

42. Ibid., 5.

43. Ibid., 14, emphasis original.

44. Tamsen Wolff, performance review of *Preaching To The Perverted* by Holly Hughes, Performance Space 122, New York, New York, May 20, 2000, *Theatre Journal* 52, no. 4 (December 2000): 557.

45. Hughes, *Preaching,* 29.

46. Ibid.

47. At least one hostile reviewer noted by contrast that Hughes' production values are spare indeed, calling the show "Less an artwork than a piece of spoken nonfiction presented with a minimal set and props." The "slight" here appears to grow out of a misunderstanding of art, since most other reviewers seem to understand implicitly that "spoken nonfiction presented with a minimal set and props" is called performance art, and has been a lively genre for decades. S. D. Trav, "Angry at Daddy," performance review of *Preaching to the Perverted. Reason* 32, no. 5 (October 2000). *Reason.com.* Available at http://reason.com/archives/2000/10/01/angry-at-daddy, accessed October 25, 2010.

48. Jacques Derrida, *Dissemination,* translated by Barbara Johnson (Chicago: University of Chicago Press, 1981).

49. Ric Knowles, "Documemory, Autobiology, and the Utopian Performative in Canadian Autobiographical Solo Performance," in *Theatre and Auto-Biography: Writing and Performing Lives in Theory and Practice,* ed. Sherill Grace and Jerry Wasserman (Vancouver: Talonbooks, 2006), 50. Emphasis original.

50. Knowles, "Documemory," 50–51.

51. Quoted in Knowles, "Documemory," 50.

52. Chris Anne Strickling, "*Actual Lives:* Cripples in the House," *Theatre Topics* 12, no. 2 (September 2002): 148.

53. Susan G. Stocker, "Problems of Embodiment and Problematic Embodiment," *Hypatia* 16, no. 3 (Summer 2001): 31–32. Even while Stocker will continue on to "choose" a biologically based approach (which I consider below), she recognizes the critical move as a choice, rather than an ontological certitude.

54. Strickling, "*Actual Lives,*" 156.

55. Strickling, "*Actual Lives,*" 155.

56. Carrie Sandahl, "Queering the Crip or Cripping the Queer?: Intersections of Queer and Crip Identities in Solo Autobiographical Performance," *GLQ* 9: 1–2 (2003): 45.

57. Sandahl, "Queering," 48.

58. Ibid.

59. Butler herself has sought to address these problems as early as 1993's *Bodies That Matter,* where she writes:

> To claim that the materiality of sex is constructed through a ritualized repetition of norms is hardly a self-evident claim. Indeed, our customary notions of 'construction' seem to get in the way of understanding such a claim. For surely bodies live and die; eat and sleep; feel pain, pleasure; endure illness and violence; and these 'facts,' one might skeptically proclaim, cannot be dismissed as mere constructions . . . But their irrefutability in no way implies what it might mean to affirm them and through what discursive means. (iv)

Here Butler's insistence on the discursive nature of the body seems to include embodied experience, a claim that remains problematic. Accordingly, her handling of pain has tended away from the physical and toward the psychological. Her essay "Burning Acts: Injurious Speech" takes on linguistic performatives that inflict pain, but specifically the psychological pain caused specifically by hate speech, which obviously has a social and historical component. Writing from the counter position within disability studies, Tobin Siebers observes in *Disability Theory* (Ann Arbor: University of Michigan Press, 2008) that:

> pain in current body theory is rarely physical. It is more likely to be based on the pain of guilt or social repression . . . When body theorists do represent pain as physical—infrequent as that it—the conventional model still dominates their descriptions. They present suffering and disability either as a way of reconfiguring the physical resources of the body or opening up new possibilities of pleasure. Pain is most often soothed by the joy of conceiving the body differently from the norm. (62)

60. Scarry, *Body,* 4–5.

61. Siebers, *Disability Theory,* 64.

62. Stocker, "Problems of Embodiment," 33. Stocker cites critiques of postmodern feminism's "anti-biologist" and anti-essentialist stance, noting

that "despite feminism's critical interrogation of 'the body,' its anti-biologism has rendered 'unthinkable' its engagement with and critique of biology" (33). Still, I tread cautiously here in deploying the biological sciences in a work of performance theory.

63. Antonio R. Damasio, *Descartes' Error: Emotion, Reason, and the Human Brain* (New York: Avon, 1995); *The Feeling of What Happens: Body and Emotion in the Making of Consciousness.* (New York: Harcourt Brace, 1999).

64. Patrick Wall, *Pain: The Science of Suffering.* (New York: Columbia University Press, 2002).

65. Paul John Eakin, "What Are We Reading When We Read Autobiography?" *Narrative* 12, no. 2 (Spring 2004):121–132.

66. Philip Auslander, "Performance as Therapy: Spalding Gray's Autopathographic Monologues," in *Bodies in Commotion: Disability & Performance,* eds. Philip Auslander and Carrie Sandahl (Ann Arbor: University of Michigan Press 2005), 173.

67. Bennett, "3-D A/B," 38.

68. Bennett, "3-D A/B," 39.

69. Ibid.

70. Bennett, "3-D A/B," 40.

71. Iris Marion Young, *"Throwing like a Girl" and other essays in feminist philosophy and social theory* (Bloomington: Indiana University Press, 1990. 153). Quoted in Stocker, "Problems of Embodiment," 49.

72. Stocker, "Problems of Embodiment," 30.

73. Stocker, "Problems of Embodiment," 46.

74. Stocker, "Problems of Embodiment," 32.

75. Susan Miller, *My Left Breast,* in *O Solo Homo, The New Queer Performance,* eds. Holly Hughes and David Román (New York: Grove Press, 1998), 120.

76. Meyer, "Have You Heard," 545–46.

77. Dolan, "Performance," 468.

78. Chris Anne Strickling, "Re/Presenting the Self: Autobiographical Performance by People with Disability" (PhD diss., University of Texas at Austin, 2003), 114–15.

79. Strickling, "Re/Presenting," 117.

80. It is worth noting that Galloway's brother-in-law is autobiographical theorist Timothy Dow Adams, who appears briefly in Galloway's memoir. I met Adams (a former department chair at West Virginia University, where I currently teach) before I came into contact with Galloway, and while I cannot presume to know anything about whose thinking influenced whose, there has no doubt been some powerful interchange of ideas about the nature of autobiographical narrative between the two.

81. Terry Galloway, Personal correspondence, 22 July, 2010.

82. Terry Galloway, *Mean Little deaf Queer.* (Boston: Beacon, 2009), 174.

83. Strickling, "Re/Presenting," 154.

84. In early 2010, Galloway underwent cochlear implant surgery, which mitigates the need for hearing aids. Nonetheless, in her memoir, she tells the story of cutting her hair specifically to make visible her hearing aids: "After hours and hours of hacking, I was almost skinheaded. My behind-the-ear

hearing aids glinted in the light and at my feet, a pile of dark hair that looked like what it was—a line in the sand" (*Mean Little deaf Queer*, 154).

85. Galloway, Personal correspondence.

86. Ibid.

87. Strickling, "Re/Presenting," 122.

CHAPTER 3

1. Lloyd Rose, "The Loving Heart of Evil: Family Betrayal Fuels 'How I Learned to Drive,'" performance review of *How I Learned to Drive*, by Paula Vogel, *Washington Post*, April 30, 1999, Co1.

2. Steven Drukman, "A Playwright on the Edge Turns toward the Middle," *New York Times*, March 16, 1997, Sunday, late edition, Arts and Leisure, final section 2.

3. Michael Billington, " How Do You Judge a 75-Minute Suicide Note?" review of *4.48 Psychosis* by Sarah Kane, *Guardian*, June 30, 2000, 5; Paul Taylor, "First Night: A Suicide Note That Is Extraordinarily Vital: *4.48 Psychosis*, Royal Court London," review of *4.48 Psychosis* by Sarah Kane, *Independent* (London), June 30, 2010, 10.

4. Roland Barthes, "The Death of the Author," in *Image/Music/Text*, trans. Stephen Heath (New York: Hill and Wang, 1977), 142–47; Michel Foucault, "What Is an Author?" in *The Foucault Reader*, ed. and trans. Paul Rabinow (New York: Pantheon Books, 1984), 101–20.

5. De Man, "Autobiography," 922.

6. David Grieg, introduction to *Sarah Kane: Complete Works* (London: Methuen, 2000), xviii.

7. Aleks Sierz, "The Short Life of Sarah Kane," *Daily Telegraph*, May 27, 2000, *In-yer-face Theatre*, http://www.inyerface-theatre.com/archive7.html, accessed August 2, 2010.

8. Graham Saunders, *'Love Me or Kill Me': Sarah Kane and the Theatre of Extremes* (Manchester: Manchester University Press, 2002), 110.

9. Ibid.

10. Ibid. emphasis original.

11. Annabelle Singer, "Don't Want to Be This: The Elusive Sarah Kane," *TDR: The Drama Review* 48, no. 2 (summer 2004): 139–71.

12. Jack Tinker, "The Disgusting Feast of Filth," performance review of *Blasted*, by Sarah Kane, *Daily Mail* (London), January 19, 1995, 5.

13. Singer, "Don't," 160.

14. Michel Foucault, *Madness and Civilization* (New York: Random House, 1965), x.

15. Ibid., x–xi, emphasis original.

16. Ibid., xi.

17. Shoshana Felman, "Woman and Madness: The Critical Phallacy," in *Feminisms*, ed. Robyn R. Warhol and Diane Price Herndl (New Brunswick, N.J.: Rutgers University Press, 1991), 6.

18. Sandra Gilbert and Susan Gubar, *The Madwoman in the Attic: The*

Woman Writer and the Nineteenth Century Literary Imagination (New Haven: Yale University Press, 1978).

19. Catherine R. Stimpson, "Zero Degree Deviancy: The Lesbian Novel in English," in *Feminisms*, ed. Robyn R. Warhol and Diane Price Herndl (New Brunswick, N.J.: Rutgers University Press, 1991), 301.

20. Grieg, introduction, xvii.

21. Saunders, *Love Me*, 112–13.

22. Ariel Watson, "Cries of Fire: Psychotherapy in Contemporary British and Irish Drama," *Modern Drama* 51, no. 2 (summer 2008): 191.

23. Sarah Kane, *4.48 Psychosis*, in *Sarah Kane: Complete Works* (London: Methuen, 2000), 245.

24. Watson, "Cries of Fire," 197.

25. Alicia Tycer, "'Victim. Perpetrator. Bystander': Melancholic Witnessing of Sarah Kane's *4.48 Psychosis*," *Theatre Journal* 60, no.1 (March 2008): 35.

26. Martin Harries, "Sarah Kane Was Not a Suicide," review of *4.48 Psychose* by Sarah Kane at BAM Harvey Theatre, Brooklyn, N.Y., directed by Claude Régy, performed by Isabelle Huppert, *Hunter On-line Theatre Review*, http://hotreview.org/articles/sarahkanewasnot_print.htm, accessed August 10, 2010.

27. Wayne C. Booth, *The Rhetoric of Fiction* (Chicago: University of Chicago Press, 1961), 74.

28. Ibid., 74–75.

29. Seymour Chatman, *Coming to Terms: The Rhetoric of Narration in Fiction and Film* (Ithaca, N.Y.: Cornell University Press, 1990), 86.

30. Susan S. Lanser, "(Im)plying the Author," *Narrative* 9, no. 2 (May 2001): 158.

31. Narratology has typically taken as standard practice the quotation marks around the author's name to distinguish the implied author of a text from the flesh and blood author in real life.

32. Lanser, "(Im)plying," 158.

33. Wayne C. Booth,. "Resurrection of the Implied Author: Why Bother?," in *A Companion to Narrative Theory*, ed. James Phelan and Peter J. Rabinowitz (Malden, Mass.: Blackwell Publishing, 2005), 77.

34. Susan S. Lanser, "The 'I' of the Beholder: Equivocal Attachments and the Limits of Structuralist Narratology," in *A Companion to Narrative Theory*, ed. James Phelan and Peter J. Rabinowitz (Malden, Mass.: Blackwell Publishing, 2005), 206.

35. Ibid., 207.

36. Ibid., 208.

37. Booth, "Resurrection," 82–86.

38. Ibid., 84.

39. Mel Kenyon, quoted in Sierz, "Short Life."

40. Kane, *4.48*, 206.

41. Ibid., 207.

42. Saunders, *Love Me*, 111.

43. Watson, "Cries of Fire," 192.

44. Adams, *Telling*, 16.

45. Smith, "Construing," 157.

46. Barthes, "Death," 145, emphasis mine.
47. Ibid.
48. Lanser, " 'I,' " 217, emphasis original.
49. Kane, *4.48*, 217.
50. Saunders, *Love Me,* 113.
51. Ibid., 114.
52. Kane, *4.48*, 209.
53. Ibid., 210.
54. Ibid., 212.
55. Ibid., 215.
56. Ibid., 230.
57. See particularly Singer, "Don't"; Tycer, "Victim, Perpetrator, By-stander"; and Watson, "Cries of Fire."
58. Kane, *4.48*, 233.
59. Ibid., 209–10.
60. Ibid., 221.
61. Ibid.
62. Ibid., 241.
63. Heilbrun, *Writing,* 13.
64. Kane, *4.48*, 224.
65. Ibid., 215.
66. Felman, "Woman and Madness," 18–19, emphasis original.
67. Ibid., 18, emphasis original.
68. Kane, *4.48*, 222.
69. Ibid., 234.
70. Ibid., 212.
71. Ibid.
72. Ibid., 213.
73. The nature of this connection varies in observing Kane's expression of admiration for Crimp's work. See Martin Crimp, *Attempts on Her Life,* in *Martin Crimp: Plays: 2* (London: Faber and Faber, 2005), 197–284.
74. Saunders, *Love Me,* 109.
75. Ken Urban, "The Ethics of Catastrophe: The Theatre of Sarah Kane," *PAJ: A Journal of Performance and Art (PAJ)* 69, 23, no. 3 (September 2001): 46.
76. Ibid.
77. Taylor, "First Night," 10.

CHAPTER 4

1. Elaine Aston, "Pam Gems: Body Politics and Biography," in *The Cambridge Companion to Modern British Playwrights,* ed. Elaine Aston and Janelle Reinelt (Cambridge: Cambridge University Press, 2000), 159; Peggy Rosenthal, "Feminism and Life in Feminist Biography," *College English* 36, no. 2 (October 1974): 180.
2. For example, neither *Theatre Journal*'s December 2000 issue devoted to women and history nor Maggie B. Gale and Viv Gardner's *Women, Theatre, and Performance: New Histories, New Historiographies* (Manchester: Manchester

University Press, 2000) devotes a single article to feminist biographies. More recent collections, including Gale and Gardner's more recent volume, *Auto/Biography and Identity* (Manchester: Manchester University Press, 2004), Lynn C. Miller, Jacqueline Taylor, and M. Heather Carver's collection *Voices Made Flesh* (Madison: University of Wisconsin Press, 2003), and Sherrill Grace and Jerry Wasserman's 2006 *Theatre and AutoBiography* (Vancouver: Talonbooks, 2006), attend more closely to biographical performance, but essays in these collections often (though not always) conflate the act of biography with the performer's autobiography, a valid approach but only one angle on a much larger picture.

3. Sheila Rowbotham, *Hidden from History: Rediscovering Women in History from the 17th Century to the Present* (New York: Pantheon Books, 1974).

4. Case, *Feminism*, 2.

5. Evelyn J. Hinz, "The Dramatic Lineage of Auto/Biography," in *New Essays on Life Writing: From Genre to Critical Practice*, ed. Marlene Kadar (Toronto: University of Toronto Press, 1992), 195.

6. Ken Mitchell, "Between the Lines: Biography, Drama, and N. F. Davin," in *Biography and Autobiography: Essays on Irish and Canadian History and Literature*, ed. James Noonan (Ottawa: Carleton University Press, 1993), 263.

7. Fiona Templeton, *Delirium of Interpretations*. Unpublished manuscript. (2000), i.

8. Joan Schenkar, *Signs of Life*, in *Signs of Life: Six Comedies of Menace*, ed. Vivian Patraka. (Hanover, N.H.: Wesleyan University Press: 1998), 44.

9. Eric Berlatsky, "Memory as Forgetting: The Problem of the Postmodern in Kundera's *The Book of Laughter and Forgetting* and Spiegelman's *Maus*," *Cultural Critique* 55 (Autumn, 2003): 102.

10. Ibid.

11. Michael Riffaterre, *Fictional Truth* (Baltimore: Johns Hopkins University Press, 1990). Perhaps, the "truth" that Riffaterre identifies as inherent in fiction provides clues to the appeal of historical narrative for feminist playwrights. Writing of fictional diegesis, he says, "As there are signs of fictionality, there must be signs palliating it, signs indicating a convention of truth, signs of plausibility that make readers react to a story as if it were true" (2). If fictionality is counterbalanced by plausibility, and plausibility is measured in terms of an audience's expectations, then the truth of a narrative lies in part in its reception, in the coherence of the narrative facts with those notions, ideologies and facts that the audience carries with them (9–10). Add to this the symbolic systems of truth that Riffaterre describes, which "provide a metalinguistic commentary that points to the truth of the context surrounding them [. . . and . . .] possess a self-contained verisimilitude" (53). The symbolic, metaphorical truth that Riffaterre speaks of can be likened to the rhetoric that these plays contain; their surrounding context is no longer the past but the present in which the audience experiences them. So half of the appeal of the "real" is that the plausibility of narrative coherence justifies the critiques that these plays levy on the present by means of the truth available in their discursive arguments. That is, even fiction provides two significant connections to

the "real": the narrative coherence that roots its subject matter to a plausible history and the discursive applicability that engages with its readerly context.

12. Schenkar, *Signs of Life*, 44.

13. William H. Epstein, *Recognizing Biography* (Philadelphia: University of Pennsylvania Press, 1987), 41.

14. Gould, "Unhappy."

15. Susan Groag Bell and Marilyn Yalom, *Revealing Lives: Autobiography, Biography, and Gender* (Albany: State University of New York Press, 1990), 1.

16. Rosenthal, "Feminism and Life," 180.

17. Ibid., 183.

18. Jamie Pachino, *Theodora: An Unauthorized Biography*, unpublished manuscript, 1997. 65–66.

19. Rosenthal, "Feminism and Life," 183.

20. Aston, "Pam Gems," 159.

21. Diamond, *Unmaking Mimesis*, 144.

22. Ibid., 146.

23. Aston, "Pam Gems," 160.

24. Carol Hanbery McKay, "Performing Historical Figures: The Metadramatics of Women's Autobiographical Performance," in *Voices Made Flesh: Performing Women's Autobiography*, ed. Lynn C. Miller, Jacqueline Taylor, and M. Heather Carver (Madison: University of Wisconsin Press, 2003), 152.

25. Of the six essays on biography found in *Revealing Lives*, Susan Groag Bell and Marilyn Yalom's volume on life writing and gender, several insist on reading biographical texts by women more as veiled autobiographies of their authors than as biographies of their subjects (e.g. "The 'Failure' of Biography and the Triumph of Women's Writing," "Biography as Autobiography," and "Biography as Reflected Autobiography").

26. McKay, "Performing Historical Figures," 158–59.

27. Anna T. Kuhn, "The 'Failure' of Biography and the Triumph of Women's Writing: Bettina von Arnim's *Die Günderode* and Christa Wolf's *The Quest for Christa T*," in *Revealing Lives: Autobiography, Biography, and Gender*. ed. Susan Groag Bell and Marilyn Yalom (Albany: State University of New York Press, 1990), 13. Trev Lynn Broughton and Linda Anderson, *Women's Lives/ Women's Times: New Essays on Auto/Biography*, (Albany: State University of New York Press, 1997), xii.

28. I use the term *biographical subject* here specifically as a shorthand for the character at the center of these plays. I do recognize, however, as I will explore, that the term *subject* is problematic, given that the biographical subject is often objectified by the omniscient narrator.

29. Elizabeth Kamarck Minnich, "Friendship between Women: The Act of Feminist Biography," *Feminist Studies* 11, no. 2 (summer 1985): 287.

30. Just as the notion of the unified self is a politically charged fantasy, so is the notion of a unified biographical tradition—a stable set of conventions—that feminism must work against. Nonetheless, these ideas are perceived to constitute a tradition of "conventional" biography; they serve as literary figureheads of life-writing authority, and feminism's responses to these conventions are not merely reactions to this straw man per se. And while examples of

traditional biography do abound (one merely need visit a bookstore shelf on presidential biographies for evidence), these plays constitute an attempt to work against a perceived set of traditional practices in a way that both espouses an oppositional ideology and provides a methodology for recovering women's lives that is viable within the framework of feminist discourse.

31. William Epstein, "(Post)Modern Lives: Abducting the Biographical Subject," in *Contesting the Subject: Essays in the Postmodern Theory and Practice of Biographical Criticism,* ed. William H. Epstein (West Lafayette, Ind.: Purdue University Press, 1991), 218.

32. Ibid., 218–19.

33. Deborah C. Payne argues that this dichotomy—Restoration actress as reified object or emergent professional—is a false one, but she does claim that the notion of emergent professionalism depends on objectification, simply in the field of taste rather than sexual desire. See Deborah C. Payne, "Reified Object or Emergent Professional?: Retheorizing the Restoration Actress," in *Cultural Readings of Restoration and Eighteenth Century English Theater,* ed. J. Douglas Canfield and Deborah C. Payne (Athens: University of Georgia Press, 1995), 16.

34. Stacy Wolf, "Desire in Evidence," in *Voices Made Flesh: Performing Women's Autobiography,* ed. Lynn C. Miller, Jacqueline Taylor, and M. Heather Carver (Madison: University of Wisconsin Press, 2003), 93.

35. Sharon O'Brien, "Feminist Theory and Literary Biography," in *Contesting the Subject: Essays in the Postmodern Theory and Practice of Biographical Criticism,* ed. William H. Epstein (West Lafayette, Ind.: Purdue University Press, 1991), 130.

36. Templeton, ii.

37. Ibid., i.

38. *Delirium of interpretations,* according to Templeton's gloss, was the nineteenth-century term accorded to what we now call paranoia or paranoid schizophrenia (ibid., i).

39. Ibid., i–ii.

40. O'Brien, "Feminist Theory," 130.

41. I could spend time critiquing how this particular choice (to present the onstage biography through images captured by the male character's camera) reproduces the processes of the male gaze in the construction of the biographical subject, but the purpose here is to examine what this technique has in common with other feminist plays that use it, no matter how much more or less successfully.

42. Lynn Kaufman, *Shooting Simone* (Woodstock, Ill.: Dramatic Publishing, 1993), 42.

43. Gabriele Griffin and Elaine Aston, *Herstory* (Sheffield, Eng.: Sheffield Academic Press, 1991), 9.

44. Paul Taylor, "Review of *Playhouse Creatures,* by April DeAngelis," *Independent* (London), September 17, 1997, Features, 20.

45. Michael Billington, performance review of *Playhouse Creatures,* by April De Angelis, *Guardian* (London), September 16, 1997, Features, 20.

46. Carole Woddis, performance review of *Playhouse Creatures,* by April De Angelis, *The Herald* (Glasgow), September 17, 1997, 14.

47. Tony Kushner, "The Art of the Difficult," *Civilization* 4, no. 4 (August–September 1997): 65.

CHAPTER 5

1. Adrienne Scullion, "Contemporary Scottish Women Playwrights," in *The Cambridge Companion to Modern British Women Playwrights*, ed. Elaine Aston and Janelle Reinelt (Cambridge: Cambridge University Press, 2000), 98.
2. Quoted in ibid., 98.
3. Aston, *Introduction*, 144.
4. Scullion,"Contemporary Scottish," 98.
5. See Lionel Abel, *Metatheatre: A New View of Dramatic Form* (New York: Hill and Wang, 1963). See also James L. Calderwood, *Shakespearean Metadrama: The Argument of the Play in Titus Andronicus, Love's Labour's Lost, Romeo and Juliet, A Midsummer Night's Dream, and Richard II* (Minneapolis: University of Minnesota Press, 1971); Richard Hornby, *Drama, Metadrama, and Perception* (Lewisburg, Pa.: Bucknell University Press, 1986); and Lionel Abel, *Tragedy and Metatheatre: Essays on Dramatic Form*, introduction by Martin Puchner (New York: Holmes and Meier, 2003).
6. Hornby, *Drama, Metadrama*, 17.
7. Ibid., 23.
8. Ibid., 100–101.
9. Elinor Fuchs, "Clown Shows: Anti-theatricalist Theatricalism in Four Twentieth-Century Plays" in *Against Theatre: Creative Destructions on the Modernist Stage*, ed. Alan Ackerman and Martin Puchner (New York: Palgrave Macmillan, 2006), 43.
10. See Ryan Claycomb, "Towards a Parodic Spectator: Metatheatre and Staged Feminist Retellings," *New England Theatre Journal* 19, no. 2 (2008): 1–18; "Staging Psychic Excess: Parodic Narrative and Transgressive Performance," *Journal of Narrative Theory* 38, no. 1 (winter 2007): 104–27; and "Re-performing Women and Reconstructing the Audience: Paula Vogel's Desdemona and Postmodern Feminist Parody," *Text and Presentation* 20 (1999): 87–93.
11. Linda Hutcheon, *The Politics of Postmodernism* (New York: Routledge, 1989). See especially chapter 4, "The Politics of Parody."
12. Fuchs, "Clown Shows," 43.
13. Ibid., 55, 40.
14. Ariel Watson, "The Anxious Triangle: Modern Metatheatres of the Playwright, Performer, and Spectator" (PhD diss., Yale University, 2008).
15. Ibid., i.
16. Ibid., 6–7.
17. We can see this phenomenon operating quite clearly in the case Suzan-Lori Parks's *Venus*, which is deeply critical of its audience's complicity in such spectatorial processes and, as a direct result (as I will argue in the next chapter), has provoked a widely varied critical response.
18. Sharon Willis, "Hélène Cixous's *Portrait de Dora*: The Unseen and the Un-Scene," in *Performing Feminisms: Feminist Critical Theory and Theatre*, ed. Sue-Ellen Case (Baltimore: Johns Hopkins University Press, 1990), 77. See also

Erella Brown, "The Lake of Seduction: Body, Acting, and Voice in Hélène Cixous's *Portrait de Dora*," *Modern Drama* 39, no. 4 (winter 1996): 634; Mairead Hanrahan, "Cixous's *Portrait de Dora:* The Play of Whose Voice?" *Modern Language Review* 93, no. 1 (January 1998): 48; Hélène Cixous, *Portrait of Dora*, in *Benmussa Directs*, trans. Anita Barrows (Dallas: Riverrun Press, 1979), 30; and Diamond, *Unmaking Mimesis*, 38–39.

19. Diamond, *Unmaking Mimesis*, 38–39.

20. Ann Wilson, "History and Hysteria. Writing the Body in *Portrait of Dove* and *Signs of Life*," *Modern Drama* 32, no. 1 (March 1989): 81.

21. Diamond, *Unmaking Mimesis*, 38.

22. Willis, "Hélène," 81.

23. Cixous, *Portrait*, 30.

24. Ibid.

25. Willis, "Hélène," 81.

26. Erella Brown, "Lake," 634.

27. Hanrahan, "Cixous's *Portrait*," 48.

28. Phelan, *Unmarked*, 146.

29. Ibid., 148.

30. Ibid.

31. Hanrahan, "Cixous's *Portrait*," 53.

32. April De Angelis, *Playhouse Creatures* (New York: Dramatists Publishing Service, 1994); April De Angelis. *Playhouse Creatures.* In *April De Angelis: Plays* (London: Faber and Faber, 1999), 153–231. Here I will rely primarily on the 1994 publication, except when major differences alter a reading of the play.

33. Throughout, I refer to the historical figure of Nell Gwyn by full or last name, while I speak of the character by using her first name.

34. Payne, "Reified." Here I use Payne's dyad as illustrative not only of the narratives that criticism uses to describe the actresses but also those with which De Angelis struggles, with quite different results, in the two versions of the play.

35. Ibid., 17. Although Payne recognizes that these discrepancies may be overstated, it seems that at the very least only the most famous actress of the age, Elizabeth Barry, had access to shares in the company.

36. The 1994 version of the play is not quite as guilty of the gross manipulations that the later version is, and for this reason, I rely on this text except when elements from the 1999 edition serve as a useful counterpoint.

37. Roy MacGregor-Hastie, *Nell Gwyn* (London: R. Hale, 1987), 39–40.

38. Nell Gwyn never appeared in Betterton's company; she acted for the King's Company, while Betterton was the leading actor and then manager of the Duke's Company. The two companies were not united by Betterton until 1682, years after Gwyn left the stage, meaning that not only did she not work with Betterton, as De Angelis presents, but she was not in the building during the 1672 burning of the Drury Lane Theatre, which De Angelis shows in Act II of the 1994 version.

39. Payne, "Reified," 16.

40. De Angelis, *Playhouse*, 1994, 25.

41. Marjorie Garber, *Vested Interests: Cross-Dressing and Cultural Anxiety*

(New York: Routledge, 1992), 86–87; Kristina Straub, *Sexual Suspects: Eighteenth-Century Players and Sexual Ideology* (Princeton, N.J.: Princeton University Press, 1992), 128.

42. Payne, "Reified," 31.

43. Quoted in Heidi Stephenson and Natasha Langridge, eds., *Rage and Reason: Women Playwrights on Playwriting* (London: Methuen, 1997), 59. Interestingly, while we have seen that De Angelis's history is not, in fact, solid as history goes, De Angelis seems to feel otherwise. In this interview with Stephenson and Langridge, she states, "I was just reflecting the history of the time!"

44. Diamond, *Unmaking Mimesis*, 146.

45. Bassnet-McGuire, 645.

46. Stephenson and Langridge, *Rage,* 60.

47. De Angelis, *Playhouse,* 1994, 24–25.

48. Ibid., 17.

49. Ibid., 60.

50. Ibid., 8.

51. Ibid., 36.

52. Marc Robinson, *The Theater of Maria Irene Fornes,* PAJ Books (Baltimore: Johns Hopkins University Press, 1999), 109.

53. Ibid., 110.

54. Ibid., 110–11.

55. Maria Irene Fornes, *The Summer in Gossensass,* in *What of the Night?: Selected Plays* (New York: PAJ Publications, 2008), 66.

56. Fornes, *Summer,* 78.

57. "THE THEATRES," *Saturday Review of Politics, Literature, Science, and Art* 53 (February 4, 1882): 143, *British Periodicals,* Proquest, britishperiodi cals.chadwyck.com, accessed September 17, 2010.

58. Fornes, *Summer,* 65.

59. Robinson, *Theater,* 115.

60. Susan Letzler Cole, *Playwrights in Rehearsal: The Seduction of Company* (New York: Routledge, 2001).

61. Fornes, quoted in ibid., 167.

62. Fornes, *Summer,* 83.

63. Ibid., 86.

64. Ibid., 88.

65. Ibid., 86.

66. Ibid., 89.

67. Penny Farfan, *Women, Modernism, and Performance* (Cambridge: Cambridge University Press, 2004), 12.

68. Ibid., 15.

69. Ibid., 12.

70. Lisa McNulty, "The Coming Woman," program for *The Summer in Gossensass,* by Maria Irene Fornes, Women's Project and Productions, directed by Maria Irene Fornes, March 31 to April 26, 1998, 2.

71. Ibid.

72. Fornes, *Summer,* 92.

CHAPTER 6

1. Saidiya V. Hartman, *Scenes of Subjection: Terror, Slavery, and Self-Making in Nineteenth-Century America* (Oxford: Oxford University Press, 1997), 56–57.

2. Charles W. Mills. *The Racial Contract* (Ithaca, N.Y.: Cornell University Press, 1997), 76.

3. Daphne A. Brooks. *Bodies in Dissent: Spectacular Performances of Race and Freedom, 1850–1910* (Durham, N.C.: Duke University Press, 2006), 4–5.

4. Diamond, *Unmaking Mimesis*, 52.

5. Hartman, *Scenes*, 57.

6. The major exception is Eberhardt's friendship with the French journalist Severine, historically notorious for both her radical politics and her sexuality. She is positioned here as Eberhardt's "scribe," an extreme exaggeration of their real-life relationship, which consisted of one meeting.

7. Garber, *Vested Interests*, 325, emphasis original.

8. Aston, "Pam Gems," 160.

9. Timberlake Wertenbaker, *New Anatomies* (Woodstock, Ill.: Dramatic Publishing, 1984), 38.

10. Verna A. Foster, "Reinventing Isabelle Eberhardt: Rereading Timberlake Wertenbaker's *New Anatomies*," *Connotations* 17, no. 1 (2007–8): 109–28. Foster takes up this point persuasively in her article, noting that post-9/11, representations of Islam, and particularly of European encounters with Islam, are more highly charged and more complexly understood than they would have been to Wertenbaker's first audiences. I take up Foster's argument in more detail later.

11. Susan Carlson, "Language and Identity in Timberlake Wertenbaker's Plays," in *The Cambridge Companion to Modern British Playwrights*, ed. Elaine Aston and Janelle Reinelt (Cambridge: Cambridge University Press, 2000), 141.

12. Sue-Ellen Case, "From Split Subjects to Split Britches," in *Feminine Focus: The New Women Playwrights*, ed. Enoch Brater (Oxford: Oxford University Press, 1989).

13. O'Brien, "Feminist Theory," 130.

14. Wertenbaker, *New Anatomies*, 52.

15. Moya Lloyd, "Performativity, Parody, Politics," *Theory, Culture, and Society* 16, no. 2 (spring 1999): 198.

16. Foster, "Reinventing," 115.

17. Ibid., 113–14.

18. In using this quote to summarize the play's subject matter, I follow the lead of Tony Kushner, who uses these same words to describe the play in "The Art of the Difficult."

19. Suzan-Lori Parks, *Venus* (New York: Theatre Communications Group, 1997), 159.

20. Jean Young, "The Re-Objectification and Re-Commodification of Saartjie Baartman in Suzan-Lori Parks's *Venus*," *African American Review* 31, no. 4 (winter 1997): 700.

21. Brooks, *Bodies in Dissent*, 5.

22. Young, "Re-Objectification," 699–700.

23. Suzan-Lori Parks, "For Posterior's Sake," interview with Una Chaudhuri, in *Program of the Public Theater, Venus,* by Susan-Lori Parks, April 2, 1996, 34.

24. Anne Davis Basting, performance review of *Venus,* by Suzan-Lori Parks, *Theatre Journal* 49, no. 2 (May 1997): 225.

25. Kushner, "The Art of the Difficult," 64.

26. Ibid., 63–64.

27. Harry J. Elam Jr and Alice Rayner, "Body Parts: Between Story and Spectacle in *Venus* by Suzan-Lori Parks," in *Staging Resistance: Essays on Political Theater,* ed. Jeanne Colleran and Jenny S. Spencer (Ann Arbor: University of Michigan Press, 1998), 276.

28. Robert Brustein, "Robert Brustein on Theater," performance review of *Venus,* by Suzan-Lori Parks, *New Republic,* May 20, 1996, 29.

29. Sanya Osha, "*Venus* and White Desire," *Transition* 99 (2008): 80.

30. Greg Miller, "The Bottom of Desire in Suzan-Lori Parks's *Venus,*" *Modern Drama* 45, no. 1 (spring 2002): 126.

31. Johanna Frank, "Embodied Absence and Theatrical Dismemberment," *Journal of Dramatic Theory and Criticism* 21, no. 2 (spring 2007): 170.

32. Ibid.

33. Carrie Sandahl, "Ahhhh Freak Out! Metaphors of Disability and Femaleness in Performance," *Theatre Topics* 9, no. 1 (1999): 16.

34. Ibid.

35. Hayden White, *Tropics of Discourse: Essays in Cultural Criticism* (Baltimore: Johns Hopkins University Press, 1978), 96.

36. Ibid.

37. Sara L. Warner, "Suzan-Lori Parks's Drama of Disinterment: A Transnational Exploration of *Venus,*" *Theatre Journal* 60, no. 2 (May 2008): 182.

38. Sarah Einstein, "Venus Inferred: The Problem of Biography in Suzan-Lori Parks' *Venus,*" unpublished manuscript, West Virginia University, May 2010, 1. While in the context of the course Einstein was my student, she is also an established writer of creative nonfiction in her own right.

39. Miller, "The Bottom," 125. We might note that the historical Baartman disappears behind the textualized trope of The Venus Hottentott in a way not unlike Ida Bauer's disappearance behind the figure of Freud's Dora, which I discussed in the previous chapter. However, unlike Cixous's Ida Bauer, performance only serves to reinforce the discursive circumscription of Baartman's body rather that offering a transgressive escape.

40. Einstein, "Venus Inferred," 5.

41. Hartman, *Scenes,* 57.

42. Brooks, *Bodies in Dissent,* 5.

43. Parks, *Venus,* 35.

44. Ibid., 65, 78.

45. Ibid., 91–98.

46. Hartman, *Scenes,* 57.

47. Ibid.

48. Elam and Rayner note the degree to which the objectification of Baartman's body continued into the present of the play's earliest perfor-

mances, as South African tribal governments and the Parisian Musée de l'Homme remained locked in diplomatic negotiations as to who would control Baartman's remains, which were only repatriated in 2002.

49. Roger Bechtel, *Past Performance* (Lewisburg, Pa.: Bucknell University Press, 2007), 243.

50. Ibid.

51. Parks, *Venus,* 25.

52. Jennifer Johung, "Figuring the 'Spells'/Spelling the Figures: Suzan-Lori Parks's 'Scene of Love (?)," *Theatre Journal* 58, no. 1 (March 2006): 46.

53. Ibid., 49.

54. Parks, *Venus,* 109.

55. Howard Kissel, "Venus Makes Spectacle of Itself," performance review of *Venus,* by Suzan-Lori Parks, *Daily News* (New York), May 3, 1996, New York Now, 47.

56. Einstein, "Venus Inferred," 7.

57. Kushner, 65.

58. Bechtel, *Past Performance,* 243.

59. Christopher Innes, "Staging Black History: Re-imagining Cultural Icons," *South African Theatre Journal* 13, no. 1 (2000): 28.

60. Sue-Ellen Case, "Classic Drag: The Greek Creation of Female Parts." *Theatre Journal* 37, no. 3 (October 1985): 317–27.

CONCLUSION

1. Dee Heddon, "The Politics of the Personal: Autobiography in Performance," in *Feminist Futures? Theatre Performance, Theory,* ed. Elaine Aston and Geraldine Harris (New York, Palgrave Macmillan, 2006), 135.

2. Holly Hughes and David Román, "*O Solo Homo:* An Introductory Conversation," in *O Solo Homo: The New Queer Performance* (New York: Grove, 1998), 1.

3. Dee Heddon, "Politics of the Personal," 139. Heddon's essay reappears substantially in her 2008 *Autobiography and Performance,* but this essay's earlier appearance seems to mark a tighter window for the cultural, political, and aesthetic shift that I am tracing here.

4. Robert Crew, "Politics of War Packs a Punch," review of *Palace of the End,* by Judith Thompson, *Toronto Star* January 18, 2008, Entertainment, E02.

5. Judith Thompson, *Palace of the End* (Toronto: Playwrights Canada Press, 2007), 8.

6. Ibid., 8, emphasis original.

7. Ibid., 33.

8. Ibid., 43.

9. Ibid., 48.

10. Ibid., 30.

BIBLIOGRAPHY

Abel, Lionel. *Metatheatre: A New View of Dramatic Form*. New York: Hill and Wang, 1963.

Abel, Lionel. *Tragedy and Metatheatre: Essays on Dramatic Form*. Introduction by Martin Puchner. New York: Holmes and Meier, 2003.

Adams, Timothy Dow. *Telling Lies in Modern American Autobiography*. Chapel Hill: University of North Carolina Press, 1990.

Alpern, Sara, Joyce Antler, Elisabeth Israels Perry, and Ingrid Winther Scobie. *The Challenge of Feminist Biography: Writing the Lives of Modern American Women*. Urbana, Ill.: University of Illinois Press, 1992.

Anzaldua, Gloria. *Borderlands/La Frontera: The New Mestiza*. San Francisco: Aunt Lute Books, 1990.

Aston, Elaine. *Feminist Views on the English Stage: Women Playwrights, 1990–2000*. Cambridge: Cambridge University Press, 2003.

Aston, Elaine. *An Introduction to Feminism and Theatre*. New York: Routledge, 1995.

Aston, Elaine. "Pam Gems: Body Politics and Biography." In *The Cambridge Companion to Modern British Playwrights*, edited by Elaine Aston and Janelle Reinelt, 157–73. Cambridge: Cambridge University Press, 2000.

Augburg, Tanya. "Orlan's Performative Transformations of Subjectivity." In *The Ends of Performance*, edited by Peggy Phelan and Jill Lane, 285–314. New York: New York University Press, 1998.

Auslander, Philip. "Performance as Therapy: Spalding Gray's Autopathographic Monologues." In *Bodies in Commotion: Disability and Performance*, edited by Philip Auslander and Carrie Sandahl, 163–74. Ann Arbor: University of Michigan Press, 2005.

Austin, J. L. *How to Do Things with Words*. Cambridge, Mass.: Harvard University Press, 1962.

Baker, Bobby. *Daily Life Series 1: Kitchen Show*. Written and performed by Bobby Baker. Filmed by Carole Lamond. London: Daily Life Ltd., 1991. VHS.

Barthes, Roland. "The Death of the Author." In *Image/Music/Text*. Translated by Stephen Heath, 142–47. New York: Hill and Wang, 1977.

Bassnet-McGuire, Susan E. "Towards a Theory of Women's Theatre." In *Semiotics of Drama and Theatre*, edited by Herta Schmid and Aloysius Van Kesteren, 445–66. Linguistic and Literary Studies in Eastern Europe, no. 10. Amsterdam: John Benjamins, 1984.

Basting, Anne Davis. Performance review of *Venus,* by Suzan-Lori Parks. *Theatre Journal* 49, no. 2 (May 1997): 223–25.

Bechtel, Roger. *Past Performance.* Lewisburg, Pa.: Bucknell University Press, 2007.

Bell, Susan Groag, and Marilyn Yalom, eds. *Revealing Lives: Autobiography, Biography, and Gender.* Albany: State University of New York Press, 1990.

Bennett, Susan. "3-D A/B." In *Theatre and AutoBiography: Writing and Performing Lives in Theory and Practice,* edited by Sherrill Grace and Jerry Wasserman, 33–48. Vancouver: Talonbooks, 2006.

Berlatsky, Eric. "Memory as Forgetting: The Problem of the Postmodern in Kundera's *The Book of Laughter and Forgetting* and Spiegelman's *Maus.*" *Cultural Critique* 55 (Autumn 2003): 101–51.

Betsko, Kathleen, and Rachel Koenig, eds. *Interviews with Contemporary Women Playwrights.* New York: William Morrow, 1987.

Billington, Michael. Performance review of *Playhouse Creatures,* by April De Angelis. *Guardian,* September 16, 1997, Features, 20.

Billington, Michael. " How Do You Judge a 75-Minute Suicide Note?" Review of *4.48 Psychosis,* by Sarah Kane. *Guardian,* June 30, 2000, 5.

Boal, Augosto. *Theatre of the Oppressed.* Translated by Charles A. McBride and Maria Odilia Leal McBride. New York: Theatre Communications Group, 1985.

Booth, Wayne C. "Resurrection of the Implied Author: Why Bother?" In *A Companion to Narrative Theory,* edited by James Phelan and Peter J. Rabinowitz, 75–88. Malden, Mass.: Blackwell Publishing, 2005.

Booth, Wayne C. *The Rhetoric of Fiction.* Chicago: University of Chicago Press, 1961.

Bornstein, Kate. "Kate Bornstein." In *Out of Character: Rants, Raves, and Monologues from Today's Top Performance Artists,* edited by Mark Russell, 48–62. New York: Bantam, 1997.

Bornstein, Kate. *Virtually Yours.* In *O Solo Homo: The New Queer Performance,* edited by Holly Hughes and David Román, 229–78. New York: Grove, 1998.

Brantley, Ben. "There's Still No Vanilla in a Finley Encounter." Performance review of *Return of the Chocolate-Smeared Woman,* by Karen Finley. *New York Times,* June 24, 1998, late edition, E1.

Brodzki, Bella, and Celeste Schenck, eds. *Life/Lines: Theorizing Women's Autobiography.* Ithaca, N.Y.: Cornell University Press, 1988.

Brooks, Daphne A. *Bodies in Dissent: Spectacular Performances of Race and Freedom, 1850–1910.* Durham, N.C.: Duke University Press, 2006.

Broughton, Trev Lynn, and Linda Anderson, eds. *Women's Lives/Women's Times: New Essays on Auto/Biography.* Albany: State University of New York Press, 1997.

Brown, Erella. "The Lake of Seduction: Body, Acting, and Voice in Hélène Cixous's *Portrait de Dora.*" *Modern Drama* 39, no. 4 (winter 1996): 626–49.

Brown, Janet. *Feminist Drama: Definitions and Critical Analysis.* Metuchen, N.J.: Scarecrow Press, 1979.

Brown, Janet. "Feminist Theory and Contemporary Drama." In *The Cambridge*

Companion to American Women Playwrights, edited by Brenda Murphy, 155–72. Cambridge: Cambridge University Press, 1999.

Brownley, Martine Watson, and Allison B. Kimmich, eds. *Women and Autobiography.* Wilmington, Del.: Scholarly Resources, 1999.

Brustein, Robert. "Robert Brustein on Theater." Performance review of *Venus,* by Suzan-Lori Parks. *New Republic,* May 20, 1996, 29.

Butler, Judith. *Bodies That Matter: On the Discursive Limits of "Sex."* New York: Routledge, 1993.

Butler, Judith. "Burning Acts: Injurious Speech." In *Performativity and Performance,* edited by Andrew Parker and Eve Kosofsky Sedgwick, 197–227. New York: Routledge, 1995.

Butler, Judith. "Imitation and Gender Insubordination." In *Inside/Out: Lesbian Theories, Gay Theories,* edited by Diana Fuss, 20–33. New York: Routledge, 1991.

Butler, Judith. "Performative Acts and Gender Constitution: An Essay in Phenomenology and Feminist Theory." In *Performing Feminisms: Feminist Critical Theory and Theatre,* edited by Sue-Ellen Case, 270–82. Baltimore: Johns Hopkins University Press 1990.

Calderwood, James L. *Shakespearean Metadrama: The Argument of the Play in Titus Andronicus, Love's Labour's Lost, Romeo and Juliet, A Midsummer Night's Dream, and Richard II.* Minneapolis: University of Minnesota Press, 1971.

Canning, Charlotte. "Contiguous Autobiography: Feminist Performance in the 1970s." *Theatre Annual: A Journal of Performance Studies* 49 (1996): 65–75.

Carlson, Marvin. *Performance: A Critical Introduction.* London: Routledge, 1996.

Carlson, Marvin. "Performing the Self." *Modern Drama* 39, no. 4 (winter 1996): 599–608.

Carlson, Susan. "Language and Identity in Timberlake Wertenbaker's Plays." In *The Cambridge Companion to Modern British Playwrights,* edited by Elaine Aston and Janelle Reinelt, 134–49. Cambridge: Cambridge University Press, 2000.

Case, Sue-Ellen. "Classic Drag: The Greek Creation of Female Parts." *Theatre Journal* 37, no. 3 (October 1985): 317–27.

Case, Sue-Ellen. *Feminism and Theatre.* New York: Routledge, 1988.

Case, Sue-Ellen. "From Split Subjects to Split Britches." In *Feminine Focus: The New Women Playwrights,* edited by Enoch Brater, 126–46. Oxford: Oxford University Press, 1989.

Chatman, Seymour. *Coming to Terms: The Rhetoric of Narration in Fiction and Film.* Ithaca, N.Y.: Cornell University Press, 1990.

Cixous, Hélène. "The Laugh of the Medusa." In *Literary Criticism and Theory,* edited by Robert Con Davis and Laurie Finke, 732–48. New York: Longman, 1989.

Cixous, Hélène. *Portrait of Dora.* In *Benmussa Directs,* edited and translated by Anita Barrows, 27–74. Dallas: Riverrun Press, 1979.

Claycomb, Ryan. "Curtain Up?: Disrupted, Disguised, and Delayed Beginnings in Theatre and Drama." In *Narrative Beginnings,* edited by Brian Richardson, 166–78. Lincoln: University of Nebraska Press, 2008.

Claycomb, Ryan. "Re-performing Women and Reconstructing the Audience: Paula Vogel's Desdemona and Postmodern Feminist Parody." *Text and Presentation* 20 (1999): 87–93.

Claycomb, Ryan. "Staging Psychic Excess: Parodic Narrative and Transgressive Performance." *Journal of Narrative Theory* 38, no. 1 (winter 2007): 104–27.

Claycomb, Ryan. "Towards a Parodic Spectator: Metatheatre and Staged Feminist Retellings." *New England Theatre Journal* 19, no. 2 (2008): 1–18.

Cole, Susan Letzler. *Playwrights in Rehearsal: The Seduction of Company.* New York: Routledge, 2001.

Crew, Robert. "Politics of War Packs a Punch." Performance review of *Palace of the End*, by Judith Thompson. *Toronto Star*, January 18, 2008, Entertainment, E02.

Crimp, Martin. *Attempts on Her Life.* In *Martin Crimp: Plays, 2*, 197–284. London: Faber and Faber, 2005.

Damasio, Antonio R. *Descartes' Error: Emotion, Reason, and the Human Brain.* New York: Avon, 1995.

Damasio, Antonio R. *The Feeling of What Happens: Body and Emotion in the Making of Consciousness.* New York: Harcourt Brace, 1999.

Davis, Tracy C., and Thomas Postlewait. Introduction to *Theatricality.* In *Theatricality*, edited by Tracy C. Davis and Thomas Postlewait. Cambridge. Cambridge University Press, 2004.

De Angelis, April. *Playhouse Creatures.* In *April De Angelis: Plays*, 153–231. London: Faber and Faber, 1999.

De Angelis, April. *Playhouse Creatures.* New York: Dramatists Publishing Service, 1994.

De Man, Paul. "Autobiography as De-Facement." *MLN* 94, no. 5 (December 1979): 919–30.

Derrida, Jacques. *Dissemination.* Translated by Barbara Johnson. Chicago: University of Chicago Press, 1981.

Diamond, Elin. *Performance and Cultural Politics.* New York: Routledge, 1996.

Diamond, Elin. *Unmaking Mimesis: Essays on Feminism and Theatre.* New York: Routledge, 1997.

Dolan, Jill. *The Feminist Spectator as Critic.* Ann Arbor: University of Michigan Press, 1991.

Dolan, Jill. *Geographies of Learning.* Middletown, Conn.: Wesleyan University Press, 2001.

Dolan, Jill. "Performance, Utopia, and the 'Utopian Performative.'" *Theatre Journal* 53, no. 3 (October 2001): 455–70.

Drukman, Steven. "A Playwright on the Edge Turns toward the Middle." *New York Times*, March 16, 1997, Sunday, late edition, Arts and Leisure, final section 2, p. 6.

Eakin, Paul John. *Fictions in Autobiography: Studies in the Art of Self-Invention.* Princeton, N.J.: Princeton University Press, 1985.

Eakin, Paul John. "What Are We Reading When We Read Autobiography?" *Narrative* 12, no. 2 (2004): 121–32.

Einstein, Sarah. "Venus Inferred: The Problem of Biography in Suzan-Lori

Parks' *Venus*." Unpublished manuscript, West Virginia University, May 2010.

Elam, Harry J., Jr, and Alice Rayner. "Body Parts: Between Story and Spectacle in *Venus* by Suzan-Lori Parks." In *Staging Resistance: Essays on Political Theater,* edited by Jeanne Colleran and Jenny S. Spencer, 265–82. Ann Arbor: University of Michigan Press, 1998.

Elam, Keir. *The Semiotics of Theatre and Drama.* London: Routledge, 1980.

Epstein, William H. "(Post)Modern Lives: Abducting the Biographical Subject." In *Contesting the Subject: Essays in the Postmodern Theory and Practice of Biographical Criticism,* edited by William H. Epstein, 217–36. West Lafayette, Ind.: Purdue University Press, 1991.

Epstein, William H. *Recognizing Biography.* Philadelphia: University of Pennsylvania Press, 1987.

Export, Valie. "Persona, Proto-performance, Politics: A Preface." *Discourse* 14, no. 2 (spring 1992): 26–35.

Farfan, Penny. *Women, Modernism, and Performance.* Cambridge: Cambridge University Press, 2004.

Felman, Shoshana. "Woman and Madness: The Critical Phallacy." In *Feminisms,* edited by Robyn R. Warhol and Diane Price Herndl, 6–19. New Brunswick, N.J.: Rutgers University Press, 1991.

Ferris, Lesley. "Cooking Up the Self: Bobby Baker and Blondell Cummings 'Do' the Kitchen." In *Interfaces: Women/Autobiography/Image/Performance,* edited by Sidonie Smith and Julia Watson, 186–210. Ann Arbor: University of Michigan Press, 2002.

Finley, Karen. *A Different Kind of Intimacy.* New York: Thunder's Mouth Press, 2000.

Fornes, Maria Irene. *The Summer in Gossensass.* In *What of the Night?: Selected Plays,* 47–96. New York: PAJ Publications, 2008.

Forte, Jeanie. "Women's Performance Art: Feminism and Postmodernism." In *Performing Feminisms: Feminist Critical Theory and Theatre,* edited by Sue-Ellen Case, 251–69. Baltimore: Johns Hopkins University Press, 1990.

Foster, Verna A. "Reinventing Isabelle Eberhardt: Rereading Timberlake Wertenbaker's *New Anatomies.*" *Connotations* 17, no. 1 (2007–8): 109–28.

Foucault, Michel. *Madness and Civilization.* New York: Random House, 1965.

Foucault, Michel. "What Is an Author?" In *The Foucault Reader,* edited and translated by Paul Rabinow, 101–20. New York: Pantheon Books, 1984.

Frank, Johanna. "Embodied Absence and Theatrical Dismemberment." *Journal of Dramatic Theory and Criticism* 21, no. 2 (spring 2007): 161–71.

Fuchs, Elinor. "Clown Shows: Anti-theatricalist Theatricalism in Four Twentieth-Century Plays." In *Against Theatre: Creative Destructions on the Modernist Stage,* edited by Alan Ackerman and Martin Puchner, 39–57. New York: Palgrave Macmillan, 2006.

Fuss, Diana. *Essentially Speaking: Feminism, Nature, and Difference.* New York: Routledge, 1989.

Gale, Maggie B., and Viv Gardner, eds. *Auto/biography and Identity.* Manchester: Manchester University Press, 2004.

Gale, Maggie B., and Viv Gardner, eds. *Women, Theatre, and Performance: New*

Histories, New Historiographies. Manchester: Manchester University Press, 2000.

Galloway, Terry. *Mean Little deaf Queer*. Boston: Beacon, 2009.

Galloway, Terry. Personal correspondence, July 22, 2010.

Garber, Marjorie. *Vested Interests: Cross-Dressing and Cultural Anxiety*. New York: Routledge, 1992.

Gems, Pam. *Queen Christina*. London: Methuen Drama, 1982.

Gilbert, Sandra, and Susan Gubar. *The Madwoman in the Attic: The Woman Writer and the Nineteenth Century Literary Imagination*. New Haven: Yale University Press, 1978.

Gilmore, Leigh. *Autobiographics: A Feminist Theory of Women's Self-Representation*. Ithaca, N.Y.: Cornell University Press, 1994.

Goldberg, RoseLee. *Performance Art: From Futurism to the Present*. Rev. ed. New York: Harry N. Abrams, 1988.

Goodman, Lizbeth. *Contemporary Feminist Theatres: To Each Her Own*. London: Routledge, 1993.

Gould, Timothy. "The Unhappy Performative." In *Performativity and Performance*, edited by Andrew Parker and Eve Kosofsky Sedgwick, 19–44. New York: Routledge, 1995.

Grace, Sherrill. "Performing the Auto/Biographical Pact: Towards a Theory of Identity in Performance." In *Tracing the Autobiographical*, edited by Marlene Kadar, Linda Warley, Jeanne Perrault, and Susanna Egan, 65–79. Waterloo, Ont.: Wilfrid Laurier University Press, 2005.

Grace, Sherrill. "Theatre and the Autobiographical Pact: An Introduction." In *Theatre and AutoBiography: Writing and Performing Lives in Theory and Practice*, edited by Sherrill Grace and Jerry Wasserman, 13–29. Vancouver: Talonbooks, 2006.

Grace, Sherrill, and Jerry Wasserman, eds. *Theatre and AutoBiography*. Vancouver: Talonbooks, 2006.

Grieg, David. Introduction to *Sarah Kane: Complete Works*, ix–xviii. London: Methuen, 2000.

Griffin, Gabriele, and Elaine Aston, eds. *Herstory*. Sheffield, Eng.: Sheffield Academic Press, 1991.

Groag Bell, Susan, and Marilyn Yalom, eds. *Revealing Lives: Autobiography, Biography, and Gender*. Albany: State University of New York Press, 1990.

Hanrahan, Mairead. "Cixous's *Portrait de Dora*: The Play of Whose Voice?" *Modern Language Review* 93, no. 1 (January 1998): 48–58.

Harding, James M. *Cutting Performances: Collage Events, Feminist Artists, and the American Avant-Garde*. Ann Arbor: University of Michigan Press, 2010.

Harries, Martin. "Sarah Kane Was Not a Suicide." Review of *4.48 Psychose*, by Sarah Kane, at BAM Harvey Theatre, Brooklyn, N.Y., directed by Claude Régy, performed by Isabelle Huppert. *Hunter On-line Theatre Review*, http://hotreview.org/articles/sarahkanewasnot_print.htm. Accessed August 10, 2010.

Hartman, Saidiya V. *Scenes of Subjection: Terror, Slavery, and Self-Making in Nineteenth-Century America*. Oxford: Oxford University Press, 1997.

Heddon, Dee. "The Politics of the Personal: Autobiography in Performance."

In *Feminist Futures?: Theatre Performance, Theory*, edited by Elaine Aston and Geraldine Harris, 130–48. New York, Palgrave Macmillan, 2006.

Heddon, Deirdre. *Autobiography and Performance: Performing Selves*. New York: Palgrave Macmillan, 2008.

Heilbrun, Carolyn G. "Women's Autobiographical Writings: New Forms." In *Women and Autobiography*, edited by Martine Watson Brownley and Allison B. Kimmich, 15–32. Wilmington, Del.: Scholarly Resources, 1999.

Heilbrun, Carolyn G. *Writing a Woman's Life*. New York: W. W. Norton, 1988.

Hinz, Evelyn J. "The Dramatic Lineage of Auto/Biography." In *New Essays on Life Writing: From Genre to Critical Practice*, edited by Marlene Kadar, 195–212. Toronto: University of Toronto Press, 1992.

hooks, bell. *Bone Black: Memories of Girlhood*. New York: Henry Holt, 1997.

Hornby, Richard. *Drama, Metadrama, and Perception*. Lewisburg, Pa.: Bucknell University Press, 1986.

Hughes, Holly. *Clit Notes: A Sapphic Sampler*. New York: Grove, 1996.

Hughes, Holly. *Preaching to the Perverted*. Unpublished manuscript, 2003.

Hughes, Holly, and David Román. "*O Solo Homo*: An Introductory Conversation." In *O Solo Homo: The New Queer Performance*, edited by Holly Hughes and David Román, 1–15. New York: Grove, 1998.

Hutcheon, Linda. *A Poetics of Postmodernism*. New York and London: Routledge, 1988.

Hutcheon, Linda. *The Politics of Postmodernism*. New York: Routledge, 1989.

Innes, Christopher. "Staging Black History: Re-imagining Cultural Icons." *South African Theatre Journal* 13. 1 (1999): 20–29.

Jelinek, Estelle. "Introduction: Women's Autobiography and the Male Tradition." In *Women's Autobiography: Essays in Criticism*, edited by Estelle Jelinek, 1–20. Bloomington: Indiana University Press, 1980.

Jelinek, Estelle. Preface to *Women's Autobiography: Essays in Criticism*. Edited by Estelle Jelinek, ix–xii. Bloomington: Indiana University Press, 1980.

Johung, Jennifer. "Figuring the 'Spells'/Spelling the Figures: Suzan-Lori Parks's 'Scene of Love (?)." *Theatre Journal* 58, no. 1 (March 2006): 39–52.

Jones, Amelia. *Body Art: Performing the Subject*. Minneapolis: University of Minnesota Press, 1998.

Kane, Sarah. *4.48 Psychosis*. In *Sarah Kane: Complete Works*. London: Methuen, 2000, 203–45.

Kauffman, Linda S. "Cut-Ups in Beauty School—and Postscripts, January 2000 and December 2001." In *Interfaces: Women/Autobiography/Image/Performance*, edited by Sidonie Smith and Julia Watson, 103–31. Ann Arbor: University of Michigan Press, 2002.

Kaufman, Lynn. *Shooting Simone*. Woodstock, Ill.: Dramatic Publishing, 1993.

Kershaw, Baz. *The Politics of Performance: Radical Theatre as Cultural Intervention*. London: Routledge, 1992.

Keyssar, Helene. *Feminist Theatre*. London: Macmillan, 1984.

Kissel, Howard. "Venus Makes Spectacle of Itself." Performance review of *Venus*, by Suzan-Lori Parks, *Daily News* (New York), May 3, 1996, New York Now, 47.

Knowles, Ric. "Documemory, Autobiology, and the Utopian Performative in

Canadian Autobiographical Solo Performance." In *Theatre and AutoBiography: Writing and Performing Lives in Theory and Practice,* edited by Sherrill Grace and Jerry Wasserman, 49–68. Vancouver: Talonbooks, 2006.

Kuhn, Anna T. "The 'Failure' of Biography and the Triumph of Women's Writing: Bettina von Arnim's *Die Günderode* and Christa Wolf's *The Quest for Christa T."* In *Revealing Lives: Autobiography, Biography, and Gender,* edited by Susan Groag Bell and Marilyn Yalom, 13–28. Albany: State University of New York Press, 1990.

Kushner, Tony. "The Art of the Difficult." *Civilization* 4, no. 4 (August–September 1997): 62–67.

Lampe, Eelka. "Rachel Rosenthal Creating Her Selves." *TDR: The Drama Review* 32, no. 1 (spring 1988): 170–89.

Lanser, Susan Sniader. *Fictions of Authority: Women Writers and Narrative Voice.* Ithaca, N.Y.: Cornell University Press, 1992.

Lanser, Susan Sniader. "The 'I' of the Beholder: Equivocal Attachments and the Limits of Structuralist Narratology." In *A Companion to Narrative Theory,* edited by James Phelan and Peter J. Rabinowitz, 206–19. Malden, Mass.: Blackwell Publishing, 2005.

Lanser, Susan Sniader. "(Im)plying the Author." *Narrative* 9, no. 2 (2001): 153–60.

Lloyd, Moya. "Performativity, Parody, Politics." *Theory, Culture, and Society* 16, no. 2 (spring 1999): 195–213.

Lorde, Audre. *Zami: A New Spelling of My Name.* Watertown, Mass.: Persephone Press, 1982.

MacDonald, Claire. "Assumed Identities: Feminism, Autobiography, and Performance Art." In *The Uses of Autobiography,* edited by Julia Swindells, 187–95. London: Taylor and Francis, 1995.

MacGregor-Hastie, Roy. *Nell Gwyn.* London: R. Hale, 1987.

McKay, Carol Hanbery. "Performing Historical Figures: The Metadramatics of Women's Autobiographical Performance." In *Voices Made Flesh: Performing Women's Autobiography,* edited by Lynn C. Miller, Jacqueline Taylor, and M. Heather Carver, 152–65. Madison: University of Wisconsin Press, 2003.

McNulty, Lisa. "The Coming Woman." Program for *The Summer in Gossensass,* by Maria Irene Fornes. Women's Project and Productions, directed by Maria Irene Fornes, March 31 to April 26, 1998.

Meyer, Richard. "'Have You Heard the One about the Lesbian who Goes to the Supreme Court?': Holly Hughes and the Case against Censorship." *Theatre Journal* 52, no. 4 (December 2000): 543–52.

Miller, Greg. "The Bottom of Desire in Suzan-Lori Parks's *Venus."* *Modern Drama* 45, no. 1 (spring 2002): 125–37.

Miller, Lynn C., Jacqueline Taylor, and M. Heather Carver, eds. *Voices Made Flesh: Performing Women's Autobiography.* Madison: University of Wisconsin Press, 2003.

Miller, Susan. *My Left Breast.* In *O Solo Homo: The New Queer Performance,* edited by Holly Hughes and David Román, 93–120. New York: Grove, 1998.

Miller, Tim, and David Román. "Preaching to the Converted." *Theatre Journal* 47, no. 2 (May 1995): 169–88.

Mills, Charles W. *The Racial Contract.* Ithaca, N.Y.: Cornell University Press, 1997.

Minnich, Elizabeth Kamarck. "Friendship between Women: The Act of Feminist Biography." *Feminist Studies* 11, no. 2 (summer 1985): 288–305.

Mitchell, Ken. "Between the Lines: Biography, Drama, and N. F. Davin." In *Biography and Autobiography: Essays on Irish and Canadian History and Literature,* edited by James Noonan, 263–76. Ottawa: Carleton University Press, 1993.

Noriega, Chon. Introduction to *I, Carmelita Tropicana: Performing between Cultures,* by Alina Troyano, ix–xii. Boston: Beacon Press, 2000.

O'Brien, Sharon. "Feminist Theory and Literary Biography." In *Contesting the Subject: Essays in the Postmodern Theory and Practice of Biographical Criticism,* edited by William H. Epstein, 123–34. West Lafayette, Ind.: Purdue University Press, 1991.

Osha, Sanya. "*Venus* and White Desire." *Transition* 99 (2008): 80.

Pacheco, Patrick. "The Karen Finley Act Reacts." *Los Angeles Times,* June 27, 1998, F1.

Pachino, Jamie. *Theodora: An Unauthorized Biography.* Unpublished manuscript, 1997.

Parker, Andrew, and Eve Kosofsky Sedgwick. Introduction to *Performativity and Performance.* In *Performativity and Performance,* edited by Andrew Parker and Eve Kosofsky Sedgwick, 1–11. New York: Routledge, 1995.

Parks, Suzan-Lori. "For Posterior's Sake." Interview with Una Chaudhuri. In *Program of the Public Theater, Venus,* by Susan-Lori Parks, April 2, 1996, 26–30.

Parks, Suzan-Lori. *Venus.* New York: Theatre Communications Group, 1997.

Payne, Deborah C. "Reified Object or Emergent Professional?: Retheorizing the Restoration Actress." In *Cultural Readings of Restoration and Eighteenth Century English Theater,* edited by J. Douglas Canfield and Deborah C. Payne, 13–38. Athens: University of Georgia Press, 1995.

Phelan, Peggy. *Unmarked: The Politics of Performance.* New York: Routledge, 1993.

Pollock, Della. Introduction to *Remembering: Oral History Performance.* In *Remembering: Oral History Performance,* edited by Della Pollock, 1–18. New York: Palgrave Macmillan, 2005.

Riffaterre, Michael. *Fictional Truth.* Baltimore: Johns Hopkins University Press, 1990.

Robinson, Marc. *The Theater of Maria Irene Fornes.* PAJ Books. Baltimore: Johns Hopkins University Press, 1999.

Rose, Lloyd. "Holly Hughes, Making Herself Decent." Performance review of *Preaching to the Perverted,* by Holly Hughes. *Washington Post,* November 6, 2000, C01.

Rose, Lloyd. "The Loving Heart of Evil: Family Betrayal Fuels 'How I Learned to Drive.'" Performance review of *How I Learned to Drive,* by Paula Vogel, *Washington Post,* April 30, 1999, C01.

Rosenthal, Peggy. "Feminism and Life in Feminist Biography." *College English* 36, no. 2 (October 1974): 180–84.

Rowbotham, Sheila. *Hidden from History: Rediscovering Women in History from the Seventeenth Century to the Present.* New York: Pantheon Books, 1974.

Russell, Mark, ed. *Out of Character: Rants, Raves, and Monologues from Today's Top Performance Artists.* New York: Bantam, 1997.

Sandahl, Carrie. "Ahhhh Freak Out! Metaphors of Disability and Femaleness in Performance." *Theatre Topics* 9, no. 1 (1999): 11–30.

Sandahl, Carrie. "Queering the Crip or Cripping the Queer?: Intersections of Queer and Crip Identities in Solo Autobiographical Performance." *GLQ* 9, nos. 1–2 (2003): 25–56.

Saunders, Graham. *'Love Me or Kill Me': Sarah Kane and the Theatre of Extremes.* Manchester: Manchester University Press, 2002.

Savran, David. *A Queer Sort of Materialism: Recontextualizing American Theatre.* Ann Arbor: University of Michigan Press, 2003.

Scarry, Elaine. *The Body in Pain: The Making and Unmaking of the World.* Oxford: Oxford University Press, 1987.

Schechner, Richard. *Performance Theory.* New York: Routledge, 2003.

Schenkar, Joan. *Signs of Life.* In *Signs of Life: Six Comedies of Menace,* edited by Vivian Patraka, 43–96. Hanover, N.H.: Wesleyan University Press: 1998.

Schmor, John Brockway. "Confessional Performance: Postmodern Culture in Recent American Theatre." *Journal of Dramatic Theory and Criticism* 9, no. 1 (fall 1994): 157–72.

Schneider, Rebecca. *The Explicit Body in Performance.* New York: Routledge, 1997.

Scullion, Adrienne. "Contemporary Scottish Women Playwrights." In *The Cambridge Companion to Modern British Playwrights,* edited by Elaine Aston and Janelle Reinelt, 94–118. Cambridge: Cambridge University Press, 2000.

Siebers, Tobin. *Disability Theory.* Ann Arbor: University of Michigan Press, 2008.

Sierz, Aleks. "The Short Life of Sarah Kane." *Daily Telegraph,* May 27, 2000. *In-yer-face Theatre,* http://www.inyerface-theatre.com/archive7.html. Accessed August 2, 2010.

Singer, Annabelle. "Don't Want to Be This: The Elusive Sarah Kane." *TDR: The Drama Review* 48, no. 2 (summer 2004): 139–71.

Smith, Sidonie. "Construing Truth in Lying Mouths: Truthtelling in Women's Autobiography." In *Women and Autobiography,* edited by Martine Watson Brownley and Allison B. Kimmich, 33–52. Wilmington, Del.: Scholarly Resources, 1999.

Smith, Sidonie. "Performativity, Autobiographical Practice, Resistance." In *Women, Autobiography, Theory,* edited by Sidonie Smith and Julia Watson, 108–15. Madison: University of Wisconsin Press, 1998.

Smith, Sidonie. *Poetics of Women's Autobiography.* Bloomington: Indiana University Press, 1987.

Stephenson, Heidi, and Natasha Langridge, eds. *Rage and Reason: Women Playwrights on Playwriting.* London: Methuen, 1997.

Stimpson, Catherine R. "Zero Degree Deviancy: The Lesbian Novel in English." In *Feminisms,* edited by Robyn R. Warhol and Diane Price Herndl, 301–15. New Brunswick, N.J.: Rutgers University Press, 1991.

Stocker, Susan G. "Problems of Embodiment and Problematic Embodiment." *Hypatia* 16, no. 3 (summer 2001): 30–55.

Straub, Kristina. *Sexual Suspects: Eighteenth-Century Players and Sexual Ideology*. Princeton, N.J.: Princeton University Press, 1992.

Strickling, Chris Anne. *"Actual Lives:* Cripples in the House." *Theatre Topics* 12, no. 2 (September 2002): 143–62.

Strickling, Chris Anne. "Re/Presenting the Self: Autobiographical Performance by People with Disability." PhD diss., University of Texas at Austin, 2003.

Taylor, Paul. "First Night: A Suicide Note That Is Extraordinarily Vital: *4.48 Psychosis,* Royal Court London." Review of *4.48 Psychosis,* by Sarah Kane. *Independent* (London), June 30, 2010, 10.

Taylor, Paul. Review of *Playhouse Creatures,* by April De Angelis. *Independent* (London), September 17, 1997, Features, 20.

Templeton, Fiona. *Delirium of Interpretations*. Unpublished manuscript, 2000.

Tertullian. "On the Spectacles." In *Dramatic Theory and Criticism: Greeks to Grotowski,* edited by Bernard F. Dukore, 85–93. New York: Holt, Rinehart and Winston, 1974.

"THE THEATRES." *Saturday Review of Politics, Literature, Science, and Art* 53 (February 4, 1882): 143. British Periodicals. Proquest, http://britishperiodicals .chadwyck.com. Accessed September 17, 2010.

Thompson, Judith. *Palace of the End*. Toronto: Playwrights Canada Press, 2007.

Tinker, Jack. "The Disgusting Feast of Filth." Performance review of *Blasted,* by Sarah Kane, *Daily Mail,* January 19, 1995, 5.

Trav, S. D. "Angry at Daddy." Performance review of *Preaching to the Perverted,* written and performed by Holly Hughes, *Reason* 32, no. 5 (October 2000). Reason.com, http://reason.com/archives/2000/10/01/angry-at-daddy. Accessed October 25, 2010.

Tropicana, Carmelita. *Milk of Amnesia—Leche de Amnesia*. In *O Solo Homo: The New Queer Performance,* edited by Holly Hughes and David Román, 17–48. New York: Grove, 1998.

Troyano, Alina. *I, Carmelita Tropicana: Performing between Cultures*. Boston: Beacon Press, 2000.

Turner, Victor. *From Ritual to Theatre: The Human Seriousness of Play*. New York: Performing Arts Journal Publications, 1982.

Tycer, Alicia. "'Victim. Perpetrator. Bystander': Melancholic Witnessing of Sarah Kane's *4.48 Psychosis*." *Theatre Journal* 60, no. 1 (March 2008): 23–36.

Urban, Ken. "The Ethics of Catastrophe: The Theatre of Sarah Kane." *PAJ: A Journal of Performance and Art*. PAJ 69, 23, no. 3 (September 2001): 36–46.

Wall, Patrick. *Pain: The Science of Suffering*. New York: Columbia University Press, 2002.

Warner, Sara L. "Suzan-Lori Parks's Drama of Disinterment: A Transnational Exploration of *Venus*." *Theatre Journal* 60, no. 2 (May 2008): 181–99.

Watson, Ariel. "The Anxious Triangle: Modern Metatheatres of the Playwright, Performer, and Spectator." PhD diss., Yale University, 2008.

Watson, Ariel. "Cries of Fire: Psychotherapy in Contemporary British and Irish Drama." *Modern Drama* 51, no. 2 (summer 2008): 188–210.

Wertenbaker, Timberlake. *New Anatomies*. Woodstock, Ill.: Dramatic Publishing, 1984.

White, Hayden. *Tropics of Discourse: Essays in Cultural Criticism.* Baltimore: Johns Hopkins University Press, 1978.

Willis, Sharon. "Hélène Cixous's *Portrait de Dora:* The Unseen and the Un-Scene." In *Performing Feminisms: Feminist Critical Theory and Theatre,* edited by Sue-Ellen Case, 77–91. Baltimore: John Hopkins University Press, 1990.

Wilson, Ann. "History and Hysteria: Writing the Body in *Portrait of Dora* and *Signs of Life.*" *Modern Drama* 32, no. 1 (March 1989): 73–88.

Woddis, Carole. Performance review of *Playhouse Creatures,* by April De Angelis. *The Herald* (Glasgow), September 17, 1997, 14.

Wolf, Stacy. "Desire in Evidence." In *Voices Made Flesh: Performing Women's Autobiography,* edited by Lynn C. Miller, Jacqueline Taylor, and M. Heather Carver, 84–95. Madison: University of Wisconsin Press, 2003.

Wolff, Tamsen. Performance review of *Preaching to the Perverted,* written and performed by Holly Hughes, Performance Space 122, New York, N.Y., May 20, 2000. *Theatre Journal* 52, no. 4 (2000): 557.

Young, Iris Marion. *"Throwing Like a Girl" and Other Essays in Feminist Philosophy and Social Theory.* Bloomington: Indiana University Press, 1990.

Young, Jean. "The Re-objectification and Re-commodification of Saartjie Baartman in Suzan-Lori Parks's *Venus.*" *African American Review* 31, no. 4 (winter 1997): 699–708.

INDEX